YOU WILL NEVER BE ONE OF US

YOU WILL NEVER BE ONE OF US

A TEACHER, A TEXAS TOWN, AND THE
RURAL ROOTS OF RADICAL CONSERVATISM

TIMOTHY PAUL BOWMAN

AFTERWORD BY
WAYNE WOODWARD

UNIVERSITY OF OKLAHOMA PRESS : NORMAN

Publication of this book is made possible through the generosity of Edith Kinney Gaylord.

Library of Congress Cataloging-in-Publication Data

Names: Bowman, Timothy Paul, 1978– author.
Title: You will never be one of us : a teacher, a Texas town, and the rural roots of radical conservatism / Timothy Paul Bowman ; afterword by Wayne Woodward. Description: Norman : University of Oklahoma Press, [2022] | Includes bibliographical references and index. | Summary: "Explores the sources and depths of rural and small-town America's reactionary political culture during the latter half of the twentieth century by describing how a young high school teacher came to be fired by the school district in Hereford, Texas, in 1975 for founding a chapter of the American Civil Liberties Union in a historically white-majority town with a growing Mexican American population"—Provided by publisher.
Identifiers: LCCN 2022003435 | ISBN 978-0-8061-9038-9 (hardcover) ISBN 978-0-8061-9318-2 (paper)
Subjects: LCSH: Conservatism—Texas—History—20th century. | Right-wing extremists—Texas—History—20th century. | Radicalism—Texas—History—20th century. | Hereford (Tex.)—Politics and government—20th century. | Hereford (Tex.)—History—20th century.
Classification: LCC JC573.2.U6 B69 2022 | DDC 320.520973—dc23
LC record available at https://lccn.loc.gov/2022003435

The paper in this book meets the guidelines for permanence and durability of the Committee on Production Guidelines for Book Longevity of the Council on Library Resources, Inc. ∞

Copyright © 2022 by Timothy Paul Bowman. Published by the University of Oklahoma Press, Norman, Publishing Division of the University. Paperback published 2023. Manufactured in the U.S.A.

All rights reserved. No part of this publication may be reproduced, stored in a retrieval system, or transmitted, in any form or by any means, electronic, mechanical, photocopying, recording, or otherwise—except as permitted under Section 107 or 108 of the United States Copyright Act— without the prior written permission of the University of Oklahoma Press. To request permission to reproduce selections from this book, write to Permissions, University of Oklahoma Press, 2800 Venture Drive, Norman, OK 73069, or email rights .oupress@ou.edu.

CONTENTS

Acknowledgments / vii

Introduction / 1
1. Defining Conservatism in the Texas Panhandle / 15
2. Coming of Age in the Texas Panhandle:
The Civil Rights Era in Rural America / 41
3. The Teacher / 57
4. Building a Civil Rights Case in the Texas Panhandle / 80
5. Mexican Migrant Labor, the American Civil Liberties Union,
and Community Guardianism in Hereford, Texas / 104
6. There Will Be No Winners down the Line:
Prosecuting a Civil Rights Case in the Texas Panhandle / 116
7. Righting Wrongs and Wronging Rights:
The Culture Wars on Trial in the Texas Panhandle / 153
Conclusion: Hereford and the Two Americas / 179
Afterword, by Wayne Woodward / 185

Notes / 187
Bibliography / 209
Index / 215

ACKNOWLEDGMENTS

Writing a history book is far from the lonely endeavor that most people might think it to be. A number of people deserve recognition for their contributions in helping me take this project across the finish line.

The first person I would like to thank is Wayne Woodward. Wayne first reached out to me with his story in the winter of 2015–16; I was initially a little unsure if there was a good story for me to tell (and whether necessary documentary evidence existed), but meeting Wayne face-to-face sold me on the importance of his experiences as a young English teacher in Hereford, Texas. Wayne and his wife, Linda, welcomed me to their home numerous times, tolerating the probing and no doubt at times tedious questions from a historian who was simply trying to get everything right. I am eternally grateful for their support and encouragement.

Numerous other people provided invaluable assistance with the research. I am grateful to Jim Whitley, Pam Whitley, Don Cooney, Robin Green, Marty Kuhlman, Jeff Roche, and Joe Rogers. Warren Stricker and Millie Vanover at the Panhandle-Plains Historical Museum helped track down a variety of sources related to Texas Panhandle history. Sidnye Johnson and her staff at Cornette Library at West Texas A&M University helped track down a number of important sources on local history. Patrick Diepen and Steve Ely helped with digital preparation of some of the images that appear in the text. I am also especially indebted to Carolyn Ottoson at Cornette, who helped me navigate the relatively unfamiliar terrain of Texas Panhandle political history.

My colleagues at West Texas A&M University (WT) have provided support and warm friendship along the way. In the Department of History, I am grateful to Berlin McIntosh, Matt Reardon, Brian M. Ingrassia, Jean Stuntz, Byron Pearson, Bryan Vizzini, Wade Shaffer, Marty Kuhlman, Bruce Brasington, Paul Clark, Elizabeth Clark, Courtney Crowley, Hillarie Easley-McPherson, and Kris Drumheller. I served as associate director for the Center for the Study of the American West (CSAW) from 2016 to 2019, which constituted the bulk of the time when I was researching and writing this book. I am grateful to Alex Hunt, A. J. McCormick, and Maureen Hubbart for their support, and to the many student interns who worked at CSAW during my time at the center. Relatedly, I've had the good fortune of having some truly excellent students at WT who have helped keep me engaged in the classroom and inspired me to continue working outside of it; there are too many to list, and though I fear forgetting some of them, I would like to thank the above-mentioned Patrick Diepen, but also Will Mulloy, Alexis Torres, Lynsie Salazar, Robin Boedeker, Katey Denney, Gabe Martinez, Jose Navarrete, and the late Stephen Green, for inspiring me to be the best historian that I can be on a daily basis.

I have had the good fortune of working with many highly supportive people at the University of Oklahoma Press. Chief among these is Kent Calder, my patient editor, who took a chance on what was admittedly an initially *very* rough manuscript and encouraged me to stick with it. I am deeply grateful to Walter Nugent, Jason Mellard, and the anonymous reader who read the manuscript in full and provided invaluable commentary. Also, a special thank-you to my colleague Brian M. Ingrassia, who read a very early version of this manuscript and asked some probing questions that helped shape and improve what I had written.

I presented a small portion of this manuscript at the 2018 meeting of the Western History Association meeting in San Antonio; my thanks to my co-panelists as well as the session attendees. That same year, I gave a talk at the Amarillo Unitarian Universalist Fellowship that was based on the research for this book. Special thanks to my former student Larry Miller for inviting me to speak, as well as to the many congregants and community members who attended that evening.

Most importantly, shortly after I began writing this book, I met a West Texan who would change my life forever. Casey Pleming and her daughter, Audrey, became the center of my world in the spring of 2017. Casey became a steadfast supporter of mine, encouraging me when I was down and congratulating me when I scored various little victories along the way. Her support remained unwavering as our relationship grew over the course of the next year, and it only continued after we were married in September of 2018. Quite simply, I would be lost without her and the little family that we started and that I cherish more deeply than words can express. Casey's love, support, and encouragement mean the world to me—for those reasons, it seems only fitting that I dedicate this book to her.

INTRODUCTION

Young Esmerelda Perales was sad. During the spring semester of 1975, when she was a student at La Plata Junior High School in Hereford, Texas, Perales learned that Wayne Woodward, her popular young English teacher, was leaving the school. Although it is unclear whether Perales understood all the major details behind Woodward's impending departure, what is clear is that she had developed a deep appreciation for him. "Well, Woody, I couldn't think of anything to say," she told him upon hearing the news. "So I thought I'd express myself in a poem. I hope you like it:"

> Your (*sic*) Beautiful
> Inside and out
> Do we love you?
> There's no doubt.
> Your teaching?
> It's very good
> We need you TREMENDOUSLY
> Is that understood?
> You showed us
> How to respect and love one another
> Please don't leave us now
> We want no other!
> Some people
> Don't want you as a teacher
> Their (*sic*) jealous of how
> God could make such
> a wonderful creature.
> You listen to us
> As none have before
> You help us out

To the very last core.
Razors pain you
Rivers are damp
Acids stain you
And drugs cause cramp
Guns aren't lawful
Nooses give
Gas smells awful
So you might as well live
We still haven't given up
Have you?

"Please read this carefully and don't leave us," Perales implored, "because there are more coming after us who may need you more than us! Does a flock of hair mean more to you than we do? Sincerely, Esmerelda Perales, '75."[1]

Perales's comment about a "flock of hair" was a reference to her beloved teacher having gotten into trouble with school administrators over his hair allegedly being too long. But having long hair was the least of Woodward's concerns.

During the spring semester of 1975, Wayne Woodward was unceremoniously fired from his teaching job. Woodward sued the school district, believing that a cabal of school administrators and community leaders in Hereford had targeted and purposefully purged him. As will be seen in this book, the ensuing drama surrounding Woodward's court case provides the perfect opportunity to explore the deep social, cultural, and political divides of the Texas Panhandle during the 1970s. Problems began immediately when Woodward started a local chapter of the American Civil Liberties Union (ACLU) in January of 1975. Hereford in those days was a majority-minority town; many of Woodward's students were Mexican and Mexican American children whose parents picked vegetables for the town's multimillion-dollar agribusiness considerations. The arrival of Woodward's ACLU chapter thus augured a social reordering—perhaps even a reckoning, of sorts—for Hereford's elite. Such a day had by then already come to other Texas towns, like Crystal City, the so-called Spinach Capital of the World, in South Texas, or in Mission, "The Home of the Grapefruit," in Texas's Lower Rio Grande Valley, both of whose power structures were challenged by labor and civil rights activists. The difference, though, was that Hereford had one particular persona non grata who embodied, on a singular level, this deep social threat. Woodward was, for the people of Hereford, a stand-in for liberal political radicalism. In reality, though, Woodward wasn't a radical at all. His court case provides further evidence of the growing "rural-urban," "local-national" divide that fractured U.S. political culture during the 1970s. American political culture has never been the same since.[2]

This book is a case study of those warring cultures in the mid-1970s United States, but instead of being set on a college campus or in the suburbs, Woodward's story is set in a small town on the rural southern plains. Social change was everywhere in the United States during those days. People everywhere had taken notice when African Americans began forging new ground in their struggle for racial equality in the years following World War II. Mexican Americans, Asian Americans, Native Americans, women, members of what is now termed the LGBTQIA community, as well as a host of other groups likewise became reinvigorated in their own quests for greater equality during the 1960s and '70s. The United States entered a new era of multiplicity and diversity—a rocky one fraught with difficulty, but one that has led to greater acceptance for many. Such a decidedly "liberal" turn in U.S. culture and politics influenced widespread reactions in pockets of the country that have received less scrutiny from historians. Many Americans in the rural United States watched with shock as an older version of America that they thought they knew seemed to come crashing down around them.[3] Many historians would argue that rural Americans' politics consisted largely of a seemingly reactionary form of protest against the destruction of older ideas. When grounding the 1960s and '70s culture wars in rural America, however—as opposed to the more common settings of bigger cities and college campuses—underappreciated elements in the history of modern conservatism come to light, as I argue in this book.

Conservative Historiography

Conservative social and political outlooks have enjoyed a renewed interest from scholars during the last several decades to the point that the historical literature has become quite robust. Recent studies of U.S. conservatism have taken more of a long-term view as opposed to understanding conservatism as principally a reactionary set of phenomena against larger changes in 1960s and '70s U.S. culture. "Recognizing the longevity of the movement," notes the historian Kim Phillips-Fein, "cuts against the idea of a sudden backlash."[4] Modern conservatism's origins in fact predate World War II, but conservatism gained political momentum after the war due in part to developments in the suburban Sunbelt, where much of the Cold War defense industry developed. The movement coalesced around ideas of anticommunism, free trade, opposition to civil rights, and traditional gender norms. Historians, though, have tended to overlook the conservative working classes in places like the U.S. South, the Midwest, or the southern plains.[5]

Phillips-Fein notes other shortcomings in conservative historiography. "Populist opposition to liberalism in the 1930s," she notes, "may have received less attention than it warrants in the recent wave of histories of the Right." Similarly, Phillips-Fein also contends that antigovernment conservatives likely had more political power during the New Deal era as well as the post–World War II era than previous historians have considered. Taking this general assessment of the field as a point of departure, Texas Panhandle conservatism thus appears less reactionary than previous historians have conceded, although it clearly was *at least* somewhat reactionary to the winds of post–World War II national politics. The entire postwar period, according to Phillips-Fein, could be recast as "more an era characterized as contest and struggle [between liberals and conservatives] all along." Conservatism's roots, she concludes, are much deeper than a simple backlash against liberalism during the post–World War II era. "The challenge for scholars of conservatism today," she writes, "is to see conservatism with a new perspective—to understand its tenacity through the liberal years, its longstanding relationship to state and economic elites, and how its history is intertwined with that of liberalism."[6]

One setting that is ripe for the study of an emerging post–World War II conservatism is the Texas Panhandle, the relatively spread-out northwestern-most portion of the state that is dotted with small towns and one mid-sized city (Amarillo). Two physiographic regions, the High Plains (or "Llano Estacado," which translates from Spanish into "Staked Plains") and the Rolling Plains, collide in the Texas Panhandle, both spilling over into the adjacent states of New Mexico and Oklahoma. The High Plains account for the western two-thirds of the region, marked by their flatness and relative aridity and known for the Ogallala Aquifer, a major source of water that lies underground. The Red Rolling Plains stretch along the banks of the Canadian River, moving through the eastern third of the region.[7] The writer Stephen Harrigan notes that the "overwhelming flatness of the land creates a top-of-the-world sensation" when driving through the High Plains, but that this gives way in the Rolling Plains to a "beautiful broken down country where the Canadian River and its tributaries have sluiced deep below the limestone caprock into red Permian clay."[8] Indeed, the natural beauty of the Panhandle's landscape is difficult to explain to those who have not experienced the region firsthand.

Woodward's story from the isolated small town of Hereford, located on the High Plains and in the western portion of the Texas Panhandle—defined here as the northern twenty-six counties in Texas, bordering Oklahoma to the east and the north, New Mexico to the west, and stopping at the southern lines of the Texas counties of Childress, Hall, Swisher, Castro, and Parmer to the south—fills a gap in the literature on U.S. conservatism. I argue that Hereford's conservative political culture was *both* deeply anchored in Hereford and the Texas Panhandle's longer histories as well as reactionary against New Deal liberalism and especially the post–World War II racial liberalism of the Democratic Party.[9] Evidence for this argument will be laid out in the coming chapters. First, Woodward's firing happened specifically because small-town conservatives during the 1960s and '70s found themselves at odds with the postwar racial and cultural liberalism that had become popular with so many young people of Woodward's age. Effectively, in their view, liberalism had previously been kept out of their towns. Second, examining the warring conservative and liberal camps in rural America offers a revealing glimpse at why so many people in small towns like Hereford allied themselves with the then emerging conservative worldview as opposed to a liberal one. What emerges in the mid-1970s as a grassroots opposition to postwar liberalism is, as I demonstrate in this book, grounded in the longer histories of Hereford and the larger Texas Panhandle. Nonetheless, it took the postwar era's jarring changes for people to coalesce into a conservative political culture at the local level. Hereford's political culture did not come together solely to oppose the nationally ascendant liberalism of the postwar era; in the longer view, as I will show, it rested on a political culture tied directly into the region's settlement by English-speaking Americans.

Conservative historiography generally overlooks people in the Texas Panhandle and on the southern plains, who rather than being victims of larger forces took an active interest over time in asserting themselves against the larger trends that they saw were then shaping the country.[10] "Conservatism," to the people of Hereford during the mid-1970s, meant protecting their town's culture and traditions from what they believed were actual threats to their own well-being that postwar liberalism could bring locally. When liberals and conservatives faced off in mid-'70s rural America, the cultural guardians of the small town would stop at nothing to win, even if it meant disregarding the constitutional rights of someone who otherwise might fit in—a straight, white, gainfully employed American male.

The Culture Wars and the Texas Panhandle

Wayne Woodward was an unwitting cultural warrior. Although Hereford's brand of conservatism dates to the turn of the twentieth century, leftover turbulence from the 1960s amplified developments that might have gone unnoticed just two decades previously. As I show in chapter 1 of this book, a conservative politics emerged in the Texas Panhandle at the level of local and regional culture as well as at the ballot box long before the countercultural era of the 1960s. Larger national developments during the 1960s and '70s, though, clearly helped rural conservatism mature into a political movement. As the historians Kevin M. Kruse and Julian Zelizer note, the United States "reconstituted itself in the 1970s and the decades that followed in ways that augmented and institutionalized" certain divisions that had begun developing during the previous decade. Arguably, Hereford's long-standing political homogeneity became more outwardly aggressive only during the 1970s specifically because this same fragmentation had become institutionalized across the country. Ultimately, by 1975, liberalism among the larger, isolated society in the Texas Panhandle could now only be tolerated up to a certain point—that of bringing the hated ACLU into town.[11]

Hereford's publicly aggressive rejection of Wayne Woodward and the ACLU fit neatly within the larger emerging conservative movement. According to the prominent 1970s conservative Paul Weyrich, "it's a war of ideas . . . about our way of life. And it has to be fought with the same intensity, I think, and dedication as you would fight a shooting war." These words rang true for countless Americans in small towns like Hereford in the wake of the turbulent 1960s.[12] As the historian Andrew Hartman notes, the 1960s universalized fracture in the United States, meaning that for the first time in U.S. history, "whether one thought the nation was in moral decline was often correlative of whether one was liberal or conservative."[13] What was at stake for the multiplicity of voices during the postwar era was the very meaning of what it meant to be an American. For many people living in rural areas in the so-called flyover states, the dominant message from the urban and coastal metropoles was one of fixed judgment: it was *their* farming practices that had caused the Dust Bowl of the 1930s, it was *their* inability to govern themselves properly that necessitated intervention by the federal government, and it was *their* Anglo-American monolithic society that was out of touch with the diversity of the emerging modern American multiethnic society of the 1960s and '70s. For people in rural communities like those in the Panhandle, the modern political fracturing between conservatives and liberals rested fundamentally on the politics of, quite simply, what it meant to be an American in a globalizing and rapidly changing world. When placing the 1960s and '70s culture wars—between liberals who sought widespread social change in the realms of racial and gender equality on the one hand, and conservatives who sought to maintain a sense of the status quo on the other—within the context of the Texas Panhandle, we see the rise of conservatism as less a movement about partisan politics, tax cutting, or evangelical revivalism, and more about defining and protecting certain tenets of Americanism expressed in local identity. According to one historian, Texas's "Radical Right have what is more an attitude than a coherent conservative ideology, and they are often at odds with conservatives outside of the state."[14] Actual policy mattered little; for Panhandle Texans, conservative politics were more about maintaining a society, or at least a sense of a version of an American society that many felt had come under threat from outside forces.[15]

Few historians have studied conservatism on the southern plains or in the Texas Panhandle. Primary among them is the historian Jeff Roche, who traces the emergence of Panhandle conservatism as being contemporaneous to the rise of political and cultural liberalism during the middle decades of the twentieth century: "Between 1933 and 1972, Panhandle voters learned to express a set of longstanding, if not actively defended, political beliefs. Usually responding to national policy debates, Panhandle conservatives came to their ideology in stages. In the process, they moved from locally oriented Democrats most concerned with their community's economic survival to nationally oriented Republicans seeking to inject their community values into a national political dialogue."[16] In this book, I build on Roche's work, which cuts off in the early 1970s, by arguing that conservative politics, upon their maturation in the region by the mid-1970s, gained expression most visibly through powerbrokers aggressively policing politics and culture at the local level to protect against perceived threats to what they considered proper social behaviors and worldviews. Such a tendency folded neatly into the longer practice in the history of the U.S. West of rural agricultural communities exercising an ethic of protecting their towns against the perceived threats of outsiders, misfits, and those who challenged local authority.

Conservatism and the Western Frontier

This book also highlights the ways in which self-ascribed notions of frontier isolationism shaped how locals reacted to post–World War II liberalism, particularly in 1975 during Wayne Woodward's court case after the political coalescence of conservatism. Even a cursory glance at Panhandle Texans' popular senses of historical memory during the middle of the twentieth century displays the premium that locals placed on notions of frontier individualism. For example, the Panhandle-Plains Historical Society (PPHS), founded in nearby Canyon, Texas, in 1921, made explicit in its constitution its own aims at celebrating frontier identity. Recorded in the first article of its constitution is the following: "[The organization] shall endeavor to present to the coming generation the life of the old settler in such a way that it shall create in them the desire to uphold, forever, the honor of the country that their forefathers wrought out of the wilderness."[17] The PPHS made one of its top priorities during the 1920s to collect and record oral interviews with the then still living "pioneers" who had settled the region during the 1870s and 1880s. Some of this undoubtedly stemmed from the fact that newcomers were still pouring into the region then, as the number of farms in the Texas Panhandle rose by 70 percent during the 1920s. As such, an interest in the so-called pioneering generation that was expiring by the 1920s seemed almost natural.[18] One of the principal investigators and gatherers of these data was the field agent for the society, J. Evetts Haley. Perhaps not coincidentally, Haley would later become one of the architects of the region's independent conservative outlook during the 1950s and '60s, as discussed in chapter 1 of this book.

Even just a cursory glance at the institution—as well as its museum, the Panhandle-Plains Historical Museum (PPHM), which opened in Canyon a few miles east of Hereford in 1933—shows the premium that locals placed on frontier identity. The so-called old-timers contributed nearly $30,000 for the construction of the original building; later Panhandle residents celebrated the fact that "from the depths of the depression . . . Plains pioneers made real sacrifices to match the state's $25,000 appropriation for" the museum.[19] Even as late as 1949, when modern conservatism had just begun to accelerate as a political movement throughout the region, a local editorialist, with regard to a building expansion plan for the museum, cheered that "men who draw a heritage of strength from the rugged culture of pioneers see near fruition of their dreams."[20]

Such efforts at maintaining the region's so-called pioneering past were at the forefront of historical memorialization in West Texas. The PPHM was just the second public museum in the state (the first being the Witte Museum in San Antonio, which opened in 1926). One local writer editorialized in 1940 that the PPHM was at the cutting edge of "Texans [having] begun to be more conscious of the importance of their historical and cultural heritage. This development follows one hundred years of neglect of Texas history and artifacts." The same writer further remarked that regional settlers played a significant role in the museum's founding, noting that "old-timers approaching their last horizons have been foremost in the effort to preserve evidences of the early lives and traditions of plains settlers." The 1936 Texas Centennial further "made Texans history-conscious."[21] By the dawn of the World War II era, then, the intellectual building blocks of public identity consciousness were firmly in place in the Texas Panhandle.

At the heart of this book is the argument that a sense of regional exceptionalism was nurtured in the Texas Panhandle—often referred to as the "last frontier" by regional boosters—because of the region's relative geographic isolation from the rest of the United States as well as locals' perceptions that the Texas Panhandle, more "western" than southern, was a place set apart. Indeed, the first chapter of this book will show how Anglo West Texans clung to a frontier individualism throughout the early part of the twentieth century that set it apart from the more "southern" attitudes of Texans in the central as well as eastern parts of the state. This exceptionalist nature of Panhandle political identity fostered a perception over time that the people of the region knew what was in their own best interests as opposed to outsiders, or even the U.S. government. As such, a sense of community guardianism in the Texas Panhandle became woven into the region's conservative social fabric, spilling out in Hereford in reaction to the coming of the dreaded ACLU to town in 1975.[22]

A sense of isolation—whether or not the Texas Panhandle or the surrounding southern plains were *actually* isolated—is an important factor in determining how the culture wars functioned in Hereford. This, perhaps, adds a layer to understanding the modern political phenomenon of people in so-called flyover states perceiving a sense of condescension from the so-called coastal elites. This viewpoint spread outward from the Panhandle, eventually forming part of the backbone of the modern conservative movement at the national level.[23]

The Southern Plains and the Sunbelt

The distinctive quality of conservative politics in Wayne Woodward's Hereford and in the Texas Panhandle—part of a larger area of the United States stretching from Florida to California known as "The Sunbelt" that boomed during the postwar era and helped birth modern conservatism—displays the region's unique contributions to the emerging national conservatism of the 1960s and '70s. The historians Michelle Nickerson and Darren Dochuk note that early postwar conservatives "spoke for one Sunbelt only." In fact, a large element of the U.S.

Southwest leaned to the political left. Issues such as "corporate accountability, responsible urbanism, environmental concern, and multicultural exchange" reigned supreme for Sunbelt liberals during the middle of the twentieth century. The key difference, of course, with their conservative counterparts was that Sunbelt liberals sought *more* government in order to accomplish their ends as opposed to less government. Nonetheless, these two camps shared two elements in common, both of which stemmed from a highly acute sense of place: a totality, an "all-or-nothing" quality to each side's political discourse, and a sense that the Sunbelt would set the political agenda for the United States as a whole.[24]

Historians of conservatism demonstrate that the Sunbelt's generally right-leaning politics set the agenda for the modern national conservative movement. Recent research has shown that the emerging conservative consensus consisted of a combination of anti–civil rights politics and suburbanization mixed with an anticommunist outlook that merged conservative-minded individuals across the Deep South and the Southwest.[25] The historian Joseph Crespino notes these larger connections in demonstrating the appeal of the Dixiecrat conservative Strom Thurmond—often known solely for his segregationist and anti-Black views—to anticommunist conservatives in Southern California during the early 1960s.[26] Such political appeal of course predated the rise of better-known conservative Sunbelt politicians, such as Arizona's Barry Goldwater, who is credited with bringing conservatives' agenda to the national level by securing the 1964 Republican presidential nomination (the Texas Panhandle contained the only congressional district in the state that supported Goldwater over the incumbent Lyndon Baines Johnson that year); or Ronald Reagan, who shot to political fame as California's Republican governor during the 1960s.[27]

The Texas Panhandle served as a political borderlands of sorts between the U.S. South and the U.S. Southwest, where the different strands of right-leaning political cultures became fused during the 1960s and '70s. Dochuk argues that the tumult of the Great Depression years and the Dust Bowl that racked the Great Plains, which sent thousands of the "Okies" to California in search of work, helped spread the "southern plain-folk" evangelism and deeply conservative political ideas like anticommunism common among the Texas Panhandle and the surrounding areas to the West Coast, thus reorienting Southern California conservatism toward the U.S. South. In doing so, evangelical Protestantism moved from the margins to the center of Southern California suburban society.[28] One of the arguments I make in this book is that the deep sense of protecting what Dochuk calls the "plain-folk values" of rural America is a distinct contribution that people in Hereford as well as other isolated rural communities made to the emerging conservative movement, given their location at the "sending-end" of the Great Depression's migratory frontier. Conservatives in Hereford and, for example, Orange County in Southern California certainly held much in common politically by the 1960s and '70s, but their experiences of the nation's culture wars differed markedly due to the differences in local circumstances between suburban coastal spaces and isolated agricultural areas in the middle of the country.

Hereford's relative geographic isolation meant that its experience of politics and culture during the tumultuous middle of the twentieth century played out differently than elsewhere, even in places where political outlooks leaned overwhelmingly to the right. One difference was in the gendered nature of its politics. The aggressive response against the ACLU's presence in the town in 1975—a major issue in Wayne Woodward's court case analyzed later in this book—came almost entirely from male actors who sought to shape politics and belonging at the local level. Such a development showed how Hereford's conservatism differed in kind from its intellectual cousin in Southern California. Nickerson, for example, writes of a "housewife populism" spanning the left and the right that shaped U.S. politics beginning in the early twentieth century. Conservative women played a crucial role, Nickerson demonstrates, in launching Southern California's well-documented contributions to conservatism's rise.[29] With Woodward's case, as will be shown, we see a more aggressive, confrontational, and mostly gendered-male response to a perceived threat to local society.[30]

The Importance of the Rural United States

Hereford thus stands as a unique case study in terms of what happened when the culture wars arrived in rural America. Ultimately, the middle of the twentieth century brought out a confrontational political culture previously unseen in the town's history. The story that follows is about how one man attempted to challenge the hegemony of the conservative, frontier-minded culture that had coalesced in Hereford by the middle of the 1970s. Ultimately, Woodward's court case shows that the divide between liberals and conservatives in the modern United States stemmed from rural conservatives' perceptions that there was not one America, but in fact, two. To the people in this book, the changes that took place in the United States during the middle of the twentieth century showed them that the rest of the country had transformed into something fundamentally dangerous, foreign, and to them, "un-American."

A word on historians' relationships with rural America is appropriate here. Implicit biases that urban elites held against rural America ran rampant in early to mid-twentieth-century historical scholarship. One need look no further than the work of the highly regarded historian Richard Hofstadter, whose characterization of late-nineteenth-century southern and western Populists as backward-thinking people evidences a certain lack of intellectual seriousness in understanding rural Americans on their own terms. Hofstadter's position has since been thoroughly debunked by other historians. Still, other aspects of rural history—namely, the development of the predominant conservative political discourse—remain poorly understood.[31] The relative lack of attention given to conservative identities and politics as well as mid-twentieth-century cultural conflict in rural America has contributed to a skewed understanding of the aforementioned phenomena as being the province of urban or suburban America. When shifting our gaze to the heartland, we begin to see some of the earliest political fracturing between liberals and conservatives in the modern United States as it happened on the ground. These deep fissures in modern American politics cannot be properly understood if historians fail to take rural America seriously. This book seeks to correct that imbalance, if in its own small way.

Finally, a longer history of rural America is worth noting. Perhaps naturally, the United States remained a locally oriented society through the time of the U.S. Civil War. Americans had reason to maintain the primacy of local community and politics; the United States was, geographically, a large country with a variety of local communities that remained, to borrow the historian Robert Wiebe's phrase, a nation of "island communities" that were largely disconnected from one another until the time of the railroad's expansion during the latter half of the nineteenth century.[32] From the end of the Reconstruction era to the outbreak of the Great War in 1914, the United States emerged as a world power, largely through wars of conquest and overseas expansion that took the nation to such far-flung places as Hawaii, Cuba, and the Philippines. Many Americans, then, had little reason to concern themselves with the goings-on of the United States overseas at least until the Spanish-American War of 1898. Such was the case in large urban spaces in the Northeast, cities devoted to manufacturing in the U.S. Midwest, emerging cities in the post–Civil War "New South," and all the small towns and hamlets in between.

The U.S. West and South—the bastions of "states' rights" and the championing of local government—have long been areas dominated by agriculture. Such was certainly the case in mid-twentieth-century Hereford. Locals looked askance at ideas that were at odds with the general sentiment of the community. Wayne Woodward's court case thus offers a compelling microhistory of events in the longue durée history of the political economies of rural communities in the United States. Questions of democracy and belonging, part of the fabric of modern conservatism, have plagued such communities for centuries.

Structure of the Book

The first two chapters of this book lay out the historical context for understanding Wayne Woodward's court case. In chapter 1, "Defining Conservatism in the Texas Panhandle," I trace the origins of twentieth-century Panhandle political identity to turn-of-the-century notions of American exceptionalism, arguing that a commonly held sense of isolation on the American frontier drove an ethic in regional identity that favored local governance and regionalism over participation in larger national politics. In chapter 2, "Coming of Age in the Texas Panhandle," I examine how the national civil rights movement cleaved Panhandle Texans into competing camps. Civil rights sympathizers found themselves vastly outnumbered by people who considered the movement a threatening menace to local society. Consequently, most Panhandle Texans' political outlooks became more outwardly aggressive to protect Panhandle communities against the seemingly dangerous threat of state-sponsored racial equality.

In the remainder of the book, I utilize Wayne Woodward's court case to understand the emerging conservative-liberal divide during the 1970s in Hereford, placing the so-called culture wars in the relatively unexplored setting of small-town America. In chapter 3, I examine Wayne Woodward's career as a teacher in Hereford, and in the following chapter, I detail in microcosm how a civil rights court case could be built in an area that was unfriendly to claims of civil rights violations. In chapter 5, I analyze the importance of Mexican and Mexican American migrant labor to Hereford's economy, suggesting that Woodward's sympathy for migrant workers threatened the town's actual material well-being, thus further painting him as an outsider in the minds of the public. Finally, in chapters 6 and 7, I examine Woodward's courtroom trial, revealing the implications that his case has for understanding the aggressive conservatism that emerged in the region and came to dominate a large wing of Republican Party politics into the twenty-first century.

Wayne Woodward's story is thus bigger than a story of civil rights or civil liberties, however historically significant such topics may be. Woodward's story hearkens all the way back to the politics of democracy, government, and free thought in rural communities that have been present throughout centuries of U.S. history. Both Woodward and his detractors sought to work out the meaning of community, democracy, and individual rights at the local level. Neither side was the first to grapple with such thorny issues, nor would they be the last. Nonetheless, it was the occurrence of this clash between two emerging modern U.S. political spheres that ultimately makes Woodward's case so important. The fracturing of America into "liberal" and "conservative" camps in the modern era continues to produce dislocations similar to what Woodward experienced in 1975, thus making his case a fundamentally American story about the politics of identity and belonging. As Americans continue to face choices between bitterly divided and warring political camps during the twenty-first century, we should not forget that such disputes are the wellspring of modern U.S. political culture—they cannot be avoided or washed away. Wayne Woodward's court case teaches us about the historical origins of our bipartisan wars during the twenty-first century regarding nationhood and belonging in modern America. First, however, we must understand both the stage and the context in which Woodward's experiences of the culture wars and the resulting court case occurred.

It is to that story that we now turn.

CHAPTER 1

DEFINING CONSERVATISM IN THE TEXAS PANHANDLE

Deep ties to the land were an important part of regional identity for many people in the twentieth-century Texas Panhandle. Because of this connection, the larger world of Wayne Woodward's 1975 drama must be appreciated on its own terms. A specific sense of isolation on the Panhandle frontier drove an ethic in regional identity that favored local governance and regional exceptionalism over participation in larger state or national politics. Panhandle conservatism has deep roots in early-twentieth-century history; indeed, the Thirteenth, Eighteenth, and Nineteenth Congressional Districts, all of which encompassed certain parts of the region over time, have long sent reliably conservative representatives to Washington, D.C., especially from the middle of the twentieth century to the present.[1]

In this chapter, I argue that a slow-moving conservatism dedicated to maintaining the Texas Panhandle's social order, which developed in relative isolation to the rest of the country, began taking shape over roughly the first half of the twentieth century. As I show in chapter 2, this conservative social and political order reacted with a newfound outward aggression to the civil rights movement during the 1960s and '70s, which provides the immediate context in which the controversy surrounding Wayne Woodward's court case occurred. Given the slowly developing conservative culture of Hereford and the surrounding areas over the course of the twentieth century, it is necessary to spend a significant amount of time analyzing Hereford and the Texas Panhandle to establish precisely why Wayne Woodward became persona non grata in Hereford during the 1970s. Woodward's particular story will be analyzed in detail from chapter 3 through the end of the book.

Historical Roots in the Texas Panhandle

The Spanish explorer Francisco Vázquez de Coronado preceded Anglo-Americans into the southern plains by over three hundred years, crossing what became the

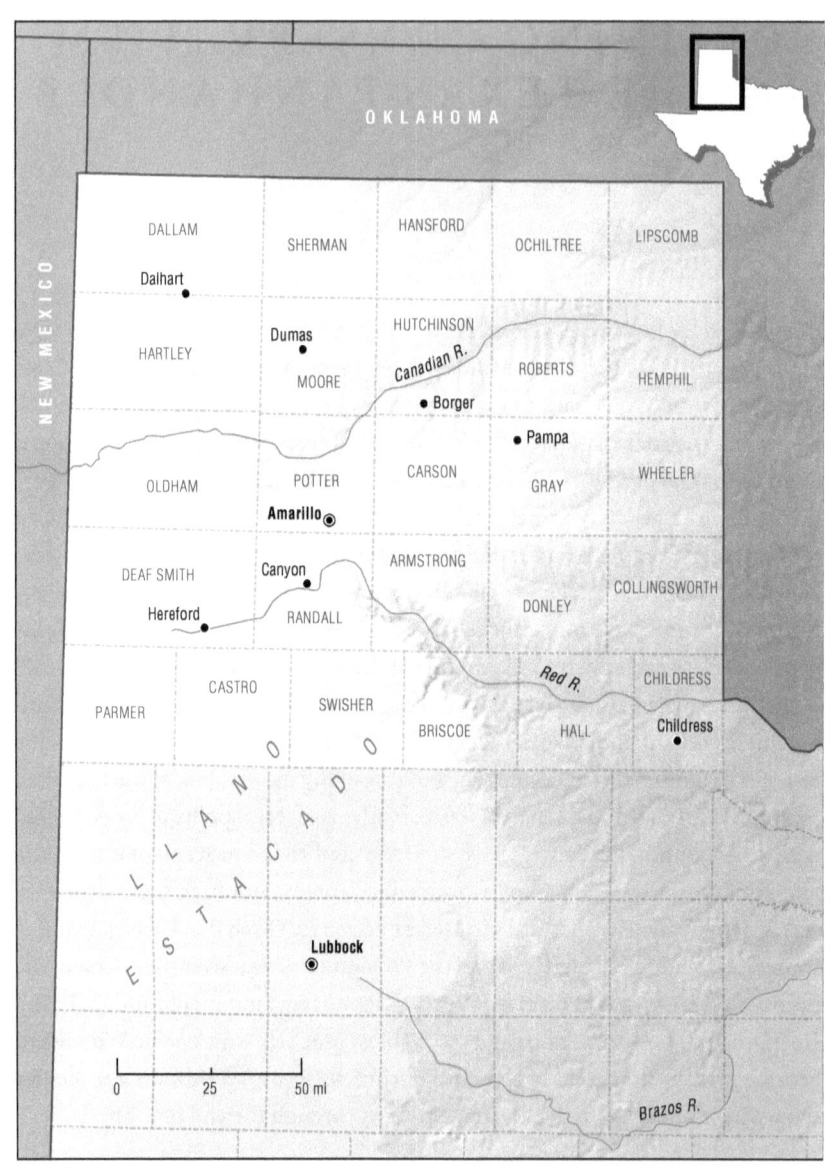

The Texas Panhandle and surrounding regions. Map by Erin Greb.

Texas Panhandle from the west and likely even the Hereford region in his illfated quest to capture the mythical city of Cíbola for the Spaniards (or, as recent research has shown and perhaps more realistically, to capture Indian slaves). In so doing, the conquistador noted the general poverty of the region's native inhabitants, who by then had lived on the southern plains for millennia.[2] What this meant for the region that became the Texas Panhandle was that its status as a frontier backwater in the viceroyalty of New Spain was all but assured for the next several centuries. Most of the northern stretches of New Spain were of limited concern to the Spanish Crown until the late eighteenth century.

Spaniards thus had no real reason to stray north onto the Plains, largely avoiding Texas as a whole until fears of French incursion led to some interest in settling the frontier. One need look no further than a map of settlements in Spanish Texas to get the impression that Spaniards not only generally avoided the southern plains but clearly did so on purpose. This behavior can be explained by citing one simple phenomenon: the growing power of what one historian has referred to as the "Comanche Empire," which emanated outwardly from the heartland of the region that Spaniards referred to as the Comanchería, a vast stretch of territory that includes the areas of modern-day Amarillo, Canyon, Palo Duro Canyon, and, of course, Hereford. Although the origins of the Comanche Empire are diverse, the establishment of a process of "colonialism-in-reverse" contributed to the region's domination by Comanches as well as their Plains Indians allies as early as 1750. Only after the U.S. conquest of Texas as well as the rest of the northern borderlands from a now independent Mexico in 1848 could any federal government conceivably focus on eliminating the "horse lords of the Southwest." Things indeed changed once the U.S. military commenced the Red River War against the Comanches and their Plains Indian allies in 1874.[3] Finally nearly fully pacified by 1875, most of the Comanches living in the Panhandle relocated to live on reservations in Oklahoma. The Red River War thus marked a clear turning point in regional history.

Things would change rapidly in the Texas Panhandle from the mid-1870s forward. Clearly, the U.S. Army had done the job of "opening" the Texas Panhandle to colonization by its defeat of the Comanches and their Plains Indian allies. Arguably, the first American rancher in the area was the famous Charles Goodnight, who left his Colorado ranch with a large herd of cattle, eventually settling about fifty miles east of Hereford in Palo Duro Canyon in 1876. Next was Thomas Sherman Bugbee, who planted a ranch along the Canadian River in the northwestern part of the Panhandle. British capital financed a number of these early endeavors, including Goodnight's own JA Ranch, funded through his partnership with the British financier John Adair.[4]

The rest of the ranches that became established in the region during the years following the Red River War were mostly large enterprises; railroad companies, foreign investors, and ranchers with large capital—such as W. M. D. Lee of the LX Ranch, Goodnight and Adair of the JA Ranch, and the Chicagoan Farwell family of the XIT Ranch—were themselves the corporate pioneers around which local communities like Amarillo, Canyon, and Hereford grew up during the early twentieth century.[5] As a result, settling the Panhandle involved as much corporatism and capital as did the explosion of manufacturing companies and related business industries in large cities back on the East Coast during the so-called Gilded Age of U.S. history.[6] Even still, the actual lives of many of the people who lived on these early ranches and farms tell a much different story.

The Frontier Roots of Panhandle Identity

Precisely at the time when large ranchers became prominent, the myth of the lone frontiersman became popular at the local level, not just because land agents promoted it but also because the new Panhandle colonists consciously abandoned easier lives back east for opportunities in this newer, more isolated space. At the turn of the twentieth century, railroad agents, ranchers, land salesmen, farmers, and merchants promoted the Texas Panhandle through booster literature, emphasizing individual self-reliance and frontier living as something the region had to offer. The XIT ranching syndicate, long past its economic prime by the early twentieth century, turned to real estate, selling off portions of its massive holdings to small farmers. Regional elites even went as far as promoting the Panhandle as "the last frontier" in national advertisements, utilizing the lure of western imagery to attract more colonists. Undoubtedly, the process of colonizing the region exposed many people to ideas about living on a modern frontier. The Texas Panhandle's population jumped from 21,274 in 1900, to 88,755 in 1910, to 114,527 in 1920.[7]

Religion also played a prominent role in the formation of regional identity. The scholar Robert Wuthnow has noted that while world religions have helped construct a multitude of outlooks and cultures, religious experience itself is fundamentally tied to place. The rural and isolated nature of the Texas Panhandle further oriented people to an "insider-outsider" ethic that would make anyone failing to identify with some form of Protestantism—let alone someone who showed little inclination to religious belief at all—a social outsider. As will be seen in later chapters, this exact phenomenon happened to Wayne Woodward in Hereford in 1975.[8]

Notably, while evangelical Protestantism was an important part of life in the Panhandle, its political voice remained somewhat muted during this early period.[9] For many Texans, religious faith was part of the fruits of individual liberty in rural areas. Texas religious leaders had preached religious faith as an expression of liberty of conscience since at least the 1920s, which, according to the historian Joseph Locke, was the decade in which the so-called Bible Belt and the politics of evangelical morality became firmly constructed by Texas conservatives and ministers.[10] The emerging conservative dialogue of the Texas Panhandle after the 1920s co-opted Protestantism into the dominant regional identity. Any public snubbing of religion, then, appeared equally to be a rejection of the emerging community itself as it was a matter of eternal spiritual damnation.

What such evidence indicates is that the roots of conservatism in the Texas Panhandle ran deeper than the typical points that many historians have recognized as the rise of "oppositional" conservative politics in the United States, namely, as responses to New Deal liberalism or more prominently the widespread cultural liberalism of the civil rights era. As such, Panhandle conservatism merely came of age as an oppositional political culture during the 1960s and '70s. Pushing its roots back to the early part of the twentieth century reveals the fundamentally ideological nature of conservatism in the region, one that would find fertile ground for widespread community coalescence during the ideologically charged times of the civil rights era.

Other evidence suggests that the particular brand of conservatism in the Panhandle is directly tied to frontier settlement. The cultural geographer Wilbur Zelinsky argues with his "doctrine of first effective settlement" that a nation or region's dominant general culture is defined by the first actual settlers who come into an area. The social, political, and cultural histories of the Texas Panhandle clearly show the predominant influence of the original ranching and, perhaps even more so, the early twentieth-century farming settlers on the development of local society over the course of the next century. In fact, the anthropologist Benjamin Lee Gorman notes five "cluster values" that became common in the Texas Panhandle, due in large part to the overwhelming percentage of its population that immigrated to the region almost entirely from East Texas, Appalachia, and the U.S. South. Those values include Protestant fundamentalism, a puritanical belief in social decorum, a sense of rugged frontier individualism, an entrepreneurial spirit, and a conservative politics that maintained an economic and political status quo. This culture only became further reinforced when the first perceived threats to the Panhandle's social culture arrived in the form of the civil rights movement and the national liberalism of the mid-twentieth century.[11]

The New Deal Threat and the Texas Panhandle

Fears of large government predated the arrival of Franklin Delano Roosevelt's New Deal during the Great Depression. Texas preachers commonly railed against socialism to their congregations as early as the first two decades of the twentieth century, arguing that it was dangerous because of its inherent materialism as well as its implications in favor of atheism. Some even couched fears of socialism in gendered terms. According to one preacher, socialism would unleash women's latent desires to dominate men. Socialist women would insist on becoming "boss of the whole goose nest."[12]

Still, voting statistics from the early twentieth century indicate that conservative tendencies in the Panhandle only rarely gained expression at the ballot box. While it is true that more than half of Panhandle Texans supported the Republican Herbert Hoover in the 1928 presidential election, this was likely a simple nativist repudiation of the Catholic faith of Hoover's 1928 Democratic opponent, Al Smith. In the 1932 election, the Democrat Franklin Delano Roosevelt won 37,503 votes in the twenty-six counties of the Texas Panhandle, carrying a whopping 87.9 percent of the vote, compared to Hoover's dismal 12 percent showing. Roosevelt's popularity carried through in the Panhandle to his reelection in 1936, when he won 89.8 percent of the Panhandle's vote compared to his Republican challenger Alf Landon's 10.1 percent. Roosevelt's popularity dipped only slightly in 1940, when he won 42,512 votes in the Panhandle, which constituted 80.2 percent of the vote, compared to his Republican challenger Wendell Willkie, who tallied 10,456 votes, or 19.7 percent of the region's electorate. Clearly, Panhandle Texans gave their overwhelming assent to New Deal policies at the ballot box during the Great Depression despite their politically latent conservative tendencies.[13] In other words, liberal Democrats were popular in the Texas Panhandle during a time of deep economic and ecological hardship.

Many ranchers, farmers, and businessmen from the Panhandle who stood to benefit from the New Deal had difficulties unifying practical policy with political ideology. A group known as the Jeffersonian Democrats feared the expansion of federal power that the New Deal seemed to represent and attempted to unseat FDR in the 1936 presidential election, just four years after he won a massive statewide majority in 1932. Despite this attempted mutiny from within the Texas Democratic Party's ranks, the president nonetheless won an easy electoral victory, defeating his Republican challenger, Alf Landon, by a 7–1 margin throughout the state. Still, grassroots efforts by Texas conservatives to oppose FDR laid the groundwork for the future social mobilization that would shake state and national politics and for conservatives' eventual abandonment of the Democratic Party in favor of the Republicans. Texas conservatives would see the benefits of such groundwork quite a bit sooner than conservatives in national politics; this came with the election of a man whom some consider to be the first prominent conservative Texas governor—W. Lee "Pappy" O'Daniel, a Democrat whom voters elected in 1938.[14]

Although a number of different phenomena ultimately fed into the burgeoning conservative identity of the mid-twentieth-century Panhandle, the growth of federal power under FDR during the Great Depression represented the first major challenge to preexisting notions of community self-reliance. For many, neighborliness was of more immediate assistance during hard times than government aid. Some soup kitchens in the region were sensitive to locals' sense of pride and independence in receiving handouts, so many of them provided meals "to go" or even on credit so individuals could avoid any potential social stigma attached to receiving charity. The only requirement to receive help in many circumstances was proof that one was a "bona fide" citizen, although how one approved such bona fides remains unclear.[15]

Despite such hardships, part of what nurtured a sense of regional exceptionalism in the Panhandle during the 1930s was its relative economic prosperity when compared to the rest of the state. For example, the Panhandle led the state in rail shipments of livestock in 1932, with $8,164,198 total, including cattle ($5,741,295), calves ($1,099,161), hogs ($873,117), and sheep ($450,626) to make up 23.3 percent of the state's total. Such relative economic health justified a sense of regional exceptionalism, further highlighting for many the Panhandle's seeming isolation from the rest of the state, region, and country.[16]

Some of the local pushback against the New Deal was fundamentally ideological. Joseph A. Hill, the president of West Texas State College in Canyon, Texas, later wrote that the Depression "precipitated a political tornado that swept away many traditional American concepts and swept in a whole flock of political and economic experiments that have vastly altered our national governmental system."[17] Other Panhandle Texans had more practical grievances against the Roosevelt administration. Chief among these came from the head of the statewide

Jeffersonian Democrats, the conservative Texas historian J. Evetts Haley, who was based out of Canyon, Texas, near Hereford. Haley—who would later be fondly remembered by some conservative West Texans as a "founding father of the Reagan Revolution"—published several essays during the Depression that contained measured and careful arguments against the New Deal.[18] First among these was an article called "Cow Business and Monkey Business," which appeared in the December 8, 1934, edition of the *Saturday Evening Post*. Haley began his attack on the New Deal by proudly situating West Texans—and by implication, really, any cattle-raising Texan—as being left in the dust while "the world has advanced . . . [meaning] that the homely virtues that we cherished are but outworn dogmas of a selfish age."[19] Haley's own ranch was large, lying in the southwestern portion of the state near the Pecos River and consisting of over 24,000 acres. Haley bemoaned that his family's ranch fare was "meager," and that they, as well as their employees, struggled for the necessities of life while people on government relief allegedly lived better. Government subsidies for cattle ranchers when the stock market crashed in 1929 led to depressed prices; now, after the general Depression had hit, a government statistician noted that there were in excess of seven million too many head of cattle—which Haley, as well as others, had held on to in the hope that prices would someday rebound. Problematically, the Agricultural Adjustment Act (AAA) of 1933 paid Texas farmers to harvest less of their cotton and corn crops, which, to Haley, not only devalued the dollar but made it nearly impossible for ranchmen to afford the necessary feed for their livestock. The ultimate solution was for the New Deal government to buy millions of head of cattle, large numbers of which were shot in the head by government agents and buried in mass graves. Fifty-three such head of cattle were killed on Haley's own ranch. This unforeseen development, to Haley, smacked of government wastefulness and cruelty.[20]

Still, despite these complaints, support for Roosevelt in the Panhandle remained strong.[21] New Deal programs did bring a great deal of relief to people in the region suffering from either the catastrophic Dust Bowl or the general economic downturn. Despite the fact that many people understood that these reforms were only temporary, some did bring lasting change. A number of farmers sought relief from the government using the justification that high tariffs had long protected the industrial sector, and thus, programs like the AAA could better be characterized, to them, as correcting a set of long-overdue imbalances as opposed to being government handouts. By 1936, Panhandle-area farmers had gotten over 20 million dollars in relief, which, however, did not come without any preconditions. For example, different laws dictated that certain amounts of acreage had to lie fallow, government agents instructed some farmers on how to "properly" till their land to avoid erosion, and farmers had to agree to government terms when renegotiating their mortgages. When World War II started and the Dust Bowl ended, many Panhandle farmers sought limitations on this continued federal domination. Panhandle farmers were grateful for the assistance they received and recognized that without it they would have lost everything. Nonetheless, the idea that the government would remain in the Panhandle long after farmers needed the help and would continue to manage local agriculture "smacked of socialism" to many. The political ideology that emerged from this would go on to form the basis of later Panhandle conservatism.[22]

Other resentments against the New Deal and national Democrats began bubbling up during the Depression. Some government representatives suggested that the economic disaster of the Dust Bowl had swept away portions of the Great Plains because individual farmers were bent on personal gain at any cost. Pare Lorentz's government-funded 1936 documentary *The Plow That Broke the Plains*, which chronicled the Dust Bowl's occurrence due to farmers overtilling the region's land and thus eroding the soils, implied that more ecologically sound farming practices could be put into place. Perhaps unsurprisingly, Panhandle farmers were openly critical of the film, labeling it government propaganda. Moreover, when the conditions that required such heavy government intervention ended, Panhandle Texans finally felt free to express their full frustration with the perceived intrusiveness of the New Deal.[23] Panhandle farmers had needed government subsidies to survive the Depression and drought of the 1930s. Once the rains came and the Depression ended, however, the continuance of New Deal programs seemed a direct affront to individualism and community sovereignty. In essence, the long-feared "big government" had arrived to stay in the region. An oppositional politics seemed necessary.[24]

Concerns over big government thus drove the burgeoning regional political culture during the 1930s to a greater degree than did any other social concerns, including race. One Depression-era challenge to the region's racial dynamics did show the looming threat that many Panhandle Texans saw as stemming from the federal government and its implied advocacy for racial tolerance. During the early part of the Depression, one of Roosevelt's most beloved New Deal programs, the Civilian Conservation Corps (CCC), came to the Panhandle to help construct accessibility to Palo Duro Canyon, an extensive natural canyon formation that Charles Goodnight had settled in during the 1870s. The CCC's main purpose was to give young men employment in building and preserving state parks and areas of natural distinction across the United States. Such an approach folded nicely into the Panhandle's political economy during the Great Depression, where people generally believed that the unemployed should work for a wage as opposed to subsisting on government handouts. In 1934, however, the CCC suddenly replaced a group of war veterans working in the canyon with a group of African American workers from East Texas. The local response was quick and nasty. Officials for the nearby city of Canyon placed a sign at the city limits that read, "Nigger, don't let the sun set on your head," warning African Americans to stay out of the town after sunset (this was in keeping with the notoriously racist construction of the so-called sundown towns that could be found throughout Texas). The presence of Black workers contested locals' notions of race and belonging, demonstrating that the federal government could, if it chose, completely remake the racial demographics of the area at will and without local consent.[25]

From the 1930s forward, local conservatives identified with a growing anti–New Deal, anti–Democratic Party backlash. Business interests across the state came together as the so-called Texas Regulars once again in an effort to defeat FDR during the 1944 election, further politicizing the Panhandle's emerging conservative culture. Meanwhile, Governor Pappy O'Daniel continued to tap into the growing sentiment against taxes and unions among the Texas right. Certain ideas that would later become popular among mainstream conservatives—such as a regressive or flat tax, or restrictions on unions' organizing efforts or their abilities to tap into political organizing—became a part of the emerging statewide conservative agenda.[26] Also, despite the dominance of the emerging liberalism of U.S. politics at the federal level, the cohesiveness of World War II as well as the coming Cold War–era polarization of the world into Black-versus-white, good-versus-evil, or capitalist-versus-communist dichotomies only further suggests the embracing of a localized version of American nationalism, despite its multiple meanings at any given point in time. Although the World War II era put a temporary damper on political disputes in the Texas Panhandle and the rest of the state, the wartime experience gave new local meaning to the concept of Americanism as embraced widely by most residents of the United States.

The Panhandle and the Democratic "Bolters"

The clear trends toward a conservative political culture accelerated in the Panhandle after World War II. First, a word on conservatism and Panhandle congressional leaders is necessary; second, it is important to explore the relationship between Panhandle politicians and conservative Democrats and Republicans at the state and national levels. Panhandle conservatives clearly played an important role in paving the way for the emerging conservative movement in Texas as well as in the greater United States.

Panhandle voting patterns during the middle of the twentieth century reflected emerging trends at the state and national levels. For example, in 1950, Hereford, along with most of the rest of the Texas Panhandle, was represented in the Texas State Senate by Grady Hazlewood of Amarillo, a reliably conservative Democrat who would hold that position for the next two decades. House Representative for Randall, Potter, and Deaf Smith Counties that year—the counties that include the cities of Amarillo, Canyon, and Hereford—was J. Blake Timmons, a young up-and-coming Democrat whose politics at this stage were more in the tradition of a standard New Deal Democrat.[27] As such, Panhandle representation in both houses of the state legislature reflected an emerging conservative-liberal divide in the state Democratic Party. The groundwork was already laid for the conservative Democrat Allan Shivers to consolidate control of the Democratic Party for conservatives in the gubernatorial election later in 1950, a rebellion in the state party that had been brewing since the New Deal.

On a similar note, the Panhandle in 1950 was represented in the U.S. House by the oil and gas lawyer Ed Gossett, who represented the Thirteenth Congressional District from his home base in Wichita Falls as a conservative Democrat with the support of West Texas's oil and gas industries, which had a strong history of opposing New Deal liberalism.[28] According to the political historian Sean Cunningham, "through all of this, the Texas Far Right reflected aspects of a radicalism with deep roots in the early twentieth-century experience."[29] Panhandle conservatives, themselves identifying more with that same early twentieth-century experience than with changes sweeping the larger state and nation, would play a leading role in developing this conservative-liberal rift in the Texas Democratic Party.

In 1954, Bruce Alger, a Dallas congressman, became the first Republican in nearly a century to win a congressional seat in Texas's Fifth District. For roughly the next decade, Alger and a cadre of other Dallas politicians waged a divisive political battle meant to cleave conservatives from the Democratic Party, which J. Evetts Haley and the Jeffersonian Democrats had attempted to do nearly twenty years previously. Still, even while Alger and his associates railed against the New

Deal and levied cries of socialism against the Democratic Party, many Texans considered him to be part of a fringe political movement.[30]

Alger as well as others like him grew increasingly distressed at the number of federal government programs maintained in the state through the turn of the 1960s, not to mention their own lack of a voice within national political circles. Alger spoke routinely on such problems:

> With the passing of each day, the real struggle taking place in our nation becomes more and more clear—the struggle between capitalism and socialism. In nearly every piece of legislation brought to the Floor of the House we are faced with the basic issues of fiscal responsibility, the further encroachment of the lives of the federal government into the people, an ever expanding Federal bureaucracy which threatens to engulf our freedoms as provided for in the Constitution, and a foreign policy which seems bent on strengthening our enemies.[31]

Many Panhandle Texans agreed. Media prognosticators in places like Amarillo and Canyon increasingly spoke out against such threats to local society throughout the 1950s and '60s. The New Deal state, they argued, now an established fact of life, had by the middle of the 1960s "been implemented by the Social Security System, medicare, educational assistance, pensions and subsidies to various groups of citizens, business enterprises and programs to aid training and employment." No threat seemed more alarming in an area built on the very notions of community and individualism, as one Panhandle editorialist stated: "Apparently, there is to be little slackening in the tug of war between the philosophy of paternalism and the tradition of individuality which has been the leavening force in the economic and political development of the United States. The debate goes on, and this offers encouragement that the American welfare state may yet be able to avoid following the tragic pattern of pursuing the ideal of social justice with the big stick of conformity and oppression."[32]

This did not represent partisan politics, but rather a seeming disjuncture between the dominant mood of urban and coastal America's relationship with interior rural areas like the Texas Panhandle. Seemingly, it was only a matter of time before the carefully nurtured rural society of the Panhandle came crashing down under the weight of a government bureaucracy that was more popular in other parts of the country. Nothing short of a political war for America was under way.

For Texans, this coming war first expressed itself within the realm of politics. Alger's presence in the U.S. House stirred up the enmity of not only his liberal Democratic colleagues but also mainstream conservative Democrats from his own state. A long-standing feud between Alger and then Speaker of the House Sam Rayburn from Bonham, Texas—a man who supported liberal Texas Democrats and contributed to the rise of Lyndon Johnson—caused ill will between the two parties; this, of course, was particularly noticeable given Rayburn's long tenure in Washington. Senator John Tower, himself a prominent Republican from Wichita Falls but politically more middle-of-the-road than Alger, worked diligently behind the scenes with Democrats to rebuild the growing rift that developed during Alger's short congressional tenure.[33] Of course, Tower could not have known that the political winds of partisanship would only blow in his favor for so long. Alger had clearly touched a nerve with voters in places like the Texas Panhandle, who feared the direction in which the country seemed to be heading.

Nonetheless, the emerging conservative movement did not yet have the resources to fully unseat the Texas Democratic establishment. Although conservative Republicans eventually would emerge victorious, their failure to convince influential conservative Texas Democrats like Governor Allan Shivers to abandon the party staved off any meaningful growth during the 1950s. In fact, it was not until after the election of John F. Kennedy that many prominent "Shivercrats" began abandoning the Democratic Party, sometimes resigning publicly. At the state level, political realignment had begun in earnest.[34]

In reality, conservative Texas Democrats' abandonment of the party had only continued slowly during the 1950s. State Attorney General John Ben Shepperd articulated the emerging outlook at a speech to the Civitan Clubs of Austin in February of 1956. What is noteworthy is that many Texas conservatives considered that the nascent movement toward civil rights had not come from within the spectrum of beliefs about white supremacy or African Americans staying away from an Anglo world, but rather from U.S. Supreme Court decisions like the *Brown v. Board* case of 1954 that seemed to chip away at the power of state and local government. Shepperd believed that "the nation is at the crossroads in federal-state relations." To him, things seemed dire: "We have come to the time for deciding whether all power will emanate from the National Government, or whether we shall continue with our constitutional system under which the states retain all authority not ceded to the Federal domain." Shepperd believed that the states and the people would ultimately decide in favor of local rule. Thus, a pair of issues seemed to be shaping the conservative agenda: getting back powers that the states had allegedly lost and checking federal authority.[35]

How to take on such a seemingly vast challenge? The only solution from within the local context in the Panhandle was to approach the problem at the grassroots level. One need look no further than the appeal of the John Birch Society (JBS) to measure the growing frustrations that many Panhandle Texans felt with national politics. Robert Welch Jr. founded the society in Indiana in 1958, naming it after a Baptist missionary killed by Chinese communists in 1945. The group maintained its headquarters in Indianapolis, but its membership included a loose network of business leaders, a number of whom—like the multimillionaire oilman H. L. Hunt—hailed from Texas. Another influential Texas member was Fred Koch, a Rice University–educated oilman who had worked in Russia during the 1930s and thus witnessed the horrors of Soviet communism firsthand.[36] Many critics pegged the JBS as a radical right-wing, ultraconservative organization, but its strong anticommunist bent along with its commitment to American national pride explains the relatively easy popularity that the group enjoyed among people living in the Texas Panhandle. Additionally, according to the political historian Darren Dochuk, the JBS "illustrated a nationwide effort by the Right to pressure the Republican center during [President Dwight D.] Eisenhower's last years in the White House" during the late 1950s.[37] Panhandle conservatives thus indirectly played an important role in fusing the emerging conservatism of the middle of the twentieth century with the Republican Party at both the state and national levels.

JBS members undoubtedly helped many conservatives win office nationwide as Republicans during the 1960s, but the party's mainstream was slow to accept the organization, especially in Republican strongholds like Southern California, where about 30 percent of the organization's roughly one hundred thousand members lived. On September 24, 1965, California gubernatorial candidate Ronald Reagan denounced the JBS as a far-right organization in an attempt to shift his appeal as a conservative Republican candidate closer to the political center. Although Reagan later softened his tone on the organization, his message came through with abundant clarity: the emerging Republican-conservative alliance was not yet ready to embrace the more isolated and radical style of JBS populism.[38] Not coincidentally, neither were Panhandle conservatives ready to come fully under the Republican banner.

Some Panhandle Texans seemed to believe at certain points that the JBS, with its popular appeal, was already outmaneuvering the Democratic Party.

In March of 1966, a columnist for the *Amarillo Globe-News* noted that the JBS had begun preparing $5 tapes of radio broadcasts that its speakers had engaged in; in response, the Democratic Party sent out four thousand mailers to local supporters urging them to spend $5 on taped speeches by prominent Democrats and to "get them on as many stations as possible and to make a special effort to have them played on any which carries the Birch program." When asked why the party sought to play five-minute speeches as opposed to the JBS's fifteen-minute broadcasts, one organization member opined that "we think five minutes makes a more effective broadcast."[39]

Perhaps not coincidentally, Panhandle political culture became more outwardly visible not only because of the patriotic fervor of the Cold War era but also because of a general ecological and economic upturn beginning during the early 1940s that allowed Panhandle farmers to thrive like never before. This improved economic status made this culturally conservative region more apt to question the policies and leadership of the Democratic Party. Many longtime Democrats threw their support behind Republicans in presidential elections during this period. Although 77 percent of Panhandle voters supported Democrat Harry S. Truman during his 1948 campaign, the tide had clearly shifted markedly by the early 1950s. Many were ready for a Republican president; even the Democratic governor Allan Shivers crossed party lines in 1952 when he endorsed Republican Dwight D. Eisenhower for the White House. Eisenhower went on to take 57 percent of the vote in the Panhandle in 1952, becoming the first Republican presidential candidate to carry the region since Herbert Hoover in 1928. Notably, Eisenhower's 57 percent of the Panhandle vote in 1952 was nearly four percentage points higher than his statewide total of 53.13 percent of the popular vote. Eisenhower had pledged his support to the state's claim of ownership to its oil-rich tidelands about ten miles off the Gulf Coast, which his Democratic opponent Adlai Stevenson argued belonged to the federal government. Clearly, conservative West Texas Democrats had concluded that elements in their own party at the national level did not have the state's own best interests at heart, nor did it respect state government.[40] Before long, many would flee the party's ranks to join the Republicans.

Naturally, certain prominent individuals drove such changes on the ground level in the Texas Panhandle, and perhaps none of them was more prominent than the aforementioned J. Evetts Haley, whose politics became even more outspoken and further entrenched on the right during this period. Haley had once been quoted as saying that the Texas Rangers should be used to stop racial integration and that violence was permissible if it brought about an end to interference against free enterprise by organized labor. Haley was a leader in seemingly every conservative organization in America at the time, including but not limited to Texans for America (a conservative group that protested what it deemed unpatriotic school textbooks), the National Indignation Convention, and in all likelihood the John Birch Society. Haley could perhaps be considered the architect of Panhandle Texans' emerging conservative outlook; his "plaintive cries to return to simple, frontier individualism ... massaged sore egos and salved raw wounds" during the 1950s. Haley shot to national prominence in the political sphere when he used his skills as a historian to draft the controversial *A Texan Looks at Lyndon,* a short book aimed at discrediting Lyndon Johnson just before the 1964 presidential election. The tactic backfired. One historian refers to *A Texan Looks at Lyndon* as a "violent polemic, [that] uses rumors, gossip, innuendo, and one-sided evidence to defame Johnson ... the book cost Haley most of his remaining scholarly reputation."[41] Haley thus embodied the mindset of the new conservatism in the Panhandle with his willingness to attack the perceived threats of liberalism to the region, despite the harm that doing so might cause to his own reputation.

Of course, it was of little surprise that a prominent Panhandle conservative would take to the pen to attack a homegrown liberal that year in particular, when the stalwart business conservative Barry Goldwater of Arizona offered the first foray of what might be considered Republican conservatism into the electoral process at the national level. Goldwater mobilized the new conservatives on a national scale in ways never before seen—the multitude of organizations and personalities that came together during the late 1950s showed that, in the words of one historian, "conservatism became something different at the end of the fifties; it became a self-conscious movement."[42] Haley clearly hoped to support such a movement, and in fact he appeared to spearhead it at the local level—the Texas Panhandle was the only part of the state in which a majority of voters supported Goldwater as opposed to Johnson in the 1964 presidential election. In fact, according to one observer, as early as 1964, "loyal Democrats were [already] becoming a minority" in the Texas Panhandle.[43]

Haley's frustrations with the Democrats in part stemmed from his own campaign for the Texas governorship earlier in 1956, inserting himself into a crowded primary contest for the Democratic nomination. Haley ran on the platform of states' rights and maintaining segregation in the wake of the *Brown v. Board* decision. Up against him were some familiar names, like Senator Price Daniel (who would go on to win the contest), liberal future senator Ralph Yarborough, and former conservative governor Pappy O'Daniel. Even the conservative regional newspaper, *The Panhandle Herald*, noted that Haley trailed in the Panhandle electorate's support behind mainstream conservatives Daniel and O'Daniel, both of whom would finish ahead of him in the election. Haley finished a distant fourth, pulling in 90,577 votes statewide, or 6 percent of the electorate. His polling numbers were similar across Texas Panhandle counties, climbing only slightly higher in some instances.[44]

Nonetheless, according to the historian John S. Huntington, Haley's shortcomings as a political candidate should not outweigh the important groundwork that he laid for grassroots organizing for conservative Texas politics between the Great Depression and the onset of the civil rights era. His appeal reached a nationwide audience long before his famous screed against Johnson. Haley's unapologetic anti–New Deal politics, as well as his embodiment of West Texas rugged individualism, constituted "an explanatory link bridging anti–New Deal ultraconservatism and the [burgeoning] mid-century conservative movement." Although Haley lost his bid for the Texas governorship, his status as a figurehead with the emerging right was clear.[45] As will become clear over the course of this book, Haley's political departure from mainstream conservatism embodied a burgeoning regional politics that rested on perceptions of isolation as well as a fundamental distrust of outsiders in the Texas Panhandle, which included the so-called radical liberals of the post–World War II era, civil rights activists, and even those who ascribed to mainstream New Deal liberalism. A few years after the 1964 election, Haley became the Republican chairman of Randall County in the Texas Panhandle.[46]

A Texan Looks at Lyndon should not be dismissed as a mere aberration. The book shows the growing appeal of antiliberal rhetoric during the 1960s. Haley had previously staked out views that, though radical in their expression, embodied the growing outlook of the Panhandle electorate. Haley had become something of a household name among conservatives when he filed a lawsuit to invalidate the federal agricultural program during the 1950s; his fame only grew with a macabre joke in 1961 calling for the hanging of Chief Justice of the Supreme Court Earl Warren. Perhaps the most important aspect of *A Texan Looks at Lyndon* was the grassroots methods of distribution that Haley followed, which mirrored the distribution methods that the conservative broadcaster Clarence Manion used in distributing broadcasts of his radio transcripts during the 1950s. Haley's book sold about 50,000 copies a day by November of 1964, many of which were ordered in bulk by rich or well-connected conservatives to give away for free.[47]

Interestingly, Haley's conservative bent provided a specific context for local communities to oust troublesome teachers without government interference. In 1959, Haley's Texans for America helped defeat a "teacher tenure" bill in the Texas legislature that would have eliminated the ability of local school boards to remove what the group described as "inept, inefficient, and even immoral school teachers."[48] Wayne Woodward, sixteen years later in 1975, was certainly the exact kind of teacher that Texans for America had in mind in 1959. The emerging Panhandle conservatism clearly had teachers like him in its crosshairs.

Conservative Aggression in West Texas during Wayne Woodward's Lifetime

The conservative antagonists that Woodward would face off against during the 1970s thus stood ready to protect local society against the threats of liberalism, which were less tolerated than they had been previously. A number of prominent events in the region preceding Wayne Woodward's struggles in Hereford put this tendency on display.

For example, in July of 1957 at Texas Tech University in Lubbock, the school's board of regents—which included the recently appointed J. Evetts Haley—terminated three professors for no other reason than their violation of local political values. Henry Greenberg, a new psychology professor, drew the board's ire due to his involvement with the U.S. Department of Health, Education, and Welfare, along with his public support of the Supreme Court's decision in the *Brown v. Board* case. Per Stensland, who was also new to the faculty, ran afoul of the regents due to his involvement with a Ford Foundation Adult Education program, which Haley as well as the other regents dismissed as "plush, academic boondoggling." Finally, the regents fired Byron Abernethy, a tenured government professor, for his standing in the liberal wing of the state's Democratic Party. Protests by students against the professors' dismissal for their supposedly liberal political views brought no recourse from the school's administrators or the board of regents.[49]

A number of the regents admitted that the firings were politically motivated, but they claimed that they had acted in the best interests of the university. Academic freedom and tenure did not seem to sway anyone's thinking. Haley expressed his own views on the "problem" of tenure at the university level. He believed that it only rewarded extremist college professors. This, to him, was anathema to the "average Texan who had a tradition and almost congenital conviction that each man should fight his battles alone." Faculty—whom Texas Tech's president referred to as "a bunch of grown-up children" in 1962—became targets when they seemingly contradicted the region's emerging social and political order. Administrations banned political groups of all stripes from campus, including the Young Democrats, Young Republicans, and the NAACP. The emerging community ethic clearly dictated a quiet, obedient sense of conformity. Entering the next decade, administrators at all of the region's main institutions of higher learning—Texas Tech, West Texas State University in Canyon, and Amarillo College—sought to eliminate allegedly troublesome elements from their respective campuses.[50] Such behavior was reflective of the emerging consensus of the protective community ethic that had been coalescing over the course of the last several decades.

Of course, the Panhandle's conservative culture continued its coming-of-age process, experiencing perhaps its most important period of growth during the tumultuous 1960s. One would be mistaken to assume that Barry Goldwater's 1964 campaign for the presidency was the catalyst, despite its importance for the national Republican Party. Panhandle residents shifted more toward a conservative populism; this is perhaps nowhere more evident than in the popularity of conservative newspaper columnists throughout the region. For example, in 1962, the noted conservative columnist Louise Evans Bruce railed against the perceived excesses of liberalism. Her positions, however, had more to do with assumed roles about government as well as people's general attitudes as opposed to certain policy elements. "What infuriates the conservative is not so much the proposal of some socialistic measure," she wrote in a 1962 piece in the *Amarillo Globe-News*, "but the arrogant, smug assumption by the people planners that state control of individuals is normal and sensible, and that anybody who opposes it is a reactionary eccentric." Bruce came to this conclusion by skimming through a recent edition of the *New York Times*. She railed against an article regarding the federal government's role in public education, in which one writer argued that the government needed to propagate a uniformity of educational standards across the county, opposition to which could only be summed up—according to her reading of the article—as "emotional and childish."[51]

Bruce spoke out against perceived threats to local government, which she also absorbed through her reading of the left-leaning *Times*. She also took the author of another piece—the Cornell associate professor of government Andrew Hacker—to task for arguing that "'except for New York and a handful of other states, legislatures have ceased to be either experimental or effective in meeting modern needs.'" Bruce responded, "If other institutions rise to take the place of the state legislatures, or even in time the states themselves, then realism dictates that we close a chapter in our political history and begin another." Furthermore, "this philosophy is sneaking up on us, as the socialist experts continue to call black white by basing their arguments on phony . . . assumptions."[52] Bruce's calls for beginning a new "chapter in our political history" provide direct evidence of the vitality that these emerging ideas about place, community, and a threatening big government had in the Texas Panhandle.

Bruce also defended other strong voices in the emerging movement, such as Alvin R. Allison, a lawyer from the small Panhandle town of Levelland and one of the Texas Tech regents who sought to purge those liberal academics who failed to understand the region's emerging sociopolitical order. Allison had spoken to the Levelland Rotary Club earlier in 1962, where he argued that "'there are a great many people who oppose Communists, but really favor communism, if it is given a respectable name like 'the welfare state.'" Such was a standard call to action among local conservatives. Allison went on: "If you want your father to take care of you, that's Paternalism. If you want your mother to take care of you, that's Maternalism. If you want Uncle Sam to take care of you, that's socialism. If you want your comrades to take care of you, that's Communism. But—if you want to take care of yourself, that's Americanism."[53] Allison's remarks were clearly representative of the new political consensus across the region.

Newspaper editorials continued to reflect this consensus as the 1960s wore on. Multiple phenomena that members of the public would take for granted in urban areas or on the coasts simply did not fit the realm of local acceptability. In March of 1963, an article in the *Amarillo Globe-Times* criticized the American Civil Liberties Union (ACLU); this same organization, as previously mentioned, would later prove to be Wayne Woodward's downfall in Hereford. A killer of five in New York State, one Frederick Charles Wood, had recently been scheduled for execution by electric chair. "'I really want to ride the lightening [sic]," Wood was quoted as saying, continuing on that he did "not welcome any intrusion into this stinking case of mine." An ACLU lawyer from New York City nonetheless attempted to file a stay of execution on Wood's behalf, noting that his sanity should be questioned along with whether his constitutional rights had been violated during his trial. Although the author made no explicit accusations against the ACLU, the implication was clear—why would any organization intervene in the case of a condemned person who wanted to die? Individual constitutional rights should not be enshrined over someone who was clearly a menace to community safety.[54] The ACLU lawyer in the case, one might have deduced, was simply causing trouble.

Local editorialists also supported Barry Goldwater with enthusiasm in 1964, as did Panhandle voters. Bruce Alger supported Goldwater as early as January of 1964 before he had even announced his candidacy. Alger warned voters against the Republican Party moving any further "to the left" than Goldwater's candidacy. He believed that Goldwater had the proper constitutional principles to move the nation forward in its fight against communism, which he argued threatened both U.S. capitalism as well as national sovereignty. Both arguments resonated well with Panhandle voters. Goldwater, in fact, later made a campaign stop at Potter County Stadium in Amarillo, where he launched into a stinging attack on the federal government, arguing that the centralization of power in Washington, D.C., had badly damaged the Texas Panhandle. The local conservative press covered the event with enthusiasm; Louise Evans Bruce was so energized that she mistakenly wrote that Goldwater's appearance marked the first time a presidential candidate had ever visited the city, forgetting, strangely, that John F. Kennedy had held a rally at the Amarillo airport just four years previously.[55]

Goldwater's message undoubtedly resonated less on the level of policy appeals and more because he represented a cultural shift for the Republican Party that was already well under way in the Texas Panhandle. Goldwater offered a more nuanced right-of-center approach for Panhandle conservatives to national politics than did the more radical reactionaries against mainstream liberalism since the advent of the New Deal. All of this energy settled on a now decades-old belief that more Panhandle Texans had grown to adopt, that love for one's country equated anticommunism. Instead of being written off as "anti-anything," more of these voters over the course of the next decade adopted the label "conservative" and voted Republican.

The Final Push toward a New Politics

The political revolution in the Panhandle was not complete, but the Goldwater campaign certainly marked a turning point in voting patterns. Despite eventually losing the campaign badly to incumbent president and liberal Texas Democrat Lyndon Johnson, Goldwater gained 47 percent of the Panhandle vote. Panhandle conservatism as a political identity did not yet have the purchase to unseat a popular Democratic politician from the state—even a liberal one. What the election did do, however, was to highlight a growing grassroots infrastructure across the Panhandle that could work to the benefit of other conservative Republican politicians. George H. W. Bush, for example, polled at a strong 54 percent in the twenty-six counties of the Texas Panhandle during his 1964 Senate campaign against the liberal Ralph Yarborough. Astonishingly, opinion polls showed that the number of Panhandle Texans who referred to themselves as "Republicans" went from 38 percent in 1964 to a whopping 82 percent just six years later in 1970.[56] Such was the essence of the revolution in conservative identity across the Texas Panhandle during the 1960s. Conservatives were finally bolting from the Democratic Party.

Not only did the Goldwater campaign prove to be a critical turning point in the coalescence of the region's conservative political culture, but President Johnson's resounding victory also galvanized conservatives. Indeed, 1964 saw Johnson's passage of John F. Kennedy's long-desired legislation to end segregation in the form of the Civil Rights Act of 1964; combining such legislation with the seemingly traitorous politics of a Democratic president from the Lone Star State was simply more than the average Panhandle conservative could handle. Kennedy had won a close presidential race against Nixon in 1960, while the 1962 gubernatorial campaign was the closest in Texas since the Reconstruction era. The bipartisan heat of the 1964 campaign between Johnson and Goldwater only further served to signify to many that divisions in the country were only getting worse. Battle lines had been drawn, meaning that Panhandle conservatives were now forced to choose sides.

This bumpy transition to modern bipartisanship was by no means a clean one. In fact, during the midterm elections of 1966, Senator John Tower, one of the leading Texas Republicans during the 1960s, from the eastern fringes of West Texas in Wichita Falls, seemed to distance himself from the party. Tower dropped the "Republican" label in all magazine and newspaper advertisements for that year's reelection bid; this despite his breakthrough victory for Texas Republicans in the 1961 race to replace Lyndon Johnson in the U.S. Senate, when he became the first Republican elected to national office from Texas since Reconstruction and marked the first official cracks in one-party rule in the state's political history in nearly a century.[57] Nowhere that year would Tower be associated with Goldwater in print; instead, Tower was pictured with Lyndon Johnson, Democratic Texas governor John Connally, and Georgia Democrat Richard Russell.[58] Although speculating as to Tower's motives is difficult, such positioning obviously stemmed from political calculations. Tower had supported Goldwater, who had suffered a bad defeat in 1964, thus necessitating a distancing from the former GOP presidential candidate. Clearly, although Tower had been an important figure in his party, ideological principle did not interfere with party loyalty. Such had been true for Panhandle voters during the preceding decades, but this would obviously change with the consolidation of Republican Party power.

Tower's popularity as a Republican, despite the vagaries of party politics, had soared in the Panhandle by the middle of the decade. In 1966, Tower easily defeated Texas Attorney General Waggoner Carr for reelection to the Senate. Only seven of the twenty-six counties that formed the Texas Panhandle voted in favor of his opponent. Clearly, Panhandle Texans voted increasingly as a unified Republican block. Such successes—as well as the positive showing that Goldwater had made combined with the increasing political polarization—seemed to be setting the stage for an all-out "liberal-versus-conservative" clash during the 1968 election season. Panhandle Republicans increasingly saw the likelihood of establishing a voice for themselves in politics outside of the state, should larger trends continue to work in their favor.[59]

Of course, the realignment of the Republican Party in the region did not occur without some significant growing pains. Grady Hazlewood, a longtime member of the Texas State Senate, was one of the first prominent Panhandle Democrats to flee to the Republican Party. Hazlewood's problems began when California governor and rising Republican Party star Ronald Reagan ran against Richard Nixon for his party's nomination in the 1968 presidential primaries. In March, during the heat of the primary campaign, Hazlewood wrote Reagan two letters: one, marked "personal," asking Reagan to come give a speech to the local meeting of the Panhandle-Plains Historical Society (Reagan had agreed to speak to the group some years previously but later backed out due to a scheduling conflict); and the other, marked "personal and confidential," during which Hazlewood made clear that a good topic for the proposed speech would be "[the Panhandle's] pioneers and the preservation of the philosophies and spirit that made our State and Nation so great." Hazlewood went on to relate that "if you are nominated for President, there will be plenty of money down in these parts." Hazlewood even pledged a $1,000 cash donation "the very minute your nomination for President is announced."[60] Reagan's eventual rejection of Hazlewood's request aside, such entreaties show that many Panhandle Texans were ahead of the curve not only in wanting to flee the Democratic Party for the Republican Party but also in supporting the eventual figurehead of the conservative takeover of the national Republican Party about a decade before many conservatives were willing to join the "Reagan Revolution." Hazlewood would find himself expelled from the Texas Democratic Party after he publicly endorsed Reagan's candidacy that August. The Texas Democrats of Wayne Woodward's time were thus split between conservative and liberal wings, with a conservative Texas Republican Party ascendant. Clearly, this seismic realignment reverberated in Panhandle party politics and further marginalized liberal points-of-view.[61]

The Texas Democratic Party maintained power throughout the 1960s and '70s despite the growing exodus. Such was due in large part to charges of extremism that the emerging right could not fend off in any adequate way.[62] Goldwater had not fully embodied the principles of Panhandle conservatism; if anyone embodied that spirit, one need look no further than Alabama governor George Wallace. Wallace once famously stood in a doorway at the University of Alabama to fight against desegregation. Interestingly, such action seemed to embolden certain elements of the emerging right as opposed to bringing an end to the governor's political career. Wallace himself, according to the *Amarillo Globe-Times,* was a resurgent militant heading toward an independent bid in the 1968 presidential campaign, while his wife, Lurleen, ran for the Alabama governorship as the de facto head of the state. According to a writer for the *Amarillo Globe-News,* nothing seemed to hurt his political prospects: "I never told you we were going to win all the battles," he said. "But I did tell you that I'd bring all these things out into the open." Wallace represented a certain pluck that like-minded voters in the Panhandle undoubtedly found appealing. He also had a knack for spinning defeats as victories. All through the gubernatorial campaign year in 1966, Wallace reminded voters of the large percentage of the public vote he received in the three primary contests in which he was a participant (his share of the vote in Maryland, Indiana, and Wisconsin had ranged from 30 to 44 percent).[63]

History would be wrong to consider Wallace a loser in 1960s politics, however, according to this same Amarillo editorialist. Federal civil rights laws had "come clamping down on Alabama" since his tenure, while the state's African American population had been registering to vote in record numbers. Wallace, though, to white conservatives, "somehow still looks like a champion." Wallace was not the perfect conservative: "outside of the racial field, he functions as a governor like an old New Dealer freshly attuned to the Great Society." Wallace regularly boasted of his spending on social programs for the poor. Nonetheless, Wallace was fond of lambasting the northern press and characterizing northerners as being out of step with the values and concerns of people in Alabama and the Deep South. Such statements, despite his seemingly more liberal spending policies, endeared him to the emerging Panhandle Republicans. Wallace needed no one to tell him what to do.[64]

The national Republican Party served to impress many Panhandle Texans, as well. Perhaps the most important figurehead in this regard was none other than California governor and future president Ronald Reagan, who capitalized on the emerging popularity of Sunbelt conservatism. In fact, Democratic governor Edmund Brown, along with California Democratic State Party chairman Robert Choate, hammered Reagan during the 1966 gubernatorial campaign for the latter's failure to fully repudiate the JBS, which many liberals considered an extremist organization. The *Amarillo Daily News,* a conservative newspaper fully in support of the upstart Reagan, quoted Choate as saying that if the Republican State Convention had adopted a platform "condemning political extremists by name, he would have been vigorously opposed to Reagan, who depends on the support of Birchers and other extremists in his campaign for governor."[65] Such a strong stance must have delighted Panhandle conservatives. Reagan went on to win the election, rising to political stardom and no doubt gaining the notice of many like-minded individuals in the Texas Panhandle.

Furthermore, it comes as little surprise that Reagan as well as California Sunbelt conservatism drew support from the Texas Panhandle. Numerous historians have established the importance of Orange County, California, as being an epicenter for the emerging conservative movement. Sunbelt conservatism emerged from various political impulses that were important to the U.S. Southwest during the post–World War II period, in particular the perceptions that the federal government had overreached its authority in terms of emerging environmentalist and regulatory policies during the decades that followed the war. Perhaps most notably, due to the increasingly common usage of air-conditioning throughout the region, the Sunbelt became a desired destination for older people from the North who preferred the region's warm climate over snowy winters and colder weather. Most of these people tended to have conservative views; naturally, then, the radicalism of even the far right also found fertile ground in the same region. George Lincoln Rockwell, head of the American Nazi Party, noted that the Panhandle had great recruiting resources. In fact, he also claimed that Randall County in the Panhandle and Orange County were the two best areas in the country in terms of recruitment.[66] As such, the ideological similarities between the inhabitants of the two regions—already established through the migratory links between the Texas Panhandle and Southern California during the Great Depression—were similar enough that emerging far-right conservatives as well as mainstream conservatives could find common cause with one another.

The Republican Party had made strong inroads among conservatives throughout the 1960s, despite the fact that the Texas Panhandle's Thirteenth Congressional District would continue to be represented by conservative Democrats until the election of the conservative Republican Mac Thornberry in 1994.[67] The local editorialist Margaret Mayer noted a Republican study that at one time a majority of Americans self-identified as Republicans. During the 1920s, many cities in the East ran as high as 80 percent Republican. Black voters were solidly Republican until the 1930s, as were many American farmers and dockworkers. Much of this large-scale shift could be blamed on the Great Depression, argued that study, but also on the suburbanization of urban America, the flight of farmers to the cities, and the GOP's simple inability to change with the tides of America, which the Democrats had capitalized on. All of this being the case, the shift from Democratic to Republican voters slowly taking place in Texas Panhandle politics represented nothing even approximating ideological disloyalty—in fact, the Republican Party had begun strategizing to take advantage of a major backlash against the liberal faction of the Democratic Party at the national level. Voters in the Texas Panhandle, with their slow abandonment of the Democratic Party, had also begun to embrace a newer, more forceful conservatism that was simply less operable within the ranks of the Democratic Party.[68]

The civil rights movement at the local level would prove to be the final nail in the coffin of the Democratic Party in the Texas Panhandle—it would also provide the necessary backdrop to Wayne Woodward's 1975 case, which highlighted the vitality of the newer, deeply political conservatism of the Texas Panhandle. It is to the story of civil rights and the increasingly confrontational, aggressive side of Panhandle conservatism that we now turn.

CHAPTER 2

COMING OF AGE IN THE TEXAS PANHANDLE

The Civil Rights Era in Rural America

Conservative ideals clearly ran deep in the Texas Panhandle by the 1960s. One historian argues that 1960s conservatives who supported violent crackdowns on protesters on the campus of the University of California at Berkeley emerged from the earlier cultural sensibilities of people who were upset at Elvis gyrating his hips on the *Ed Sullivan Show*.[1] Such an overly simplistic characterization fails to take seriously, however, the complicated and long-existing forces in places like the Texas Panhandle that had taken many decades to meld into a new conservative outlook. Notions of frontier individualism and self-reliance had, according to many Panhandle Texans, increasingly come under fire during the previous decades. As the previous chapter has shown, Panhandle Texans joined forces with the emerging conservative movement over the course of the mid-twentieth century to protect themselves against perceived threats to their communities.

Panhandle conservatism thus predated the post–World War II period; it was also, however, deeply reactionary to the rise of national liberalism and civil rights politics during the 1950s and '60s. This chapter argues that the tumult of the 1960s sparked a visibly aggressive response from Panhandle conservatives who were intent on protecting their own communities against certain perceived threats. Our story thus briefly shrinks down to the immediate world of Wayne Woodward and his friends and contemporaries in the Panhandle during the civil rights era, before turning to Woodward's own specific struggles in Hereford. Panhandle conservatism shifted during the 1960s due to one dominant human emotion: fear. The national civil rights movement was central to all of this, as it resonated negatively with most Panhandle conservatives. Of course, negative reactions against civil rights and racial equality were not unique to the Texas Panhandle, but reactions to the movement in the region must be understood from within the locally oriented outlook that had developed over the previous decades. Changes shaping national and global society threatened to come crashing into the Panhandle, seemingly challenging the dominant localized culture that had developed since the region's settlement by English-speaking Americans. These same changes would spark a response in Hereford, Texas, in 1975, when a young Wayne Woodward naïvely announced the opening of a new local chapter of the American Civil Liberties Union. Wayne Woodward and other young Panhandle liberals came of age in a period when conservatism grew increasingly confrontational in rural America.

Liberals in a Sea of Postwar Conservatism

Wayne Woodward, perhaps showing early signs of his burgeoning outsider status, showed an acute awareness of the region's political culture from a young age. One of his earliest memories was walking into the Kress department store in downtown Amarillo during the 1950s, where he recalled seeing "Whites" and "Negroes" signs above the restrooms. Later, while riding the city bus with his mother, he asked her why Black passengers had to sit at the back. "That's just the way it is," she replied. He next became aware that Black and Latino students in the city seemed to have their own schools. By 1963, when he graduated from high school, he could not recall having seen a single person of color at any of his schools.[2]

Woodward was hardly a far-left liberal, and neither was his mother. But the tendency that he and others like him had for questioning the Texas Panhandle's conservative culture—a theme explored further at the end of this chapter—marked them as different. Woodward innocently asked questions about the social order that surrounded him. As will be seen later in this book, this would remain true through the middle part of the 1970s when he was a young man. However, young people like Woodward who questioned the region's social order during the tumult of the post–World War II years were relatively few and far between.

Panhandle society remained overwhelmingly politically homogeneous during those years. The strong anticommunist fervor of Panhandle politics elicited, almost naturally, a positive response to the Lyndon Johnson administration's escalation of the conflict in Vietnam after 1964. The aforementioned conservative editorialist Louise Evans Bruce tapped into local frustrations with war critics by calling them out in print. One such unfortunate soul was the famed British philosopher Bertrand Russell, who was a noted critic of the war (as well as unrepentantly nontheistic). Russell proposed to hold a mock trial of President Johnson for his Vietnam policies in December of 1966; Bruce implied a certain hypocrisy on Russell's part in reminding her readers of his statement in 1948 that the United States would be well served to make a preemptive strike on the Soviet Union before its successful development of the atomic bomb (which the Soviet Union did acquire the next year). Bruce's attack on Russell did not stem from any personal or ideological vendetta; instead, it was meant to elicit a visceral response among her readership that the wider, changing, "liberal" world was out of touch with the mindset of the typical Panhandle citizen. Bruce knew her readership well.[3]

Naturally, then, the ACLU did not escape Bruce's wrath nor that of the emerging regional political hegemon. Conservative cold warriors commonly criticized the conscientious objector status that federal law allowed some men who faced the military draft to take during the Vietnam era. In May of 1966, the ACLU sought to expand such objections to people who opposed the war on "moral, philosophical, or religious ground." This, argued Bruce, was cowardice of the first order as well as an insult to the men fighting to stop the spread of communism in the jungles of Vietnam. "To put it another way," wrote Bruce, "the ACLU is going to do its utmost to insure [sic] that anyone who doesn't want to fight in Viet Nam won't have to endanger himself or the Communists there." If successful, she continued, such an action would set a precedent such that only a few patriotic men would willingly respond to any call to arms, thus weakening the United States diplomatically. Fortunately, the ACLU had not attempted such a tactic two decades previously when the United States took it upon itself to oppose the spread of fascism emanating outwardly from Nazi Germany.[4]

The importance of such negative local perceptions of the ACLU to Woodward's later courtroom drama cannot be understated. Panhandle Texans did not oppose the ACLU out of a sense of partisan politics or due to any vague charge of the organization perpetuating anything akin to a liberal political bias. The implication is clear—the ACLU, to the local citizenry, was fundamentally anti-American. Clearly, the emerging dominant political identity of the Texas Panhandle defined community membership on the basis of an agreed-upon sense of Americanism, whose tenets included a belief in local government, personal responsibility, anticommunism, and an intense sense of American nationalism. Woodward would find himself in trouble in large part because he did not fit this emerging social cohesion. By his own admission, as will be seen later, Woodward did not necessarily self-identify as a "liberal" at all, despite seeking to change things locally. Support for the ACLU simply did not translate to the kind of American ideals to which most Panhandle citizens of the time subscribed.

Significantly, such elements remained latent within the larger structure of the Texas Panhandle's shifting political outlook. The ACLU only needed to be challenged when it actually gave the impression of infiltrating local society. Otherwise, it remained something of an abstraction. The same can be said for the initial racial unrest of the civil rights era. Issues like integration or civil rights had not yet been confronted by Panhandle conservatives in any meaningful way, due in large part to the fact that the region's African American population remained relatively small. People watched riots and protests in other areas on their televisions; the fact that none had yet happened in the Panhandle indicated to many people that African Americans on the southern plains were happy with their lives.[5] Any discontent, then, could translate as stemming from the work of outsiders seeking to disrupt local society.

Nonetheless, the slow arrival of the civil rights movement along with its emphasis on protecting individual civil liberties—embodied by the very fabric of the ACLU's code—was a watershed moment marking the coalescence of the Panhandle's aggressive conservatism into a viable movement. African Americans themselves raised issues, particularly on the campus of Woodward's college, West Texas State University in Canyon, Texas, during the late 1960s. The university had long prohibited interracial dating, an issue that students had then begun to challenge. Also, usage of the racial slur "nigger" was common—so common, in fact, that many who used it loosely found themselves shocked when African Americans took offense to whites saying the word. Finally, West Texas State's chapter of the Kappa Alpha fraternity found itself in trouble during the late 1960s for its tradition of "Old South Day," which perpetuated demeaning stereotypes of African Americans. Importantly, when white college students and locals were challenged for such ideas and behaviors, their reactions were not necessarily those of ethnocentrists defending a racial hierarchy or status quo, as was often the case in other places like the Deep South. Their visceral reactions instead came from a set of seemingly innocuous traditions—innocuous to them, at least—being challenged. Naturally, again to them, any person who operated inside of the community ethic would see that no actual harm was meant in maintaining such institutions and attitudes. Instead, what had once been acceptable traditions now drew condemnation from people who seemingly had no understanding of generations of local tradition. This explains what others might judge to be their apparent lack of sympathy for African Americans' issues. Few would have challenged, for example, the principal of local Tascosa High School in Amarillo, who instead of addressing racism at his school banned the usage of rakes—a type of comb that African Americans used for Afro hairstyles—because he worried that Black radicals at the school would use them as weapons.[6]

While some actions among the emerging right can be dismissed as the products of explicit racism, such characterizations do not entirely strike at the heart of locals' motivations in restricting the rights of minority citizens. Paranoia about the looming specter of state control also lay at the heart of many racially discriminatory actions. In 1965, the local state senator Grady Hazlewood from Amarillo proposed a discriminatory constitutional amendment that he entitled "The Rights of Man," drawing on the language of the famous skeptic and patriot Thomas Paine from the American Revolutionary War era. Prompted by "recent Supreme Court actions," Hazlewood's bill would prohibit the state of Texas from interfering if a property owner refused to rent or sell to someone for any reason whatsoever, including the potential purchaser or renter's ethnicity. The amendment, however, immediately went nowhere in the legislature. One of his colleagues in the senate, George Parkhouse of Dallas, remarked that "all this is going to do is put Texas on the wire services." The amendment eventually withered away. Clearly, the lack of support that Hazlewood's amendment received shows that even as late as 1965 such an anti-government and subsequently racist proposal gained little traction with other state political leaders, perhaps even those Texas conservatives from outside the Panhandle. The emerging conservative culture of Hazlewood's home region was clearly somewhat out of step with the political winds of the rest of the state.[7]

Other forces prevailed to make such issues as civil rights legislation seem even more threatening. Within two weeks of the passage of the Voting Rights Act in 1965, the city of Watts, California, burned in dramatic rioting. Fears of such spontaneous rioting spread almost everywhere. In 1970, after the riots and deaths of four anti-Vietnam protestors at Kent State University in Ohio, the governor of Texas shipped riot gear to the Randall County Sheriff's Office in the event of a riot at the West Texas State University campus. For many in the Panhandle, events such as these reinforced ideas about communists taking over the country, which dated back at least to the Red Scare of the immediate post–World War II era. To them, ideas related to cultural liberalism could eventually arrive in the Panhandle and cause their own cities to burn.[8]

Hazlewood's ideas gained widespread purchase among Panhandle Texans. Louise Evans Bruce bemoaned that certain civil rights or human rights commissions would be attached to local government to ensure fair treatment for all. During the 1960s, further pushes toward what she referred to as "supra-governments" would occur due to the passage of civil rights legislation by the U.S. Congress. Bruce enunciated her fears in the pages of the local Amarillo newspaper, where she wrote that "a common practice of such groups is to seek quasi-governmental status by being attached as an 'advisory commission' to an elected body—Legislature or Commission—or to an established governmental agency." Bruce believed that complaints about the legality of certain policies best went to the courts, not to such special advisory commissions. Such complaints, she argued, should be heard in open among the public or through the activities of the court system. "Happily in Amarillo," she continued, "we have no housing ordinances, no employment ordinances, no hotel-and-restaurant ordinances, no school regulations, no specialized legislation thwarting any group living, working, playing as it pleases—within the limits of decency and good citizenship." In other words, Bruce believed that the people of Amarillo were above such things as enforcing "separate but equal" policies, hence governmental enforcement of equal rights policies was not necessary. Her structure was the hallmark of "good government." Bruce never advocated for segregation for its own sake, but rather for traditional forms of government that functioned "openly, fairly and impartially under the laws and ordinances accepted by community consensus."[9] Protecting community self-determination was of the utmost importance.

School Unrest in the Texas Panhandle

Activities in area schools foreshadowed the backlash that Woodward would face in Hereford during the 1970s. At West Texas State University, administrators sought to keep the students quiet to keep order during periods of social unrest. Under T. Paige Carruth, dean of students, and James P. Cornette, president of the university, the university passed new rules in the fall of 1964 that "forbade campus organizations from endorsing political candidates . . . and they were not allowed to distribute campaign literature or 'deal with political personalities.'" The stifling of political voices on campus still remained largely bipartisan. A group of students under a young history professor named Edgar Sneed, who came to West Texas State in 1968, tried to organize a chapter of the national Students for a Democratic Society (SDS), an organization that had its roots in the politics of the New Left of the 1950s, who sought to push the liberalism of the New Deal generation to include cultural issues related to women and ethnic minorities. The group faced a lot of hostility from local police, the FBI, and the local press—more than any of their conservative or Republican organizational counterparts—all of whom lambasted the organization. The FBI even spied on them for a time. Perhaps unsurprisingly, Woodward himself experienced a political awakening of sorts due to his exposure to this very same group of people, which will be explored later in this chapter.[10]

West Texas State University officials feared the SDS. Although the group's intention was to promote equal rights, locals tended to associate it with violent events committed by radicals that people saw taking place in the news. Carruth, exemplifying such hysterics, remarked that the SDS had the goals of wiping "out all institutions of society as we know them today . . . [and playing] heck with our accepted moral structure. They advocate free love, for instance, or wear long hair, dirty clothes." The local chapter's membership never exceeded forty people. Some recalled that there were more people who appeared to be undercover police as well as other agents at its first campus meeting than there were actual potential members. John Rhinehart, a West Texas State student leader for the group who graduated in 1970, later learned under the auspices of the Freedom of Information Act that the FBI had assembled a large file on him.[11]

Such actions by university administrators stemmed from the policy of in loco parentis, whereby college administrators made rules for students in place of parents. Although activists had successfully challenged this policy on college campuses across the country since the 1950s, in loco parentis remained a useful tool.[12] Educational institutions like West Texas State, where Woodward was a student, and La Plata Junior High School, where Woodward later gained employment as a teacher, emerged as the battlegrounds in the Panhandle where school administrators sought to stifle unrest. Dean Carruth at West Texas State serves as an almost perfect example, foreshadowing the kind of unfair treatment that Woodward could expect a decade later in Hereford. In mid-February of 1966, a district court judge ordered university officials to reinstate a junior who had been expelled earlier that month. The student, twenty-one-year-old Darrell Aldridge, charged that Carruth's actions leading up to his expulsion were "wholly arbitrary, capricious and unreasonable." Aldridge had been placed on academic probation on January 25 after having been caught returning to campus on January 14 having consumed some beers with his friends. Aldridge, according to Carruth, was said to have driven another student's car that day, operating it "in an extremely reckless manner and at an excessive rate of speed." Aldridge's disciplinary record as a student had been clean since his admittance to the university as a freshman. The young man alleged in court that Carruth informed him orally that his good standing during probation depended on him *not* driving a car—even in his hometown of Lamesa, Texas, over one hundred miles away from the university campus. Aldridge ignored the order, driving his car for a few hours on the streets of Canyon during the winter break. A Canyon policeman pulled him over at one point, but the young man received no citations. Aldridge subsequently registered for the spring semester but later learned that Carruth had expelled him from the university, a decision that West Texas State University president James P. Cornette supported.[13]

Clearly, Carruth's and Cornette's actions were illegal: Aldridge charged that his right to an education could not be dependent on such an arbitrary exercise of authority; that he could not be disciplined for committing a minor traffic violation (driving recklessly); that as an adult citizen of Texas he could legally consume alcohol if he so chose; and that university officials were out of line in telling him that he could not operate a vehicle and certainly overstepped their boundaries in trying to keep him from driving in his hometown.[14] One can only explain Carruth's and Cornette's actions as being part of the exercise of arbitrary power at the local level. The two men, quite simply, saw it as their duty to ensure a certain level of social cohesion and order on the school's campus. Strikingly, two university officials implicitly placed their devotion to their own perceptions of acceptable behavior on campus and in the town of Canyon above even the constitutional rights of a young American citizen. As will be seen, the same thing happened to Wayne Woodward just a few years later in nearby Hereford. An almost Puritanical devotion to promoting local order meant more to Carruth and Cornette than individual constitutional liberties.

Carruth's and Cornette's overbearing control of the Aldridge incident was far from an isolated overexertion of power by local officials. In fact, such incidents were common. Carruth himself seemed to overstep his authority somewhat regularly. For example, in 1969, the aforementioned Rhinehart found himself challenged by Carruth because of his style of dress. Rhinehart wore what can be described as a hippie "uniform"—a mustache, blue jeans, T-shirts, Army surplus jackets, and shaggy hair. When Rhinehart sought to redeem a federal loan that was rightly his, Carruth denied him the loan on the grounds that someone with this student's political agenda should not be taking advantage of acquiring federal money. After discussing his options with his peers and professors, Rhinehart shaved, dressed conservatively, and pleased Carruth to the point that the dean was willing to release him his loan money. After receiving his money, Rhinehart "reverted" to his countercultural appearance. An editorial in the *Canyon News* applauded Carruth's efforts to deny an SDS member a federal loan, to which he was nonetheless entitled by law. Carruth, defending his actions, later stated that his response might have been "blown out of proportion." Nonetheless, later that same year, the West Texas Chamber of Commerce lauded the university for its "climate conducive to learning and education fabricated from the teaching of fundamental values of restraint, discipline, morality, constitutional government, respect for law and order and patriotism."[15]

Why engage in such efforts? Why would men in positions of power try to control not only people's behaviors on an individual level but also the very physical appearance of grown adults? The answer is quite simple: anything that deviated from the norm stood out as threatening, and this fear grew particularly acute in towns across the Texas Panhandle during the 1960s. Part of conserving life in the Texas Panhandle was keeping the national tumult of the 1960s at bay—this could be done, of course, by diminishing not only the countercultural "look" that so many of the older generation abhorred but also the widespread challenges to authority taking place on school campuses throughout the country. Respect for authority was of paramount importance. People's conformity to a preset standard of prevailing social norms had become of tantamount importance in the region as the new conservatism had begun to take shape. One could simply *identify*, by sight, who belonged in local society and who did not.

Local high school students also challenged social conventions. Long hair, public protests, and baggy clothes all became normal on school campuses. A local newspaper editor, Ben Ezzell, experienced the following when it came to his high-school-aged daughter, saying, "[I] had to defend [her] when she was kicked out of school for wearing a black armband to protest the [Vietnam] war." Her case went before the local school board, which backed off when faced with a lawsuit for violating a student's right to free speech. "In other parts of the Panhandle," he added, "teachers handed out striped red, white, and blue armbands for the students to wear on Moratorium Day. Those with black armbands were suspended or expelled." The appearance of such young people across the area was scandalous to many older Panhandle Texans. Radicals, Black militants, and even hippies, although vastly in the minority, began appearing across the region. The chaotic world of the 1960s came crashing in with a frightening quickness, and Panhandle

Texans were forced to bear down in the only way they knew how—by striving to protect threats to community well-being.[16]

Even still, one should not mischaracterize Panhandle conservatives as necessarily seeking to politicize any of the above-mentioned issues. The sentinels of local or community identity seemed more interested in maintaining an older, more rural mindset that would protect local communities against threats from the rapidly changing larger world. Only then would the Panhandle be safe. Local voters finally discovered their national hero during the 1968 presidential election: former vice president Richard Nixon, who was the Republican Party's nominee. The area was apparently under siege: hippies, radicals, the SDS, and Black activists all threatened to remake the area's social makeup, most threateningly on its school campuses. What made this worse, according to the typical voter, was that these forces came from the "outside," meaning the larger country. Consequently, anyone, such as a young man like Wayne Woodward whose natural inclination was to question authority, would find himself or herself labeled an "outsider." Nixon was overwhelmingly popular in the Panhandle: he won 78 percent of the vote during his reelection bid in 1972.[17] No presidential candidate had so thoroughly swept the Panhandle electorate since Roosevelt in 1936. Voters were thus no longer marginalized political activists but rather proud Republicans, supporting a man who had a tremendous amount of experience in government, who had run with an appeal to the so-called silent majority of quiet Americans who did not participate in the turbulent 1960s counterculture. Since 1972, the Panhandle persisted as one of the most solid blocks of support for Republican Party politics in the entire country, let alone the state of Texas.

One element that often goes overlooked in the literature on modern conservatism's rise is the backlash politics of the early 1970s. For example, in 1970, the conservative Lloyd Bentsen defeated the liberal Ralph Yarborough as well as the more moderate George H. W. Bush in a senatorial race by portraying himself as the backlash conservative option against mainstream liberal Democratic and middle-of-the-road Republican Party politics. Furthermore, as the historian Sean Cunningham notes, conservative backlash politics took a sharp antiliberal and antiestablishment turn throughout the Nixon administration. The Watergate Scandal of 1972–74, in fact, paradoxically benefited Texas Republicans—it seemed to prove that establishment Republicans had lost their way.[18] Consequently, the early 1970s—the time when Wayne Woodward ran afoul of Hereford powerbrokers—was the same decade in which local elements now swirling together would have rejected a political nonconformist as a vile threat to the community.

What did it mean to be a conservative in the Texas Panhandle of the 1960s and '70s, then? Locals were well aware of the charges that moderates and liberals made against them, namely, that they were lunatics and crackpots. The conservative commentator Joseph Alsop noted in a 1966 speech covered by the *Amarillo Globe-Times* that in the United States, "the word 'conservative' has been strangely debased to stand for crackpot Texas millionaires, hot-eyed, Birch Society members and Southern racists." For him as well as many others, though, it had now been reclaimed in the "normal political lexicon." He continued, arguing that "'conservative' is still an honorable word, meaning a practical, national-minded man who holds to the old ways while being willing, maybe a bit grudgingly, to support great innovations when the national interest demands them."[19] In other words, conservatives were traditionalists who simply wanted to be left alone. Clearly, the changing nature of government as well as the tumult of the middle of the twentieth century helped people in the Texas Panhandle articulate this shared sense of values in unprecedented ways. Alsop would be the first to admit, though, that such ideas were grounded in the very fabric of Panhandle communities. The older world was better. Conservatism had come of age in the Texas Panhandle to protect itself against threats coming from the greater part of urban or coastal America, as well as the outside world more broadly.

Growing Up "Liberal" in the Panhandle during the Civil Rights Era

Importantly, the new conservative political ethic's emphasis on community values as well as belonging meant that some people at the local level simply would not fit in. Panhandle Texans prided themselves on their friendliness and neighborliness, but outsiders—people who fit with the above-mentioned trends of the 1960s and '70s, or people who more generally simply sought to change the area's sociopolitical order—sometimes found themselves shunned.[20]

Wayne Woodward was one such individual.

Woodward was born in Freeport, Texas, in 1944, but he moved to Amarillo, the region's largest city, when he was four years old. Woodward's childhood was a relatively normal one for a boy born in Texas at that time. His father was a conservative whose speech was peppered with racial epithets. Woodward's mother was a liberal from the Texas Hill Country who had sympathies with the poor as well as prisoners in chain gangs, which had been common in Texas since the early twentieth century. Woodward's father passed away in a car accident when he was young, so he spent the rest of his childhood and adolescence being raised by his mother. Notable, however, given his mother's politics—which were in line with the liberal leanings of Lyndon Johnson, who was born and raised in the same area—was the fact that Woodward grew up in an essentially apolitical household. When politics did come up, it was usually within the context of a presidential election. Woodward's father was shocked, for example, when his mother supported Democrat Adlai Stevenson over Republican Dwight Eisenhower in the 1956 election. Nonetheless, as stated earlier, Woodward himself would later admit that he did not grow up "liberal" in any traditional sense of the word. His political awakening would be some time in coming. He did, however, have a tendency to question authority and to talk back to authority figures, which certainly did not serve him well in Hereford after beginning his career as a teacher.[21]

Woodward, as stated earlier, recalled segregation and racism growing up in Amarillo. Segregation was quite simply a fact of life that few whites in the city questioned. Segregated buses and water fountains were common; restaurants and public institutions were also segregated. Woodward attended Tascosa High School in Amarillo during the 1960s, which of course was also a segregated school. Tascosa's mascot was the "Rebels," complete with Confederate iconography. At one point, Woodward attended a football game against another local school, Palo Duro High School, which was one of the few schools in the area that was already integrated. When one player scored a touchdown for Palo Duro, an audience member nearby remarked that the touchdown should only count for half, since the player who scored it was Black. Despite this, Woodward could not recall being aware of a single public incident involving an organization like the Ku Klux Klan while growing up in the Panhandle. Given the region's overwhelmingly Caucasian demographic makeup, the Klan perhaps served little purpose in an isolated area like the urban Texas Panhandle.[22]

Woodward was never conscious of being treated differently because of his views or beliefs, but this was in large part due to the fact that he would not experience anything resembling a political "awakening" of sorts until his college years. Of course, he was still quite conscious of issues related to race. A Black student tried to join his fraternity, Sigma Nu, at West Texas State, but that effort was quickly quashed. Similarly, at a Sigma Nu party at a nearby Holiday Inn hotel, Woodward asked a Black waiter who seemed to be a good dancer to show him some of his moves—he later found out that the waiter had been fired for fraternizing with a white patron. As he came of age, then, Woodward took notice that society was unfairly cruel to African Americans and other ethnic minorities.

Woodward's experience of an "awakening" at college during this time period was not unique to him, even in a place as overwhelmingly conservative as the Texas Panhandle. Marty Kuhlman—the son of a local wheat farmer and German immigrant—grew up in the region during this same time, which naturally steered him toward a more conservative outlook. Kuhlman himself was exposed, for example, to the typical racial points of view that were common among Caucasians in the Panhandle, but he would later admit that as a young boy he never really understood why whites believed the things they did about Blacks. Typical of most young Panhandle Texans during the middle of the twentieth century, Kuhlman also believed in the ideals that people should be responsible for their own well-being and that government handouts had no place in society (a common idea, as already established, after the local turn against New Deal programs after the Great Depression ended). College, however, changed him. Only when he was a student at West Texas State during the 1970s did Kuhlman learn that the U.S. South was built on the backs of slave labor. When Kuhlman revealed to his roommate that he voted for Jimmy Carter instead of Ronald Reagan during the election of 1980, his roommate refused to speak to him.[23]

Despite the broadened horizons that young men like Woodward and Kuhlman experienced during their respective tenures as students at West Texas State University, Woodward himself was really in his midtwenties when he "woke up" up politically, which he attributed to the help of several history professors at Amarillo College and West Texas State, as well as a number of his friends whom he had met at both institutions. Several of his friends encouraged Woodward to become more politically engaged and active. History professors made him realize, for the first time in his life, that he was not fully in touch with life in the Panhandle, particularly its political culture. Of course, Woodward's engagement with the student activism of the time only made him more of an outlier in terms of his political affiliations. His friend Don Cooney was vocally critical about U.S. involvement in the Vietnam War; a few years later, when Woodward accepted his teaching position in Hereford, Woodward invited Cooney to speak to his class about the war. He knew that bringing in an antiwar speaker like Cooney would curry little favor with the school administration or his colleagues, so Woodward invited Cooney under an assumed name, told his students he was a Harvard professor, and snuck him into his classroom through a back door in the school building. Such extreme measures, though comical, were necessitated by the burgeoning political climate in the Panhandle during the 1960s and '70s, which, as has already been demonstrated, tolerated little criticism of U.S. involvement in Southeast Asia as well as the defense of the free world against communism.[24]

What, then, did it mean to come of age in the Texas Panhandle during such tumultuous years as the 1960 and '70s? Liberalism and large government frightened many people, which is understandable given the larger context of the region's history. As stated in the previous chapter, the Panhandle had remained isolated since the vanquishing of Comanche power and through the settlement of the region by cattlemen, farmers, and others who had deep roots in rural communities in the U.S. Midwest and larger western regions. Reactions against the seeming intrusion of the New Deal, combined with the tumult of the Vietnam War and social movements after World War II, put on full display that the world was bent on crashing in on this isolated space. In these circumstances, the new conservatives helped locals navigate the rapid changes taking place in the larger country. Conservatism had deep roots in the Panhandle, but its coalescence during the postwar era reveals a political outlook driven not by partisanship but rather by a sense of new beginnings. In this way, Panhandle conservatism had more in common with newer forms of identity politics like feminism, civil rights organizing, ethnic identities, and the New Left than previous historians have realized. Naturally, not all people at the local level would fit the shifting sands of place-based belonging that swept through the region. While many would find comfort, belonging, and purpose in the new conservatism, others would find themselves at odds with this new culture. Wayne Woodward was one of those people; Marty Kuhlman later became one of those people. They were a minority in the area.

Social outsiders tend to gather together, and such was the case for Woodward and several people with whom he became close during his formative college years. Don Cooney was one such person. Cooney was born in Chicago, Illinois, to a conservative Catholic family that relocated to Amarillo. His father's politics, perhaps unsurprisingly, were similar to Woodward's father's—later in life, Cooney's father had a wall of photographs dedicated to the iconic Ronald Reagan, which he lovingly dubbed "St. Reagan's wall." Politically, Cooney's father certainly fit in well in the Texas Panhandle—he had once credited Franklin Roosevelt for saving capitalism during the Great Depression, which he had experienced as a young man in South Dakota, but his views on Roosevelt as well as liberalism in particular had shifted during the intervening decades.[25]

Just because Cooney grew up in a conservative household did not mean that he fit in well with his peers in Amarillo. Cooney attended a Catholic school for six years before transferring to a public high school, at which point he became increasingly cognizant of the differences between himself and others. Most of the other students were native Texans who grew up in evangelical Protestant churches; their understanding of Catholicism did not even recognize people like Cooney as Christians. Much of this was reflective of Amarillo's still-relative status as an isolated area in the middle of the United States. Racial prejudice, as stated, was an accepted part of this still-isolated Texas culture. As a young man, Cooney noted the somewhat latent tendencies of conservatism coming to the fore during the 1960s. Much of this had to do with Lyndon Johnson; not only was Johnson a Texas Democrat as well as a liberal, but his signing of the Civil Rights Act in 1964 as well as the Voting Rights Act in 1965 represented under-the-surface threats to notions of white supremacy in the Texas Panhandle. Johnson also failed to endear himself to Panhandle voters when he announced the closure of the Amarillo Air Force Base after his 1964 election. Still, Blacks' agitation for rights, in Cooney's words, "drove them crazy." Concurrently, protests against the Vietnam War during the late 1960s struck many Panhandle voters as unpatriotic and abhorrent. As an outsider—though not necessarily someone who had liberal tendencies as a young man—Cooney, perhaps like Woodward, was well suited to note these tendencies among the vast majority of the people whom he encountered on a daily basis.[26]

Hippies were not common in the Texas Panhandle during the 1960s, but nonetheless, Cooney self-identified as one. As a young man, he was very much influenced by the culture and music of the times. Also, unlike many of his peers in the Panhandle, he was opposed to the Vietnam War. For Cooney, the war was what really turned him against the Panhandle's larger conservative culture. Cooney was a Marine Corps reservist who never actually had to go to Vietnam, which in his case might have saved his life, as most of his platoon was wiped out just six months after its deployment. Like many young men at the time, Cooney developed a problem with alcohol, but the war itself was a major turning point in his outlook on everything and made him want to change things when it ended. The music got more radical, of course, and Cooney absorbed all this, and it started to make sense to him. He was eventually discharged due to his "conscientious objector" status. After the war, he relocated to Austin, Texas, which was the only real bastion of liberal thinking and antiwar ideas in the state. He also joined the New American Movement, which was a democratic socialist organization. Cooney was in and out of Amarillo at the time; perhaps unsurprisingly, none of the antiwar protests taking place in the state occurred in Amarillo, due in large part to the area's monolithic conservative culture. Cooney later recalled that the American Nazi Party—which, again, had at least some following in the Texas Panhandle—organized many counterprotests against antiwar demonstrations in Texas, although Cooney could not recall that any violence occurred during any of the demonstrations. Although the American Nazi Party was by no means widely popular in the deeply conservative Texas Panhandle, its pro-war stance still would have been in line with the overwhelming majority of the more mainstream conservative population in places like Amarillo and Hereford.[27]

As in Woodward's case, however, it is striking how little any of Cooney's misfit status in Amarillo had anything to do with politics. Politics seemed only a secondary concern that came from looking at society from an angle that was unpopular. Cooney himself was not as outspoken as his friend Woodward, but he nevertheless cheered Woodward on as the latter attempted to rile up locals. In the earlier incident when Woodward snuck Cooney in through the back door of his school as an anti–Vietnam War guest speaker disguised as a Harvard professor, Cooney recalled the thrill of participating in the event as well as how rewarding it was when students, who at first suspected him of being a communist sympathizer, eventually admitted that perhaps the Vietnam War was not a well-thought-out conflict. Of course, however, their politics were not palatable—parents who heard about such antics complained to school officials, which was the start of Woodward's problems at the school. Cooney himself admitted that Woodward would not have run afoul of locals if ultimately his politics were more in line with the conservative nature of the Panhandle's political culture.[28] Nonetheless, because of the tenor of the times, local responses to misfits like Cooney and Woodward would become more martial and increasingly aggressive.

A generation of people like Woodward, Kuhlman, and Cooney grew into adulthood in the Texas Panhandle just while Panhandle conservatism itself also came of age politically. Any one of them who chose to stay in the Panhandle into the 1970s would have to contend with a regional culture with which they remained at odds; one that, indeed, might forcefully reject them in ways that simply had not occurred before the 1960s. Woodward, perhaps most visibly, made that choice. It is to his story that the rest of this book now turns.

CHAPTER 3

THE TEACHER

Hereford, where Wayne Woodward lived and worked, was not an atypical Texas Panhandle town. Much like the rest of the area, Hereford—a small farming and ranching community about thirty miles west of Canyon, Texas, where Woodward attended college—was settled and incorporated rather late, in keeping with the local sense of the region being part of the last frontier of the United States. The town was founded in 1898 along the lines of the Pecos and Northern Texas Railway; initial settlers called it Bluewater due to its proximity to the Tierra Blanca Creek just to the south. Federal postal authorities soon notified locals that there was already a Blue Water, Texas, so locals changed the name to Hereford after the cattle type brought to the area by its first ranchers. Hereford's first school was founded in 1900, with the area's schools being constituted as an independent school district a few years later in 1908. By 1913, enrollment in the district included 445 students and thirteen teachers in two school buildings. The district grew steadily from that point forward until the middle of the twentieth century.[1]

Hereford thrived as a railroad town during the early twentieth century. By 1900, the town already counted 532 residents. The *Hereford Reporter*—later known as the *Hereford Brand*, the same local newspaper that would cover Woodward's court case—began publishing in 1901. By 1906, after some delays, Herefordites voted to incorporate their town, which in turn paved the way for modern civic development. One of the reasons for Hereford's early success at attracting settlers was its plentiful groundwater supply (unusual levels of fluoride in the town's water led locals to dub Hereford "the town without a toothache," which also allowed local producers to market the town's water supply worldwide by the middle of the twentieth century). Although the town also developed a strong reputation for livestock raising, dryland farming gave way to irrigated farming by the 1930s and '40s after locals tapped into the underground Ogallala Aquifer water supply. The local vegetable industry that became so prominent during Woodward's time had its origins in the founding of the 1939 Hereford Potato Growers Association. Still, despite such rapid development, Hereford's population remained small—only 5,207 people lived in the town by 1950.[2] The insulated nature of this small town in the Texas Panhandle stemmed from a mixture of the settlement's relative success during the early twentieth century and the fact that its demographics were largely homogeneous. Most people in Hereford were Caucasians as late as the early 1960s, though the importance of a demographic change that swept through the town around that time will be addressed later.

Wayne Woodward first came to work in Hereford in September of 1969 when the school district hired him to teach seventh- and ninth-grade English.[3] Woodward had taught the previous year at a school in Shoshone, California, a town of about five hundred people in Death Valley. He taught world history, U.S. history, and world geography to middle school and high school students. Woodward had grown up in the Texas Panhandle and wanted to see something of the rest of the world, but after a year in Death Valley, he decided he didn't like rural California. A friend got him an introduction to interview for a position at La Plata Junior High School in Hereford. The school did not have any openings in history, but it did hire him to teach English.[4] As was standard throughout the Hereford Independent School District, as well as many others across the state and country, Woodward received annual contracts that could be renewed by the school board, allowing him continued employment.[5]

Woodward drove into Hereford during the 1969 "summer of love," which was the height of the hippie revolution. He wondered if arriving in Hereford with California license plates on his car might mark him as a hippie or a subversive. To their credit, the people of Hereford did not seem to view him that way, at least initially. Not long after moving to town, someone asked him to join a local chapter of the Lions Club as well as the Kiwanis Club, both of which were international civic service organizations. Woodward remembered a friend's father in Amarillo who had been a member of the Lions Club, and he had "talked horribly about minorities." With that experience having soured his impression of the group, Woodward politely declined both invitations. After that, he was basically left alone.[6]

Woodward's students, for the most part, liked him. Personal notes that students gave to him over the years serve as a testament to their general devotion. One seventh grader told him that he was "the best teacher I ever had" and that "I want to have you in the ninth grade." Another student reported that Woodward was "a good teacher because he likes teaching kids[,] he cares about them[,] he's not a grown up that pushes you aside or thinks a child is to be seen not heard. He cares or he wouldn't have spent more than half his life learning [sic] kids. He's not like teachers who are just here to make money and pass time." Students routinely reported that Woodward was fun, fair, and engaging. Woodward treated his students more like adults as opposed to children, to which many of them responded positively. He asked for their opinions and took them seriously as people: "I really think this is the best English class I have ever had. I [am] free to say what I want in here. I don't have to hide any of my feelings, and I think that's great. I've enjoyed the books that we read in here too. Most of them have been real good. I like the way you teach too, it is never boring and usually English classes are boring."[7]

Even the students who provided critical feedback regarding Woodward's teaching admitted his pedagogical talents: "Some people can get away with murder and some can't do a thing. Like Doug doing math in here or Steve talking all the time. I think its [sic] a good class but we need more discussions about important things that are happening in this world, don't have it be such a routine thing. I know your [sic] held down quite a bit but we do need more of a difference in routine day by day."[8] Woodward was clearly the kind of teacher that most schools would strive to attract—he was intelligent, young, interested in his students, and able to get them to think critically about important topics. Perhaps most important, Woodward was also a talented male teacher in a field generally dominated by women. Put simply, things seemed to be going well during his first few years in Hereford.

Signs of Things to Come

None of this is to say that Woodward's early teaching years were without difficulty. Pat Hughes—an assistant principal who was later promoted to principal, at which time he would become Woodward's chief antagonist—appears to have disliked Woodward from the start. Hughes was a big man with a thick West Texas drawl; he seemed to naturally distrust Woodward, who was a little younger, more laid back, and perhaps most importantly, a member of the 1960s generation. Additionally, Woodward's natural bent for outspokenly questioning authority ran him afoul of Hughes on multiple occasions. Hughes, for example, had the tendency to listen in on Woodward's classroom through the school's PA system. The problem, though, was that

Woodward was attuned to a certain buzzing or clicking sound that the system made when Hughes turned it on from the principal's office. Woodward—as a joke—once coached his students to exclaim in unison, "Good morning, Mr. Hughes!" one morning when this happened. Naturally, Hughes was not amused.[9]

Politics occasionally crept into school business. In 1972, the superintendent of schools, Roy Hartman, circulated a petition for teachers to sign who were in opposition to the recently reintroduced Equal Rights Amendment (ERA) to the U.S. Constitution. The ERA had first been introduced in 1923, when it failed in Congress. The renewed intent was to provide a constitutional amendment that guaranteed gender equality in the United States. Conservatives generally opposed the amendment on the grounds that it challenged traditional gender roles. Several teachers, including Woodward, refused to sign Hartman's petition. Woodward himself believed that Hartman likely circulated the petition at the behest of locals in fear that if he failed to do that, he might potentially lose his position as superintendent. Such an impulse exemplifies not only the region's homogeneous political outlook but also locals' desire to enforce a certain conformity in contrast to the cultural liberalism sweeping through the rest of the country.[10]

Problems with the younger generation's physical appearance—as outlined in the previous chapter with the incident relating to a West Texas State University student whom a dean denied access to a federal loan until the student agreed to stop dressing like a hippie—also occurred with Woodward. In one incident, Hughes instructed Woodward to get a haircut because his hair hung below his ears. Woodward, ever the one to question Hughes's authority, pointed out that Hughes's hair—which he wore slicked back—was in fact probably even longer than his. Hughes responded by daring Woodward to grab his hair to see whose was actually longer—one can imagine the shock on Hughes's face when Woodward *actually* reached across the desk and did just that, although he did find that Hughes's hair was shorter than he thought. The tension in the room must have been palpable.[11] Ever desirous of people respecting social order at the local level, men like Hughes did not tolerate a younger generation that not only questioned authority but also seemed to have an actual disdain for authority figures. Woodward's response, to Hughes, showed that older notions of unquestioned respect for authority ran counter to Woodward's expectations. Woodward questioning his supervisor undoubtedly helped transform him into a microscopic embodiment of the social changes taking place in the larger country—the exact changes that men like Hughes hoped to reject in their quest to keep big government and cultural liberalism out of the Texas Panhandle.

Culture aside, politics were again an occasional problem. In the fall of 1973, seventh-grade life science teacher John Murdock sent a telegram to the local U.S. congressional representative George Mahon stating that Richard M. Nixon's continued inhabitance of the White House was a national disgrace in the wake of the ongoing Watergate scandal. Murdock informed Mahon that if he wanted to maintain his vote, he should make any possible effort to remove Nixon from office. Several other teachers, including Woodward, signed the note, which Woodward sent to Washington, D.C., on his lunch break (Woodward also sent the same message to U.S. Senators Lloyd Bentsen and John Tower). Later that afternoon, Hughes interrupted Woodward's class to take him into the library for a private discussion. Someone at an administrative staff meeting had complained to Hughes that Murdock and Woodward had circulated a petition calling for Nixon's resignation; after arguing over whether the note should be classified as a petition or a telegram, Hughes informed the teachers that he should have been consulted on the matter first. Hughes met with them again a few days later under the pretext that the teachers should not be sending out telegrams on school hours, period.[12] Woodward had thus come to Hughes's attention as a teacher whom he needed to control in his role as school principal.

Woodward himself recalled another incident in 1973 that was indicative of the cultural clashes taking place at the school. During the spring semester of that year, Hughes called Woodward into his office for a meeting with Superintendent Hartman. One of the school board members had somehow deduced that Woodward was an atheist, which was upsetting, especially given the fact that the board member's own daughter happened to be one of Woodward's students. Although Woodward could not later recall the names of the board member or the student, he did recall wondering whether the board member or his wife talked routinely to their daughter about him.[13] His personal religious views were of such a concern to the administration that he clearly, in their view, needed some kind of disciplinary intervention perhaps in the hopes of either releasing him if he was actually an atheist, or changing his mind so he could fit in better with the conservative Christian culture of the town. Additionally, Woodward later recalled that either Hughes or Hartman told him "not to tell students I don't go to church," as this information was simply too shocking for them to hear. Furthermore, Woodward later realized that when the administration had built up a case to terminate him, their instructions to keep his lack of church attendance a secret—especially given the legal defense's contention that a multiplicity of actions led to Woodward's later firing in the spring of 1975—could in fact be legally defined as religious discrimination.[14] Either way, this small incident was indicative of the fact that as early as 1973 there was some concern among school and community leaders that Woodward was a dangerous person who did not fit in with the larger town.

Despite the potential for drama stemming from such incidents, Woodward never felt as if he received wholly unfair treatment from Hughes and Hartman before his sixth year of teaching. In fact, the Hereford School Board renewed Woodward's teaching contract on an annual basis without any major concerns.[15] The years thus passed with hardly any incidents of note, until Woodward made a fateful decision in January of 1975—he decided to start a local chapter of the American Civil Liberties Union (ACLU).

The ACLU in Rural America

To fully appreciate the severe shift this represented to Panhandle conservatives of the 1970s, a word on the ACLU is in order. The ACLU was founded in 1915 by a number of prominent Progressive-Era activists, perhaps most notably Jane Addams, the founder and proprietor of Hull House in Chicago, as well as Lillian Wald of the Henry Street Settlement House of New York. Both women advocated for working-class people's rights. Such antecedents alone would be enough to make any Panhandle conservative cringe. Wald and Addams—and thus, the ACLU—could be perceived through the lens of radicalism due to their dedication to social justice for the poor, mostly immigrant working classes in early twentieth-century American cities. Roger Baldwin, who joined the organization in 1917, routinely opened letters to fellow ACLU members with the salutation "Dear brother" or "Dear comrade." Indeed, as one historian notes, the organization's board of directors during these early years "looked like a broad-based radical coalition of Communists, Socialists, labor unionists, liberal intellectuals, social concerned clergymen, and parlor pinks."[16] Additionally, the organization's "first annual report called for 'a union of organized labor, the farmers, radical and liberal movements.'"[17] The ACLU was thus born of the strain of early twentieth-century leftist politics that mid-twentieth-century Panhandle conservatives consciously sought to reject. Perhaps ironically, this rejection of the ACLU existed despite the fact that the People's Party, known colloquially as "the Populists," enjoyed some level of popular support in the Panhandle, sending delegates to the party's convention in Waco way back in 1894. Although the People's Party rose to prominence and then disappeared several decades before the ACLU's founding, left-leaning or potentially even radical politics themselves had obviously not always been so resoundingly rejected in the Texas Panhandle as they were by the 1970s.[18]

Given the ACLU's radical bent, it comes as no surprise that locals in the decidedly anticommunist Texas Panhandle who were familiar with the organization might have reacted so swiftly against the founding of an ACLU chapter in one of their own communities. Of course, perhaps the ACLU's then more recent battle in favor of ratifying the Equal Rights Amendment—which, as stated previously, was clearly anathema to Hereford's political culture—would have been enough to create an onslaught of judgment and social marginalization for Woodward in January of 1975.[19] Either way, Woodward's well-intentioned founding of an ACLU chapter in Hereford marked a drastic falling-out with the school administration as well as members of the local community.

Radical roots aside, to many, the ACLU had long stood as an organization that simply sought to protect Americans' civil liberties. Such was the idea that Woodward had when launching the Hereford chapter of the organization. As shown earlier, Woodward's own politics had leaned to the left since his time in college during the 1960s; nonetheless, it would be mistaken to argue that Woodward self-identified as anything resembling a "liberal activist" during his tenure at La Plata Junior High School. Woodward was, at this stage of his life, a young man who was admittedly somewhat naïve. Just how little Woodward understood the local political climate can be seen by the fact that he took it upon himself to announce to a local radio station that the ACLU chapter was now in existence, should anyone wish to join. Woodward was thus completely unaware of the fallout that such an action could incur, nor was he aware that the politics of most radio outlets across the Texas Panhandle skewed too far to the political right for any media outlets in the region to consider a new ACLU chapter as anything but radical liberalism infiltrating the Panhandle.[20]

Perhaps the issue would have faded had Woodward done nothing else. Unfortunately, he made one additional mistake. Woodward mentioned the ACLU in class to his students around the same time that he contacted the local radio station. After class was over, one student, Pam Whitley, asked Woodward if he had any literature on the organization, to which he replied in the affirmative. The next day, Woodward brought Whitley a membership pamphlet. Whitley's friend Cindy Ford was sitting next to her and also asked for a pamphlet. When Ford's father discovered what had happened, he lodged a complaint with school board member Roy Martin. Parental complaints to board members about teachers were relatively common in Hereford, but notably, this was the only complaint ever lodged about Woodward during his six-year tenure at the school.[21]

Clearly, the school's administration had tolerated Woodward's politics up to this point. In reality, what harm could come from complaining to one's legislators about a corrupt president (Nixon) needing to be removed from office (Hughes's complaint about Woodward doing so on school time aside)? Starting an ACLU chapter, though, was a different matter. When Woodward announced the founding of his chapter, the psychological alarm bells of identity and the distasteful looming presence of cultural liberalism went off in the minds of many. Woodward, of course, would have had no way of knowing any of this at the time—he had unconsciously marked himself as a threat amid the region's now popularized conservative ideals. Unfortunately, the downhill slope would prove quite steep.

A few weeks later, on February 4, Hughes called Woodward into his office. Hughes wanted to know what a recent Hereford ACLU meeting was all about. Woodward informed him that he was free to attend future meetings. In response, Hughes said, "No, I better not do that, I would have more people mad at me than I do now." Woodward later recalled that "he asked me to name the members of the A.C.L.U. (here) and I did."[22] Three days later, on February 7, 1975, Hughes walked into the office of Superintendent Hartman to discuss Woodward. During the conversation, Hughes explained to Hartman that Woodward was "determined to express a hostile attitude to efforts of the school administration to carry out board policy by his attitude and refusal to accept decisions by his superiors." Furthermore, according to Hughes, Woodward had "apparently used material in the classroom which has not been cleared for use through normal school channels prior to their actual use." Hughes thus made recommendations to Hartman regarding Woodward's appointment at the school, which would be delivered to the teacher five days later in the form of the following typed letter:

Dear Mr. Hartman:

This letter is to confirm our conversation in your office on the seventh of February.

It appears to me that Mr. Woodward is determined to express a hostile attitude toward efforts of the school administration to carry out board policy by his attitude and his refusal to accept decisions by his superiors.

Mr. Woodward has apparently used material in the classroom which has not been cleared for use through normal school channels prior to their actual use.

I would recommend that Mr. Woodward's contract not be re-newed until such time that he proves to me that he is supporting the school policies and using material in his room which has been approved by the proper personnel. At the school board meeting in May, I will make the recommendation concerning Mr. Woodward's contract, until that time I consider him to be on a probationary basis.

Sincerely,
Pat Hughes.[23]

Woodward had thus gone from being a popular teacher in good standing to being placed on a probationary status seemingly overnight. The timing—just weeks after the revelation of Woodward's involvement in establishing a local ACLU presence—was telling.

Five days later, Hughes sent Woodward a note to meet him in his office at 2:30 P.M. that day. Woodward had been busy, so the meeting was delayed until 3:45. At the meeting, Hughes simply handed the letter to Woodward. Hughes asked Woodward if he had anything to say on the matter after he read the letter, to which Woodward replied, "I'll hand this over to my lawyer," and he got up and walked out of the room.[24]

The letter made young Woodward, who was about thirty years old at the time, feel like he had been hit with a sledgehammer. Nevertheless, he was not entirely surprised. Sometime during the preceding weeks, Hughes had called Woodward and his colleague Bruce Logan, a history teacher, into his office, ostensibly to discuss issues pertaining to hairstyles as well as the school's dress code. The conversation turned quickly to whether either of the teachers had solicited student membership in the ACLU, which both, of course, denied. Logan, in fact, had already denied his own membership in the ACLU outright to Hughes and immediately resigned from the organization, but he felt that Hughes was perhaps trying to entrap him by requestioning him. Woodward was also frightened. Hughes had informed Woodward that he would be evaluated again at the end of May; additionally, Hughes had begun calling in the school's vice principal to all their meetings. During one meeting, the vice principal informed Woodward that he would "hunt for anything he could find to get me out and would be watching me every day." Woodward later told a friend that he "may be paranoid but I don't like the idea of me meeting with both of them at the same time, I feel that they will distort the truth in our meetings."[25] Indeed, both young men had clear reasons to feel not only concerned but also intimidated.

Notably, Logan had received a similar letter addressed by Hughes to Hartman on the same day as Woodward had, although his letter was far less severe in tone:

Dear Mr. Hartman:

This letter concerns the recommendation of Mr. Bruce Logan for the 1975–76 school year. I have suggested several changes to Mr. Logan regarding his method of handling students, attitude toward school policy and his criticism of his fellow teachers.

I am confident Mr. Logan will make these changes by May. I will make the recommendation concerning his appointment for the coming year at that time.

Sincerely,
Pat Hughes[26]

One might surmise that Logan's immediate response of resigning from the ACLU had already proven satisfactory to Hughes. Still, Woodward questioned whether it was permissible for the teachers to be members of such an organization on a weekend or after-school basis. Woodward asked, "Do you mean that I can't do what I want on the weekends?" Hughes apparently responded with, "Yes, as a teacher you . . . have to fit a mold. And . . . teachers have to do some things that other members of the community don't have to." As long as their membership in such an organization was not a distraction to the students, Logan chimed in, he did not understand why it was a problem. Hughes responded that being a teacher was a "24-7 job."[27] Hughes also told both teachers that they should completely support decisions made by the school board whether or not they actually agreed with them. The question of loyalty to the school board came up repeatedly during the discussions of whether Logan's contract would be renewed, which eventually it was.[28]

While the true nature of Woodward's problems with the school district stemmed primarily from his status as a freethinker who had a penchant for questioning authority, Logan's outsider status, he believed, stemmed from his own seeming cosmopolitanism. Woodward's lawyer in his upcoming court case, Robin Green, later told the two men that "missionaries and prophets have never been welcome in their own hometowns," meaning that Logan, who despite being only twenty-nine years old at the time, had traveled the world and had a lot of experiences. As such, he was not fully welcomed by the school's administration because he was an outsider. Logan noted that he was a ninth-grade world history teacher but that he had recently been contracted to start teaching seventh graders due to a need at La Plata; also, he had assigned Socrates and Thomas More, had a good rapport with the students, and "turned the lights on in some of their heads." This, he argued, seemed to bother Hughes, Hartman, and the school board. Logan believed that the administrators wanted him teaching at a junior college or a university because he was "messing with [the students'] minds."[29]

Logan, in his conversation with Green and Woodward, diagnosed the problem with lucidity:

> I think that what you're fighting is something that I can see present all through history ... the inhibiting of agriculture and civilization in largely agricultural communities ... the same thing was true back in Rome ... during the reign of the Franks and the Maraviches ... when you predominately remove yourself from the metropolis ... you're in a situation where the rapid interchange of ideas is just absolutely stymied ... I think you're fighting geography here as much as the ideas ... I think it's all a messed up sociological phenomenon. You start with these little country towns ... it's true almost every place you go. I've lived in an agricultural area ... it was a lot like that.[30]

In other words, the problems that the young teachers faced in Hereford were simply a contemporary iteration of a problem that was as old as humanity itself. Logan believed that the powerbrokers were paranoid or threatened by the ACLU in particular. Logan had only one direct conversation with the administrators about the ACLU, wherein they intimated that it would be a good idea if he just quit the organization. As further proof of this paranoia, Logan also related that he had been accused of various "isms" during his time in Hereford, such as atheism or communism. The school's counselor, Mary Duvall, told Logan that "Hereford's just not a radical town. It just doesn't need to be changed. We're a conservative community and it shouldn't be changed."[31] Woodward and Logan simply never could gain acceptance as full members of the community.

Hughes, as an agent of the local populace, clearly had a problem with an ACLU presence not only on the campus but also in the larger town. Naturally, though, as far as Woodward knew, he had not done anything wrong that could jeopardize his career. Woodward may have had a few minor issues with authority figures, but Hughes had never given him any reason to suspect that the administration was dissatisfied with his job performance, at least up to this point. Hughes had, in fact, visited Woodward's classroom before, and he had previously noted with apparent surprise (probably given the nature of their working relationship) that not only was Woodward extraordinarily professional in front of his students, but that he had a good rapport with them as well. Every time Hughes visited Woodward's classroom, Hughes noted that Woodward presented the material well and that in general terms Woodward was "doing a fairly good job." Hughes, in fact, later went on record as saying that his complaints about Woodward did not stem from anything that was going on in Woodward's classroom. Likewise, he had never received any complaints from students or parents about Woodward's teaching.[32]

Upon learning that his contract was probably not going to be renewed, Woodward requested a hearing to determine the charges against him and to demonstrate, in his view, that Hughes and Hartman were motivated by their objection to his association with and activities on behalf of the ACLU. No one—save Hughes and Hartman, later—could argue against the fact that Woodward had only truly run afoul of the administration upon announcing his founding of the local ACLU chapter.[33] Woodward's reliance on a lawyer, Hughes and Hartman would later counter, caused the lines of communication to break down to the point that Woodward could no longer be employed at La Plata. Woodward thought that this charge, however, was highly debatable. Also, Woodward could make little sense of the charge that he had passed out materials in class that required Hughes's preapproval. Hughes had asked some of Woodward's students if he had passed out ACLU materials in class. They responded that he had not, but that he had written an address on the chalkboard in his classroom where interested students could obtain ACLU materials. Hughes complained about Woodward not clearing material through him, but the only material that *had* to be cleared through him—according to Hughes—was controversial material. School rules did not require teachers to clear tests or copies of any short stories with the principal. Again, the charges that he had behaved improperly in some way did not seem to add up.[34]

The issue of Woodward passing out materials that were not yet approved could only have stemmed from providing Whitley and Ford with ACLU pamphlets at the students' own request. As stated earlier, Whitley had taken an interest in the ACLU after a class discussion on the organization and requested that Woodward provide her with some additional information on the group, which he did, but it was during a so-called passing period between classes. Although there is no direct evidence about what Hartman, the parents, or the other board members thought about the ACLU, the fact of such a seemingly innocuous incident between a teacher and a student going all the way up to the top of the administration in the school district clearly indicates the grave reaction locals had to the organization's presence. Allegedly, Hartman had privately ordered Hughes to "get rid of" the ACLU problem.[35]

Other corroborating evidence suggests that the letter was, in fact, motivated by Woodward's ACLU participation. Around the time that Woodward received his letter, Hughes called one of his students, Kathy Wilson, into the principal's office for a discussion. Mary Duvall, the school's counselor, was also present. Hughes asked Wilson if Woodward had ever said anything to upset the students, to which she replied in the negative and offered that she believed Woodward was a good teacher. The duo asked specifically if Woodward had ever shown the students any literature from the ACLU, to which Wilson once again said no. Wilson went on to offer that he had never talked about the organization in class; if he had said anything to a student at all it was because, in her view, the student (Whitley or Ford) had specifically asked him. Finally, either Duvall or Hughes also asked if Woodward had ever said anything demeaning about God in class, to which Wilson, once again, replied in the negative. Wilson ended the discussion by informing the principal and counselor that she was aware of Woodward's situation of potentially not being rehired and she believed it was a mistake.[36]

Although it seemed fairly obvious that he had been targeted because of his membership in the ACLU, Woodward agreed, after Hughes conferred with him, not to pass out any more ACLU materials in the future. Woodward did state that he had a legal right to do so, but that he would refrain from passing out ACLU pamphlets in the future anyway to meet Hughes's wishes. Nonetheless, his seeming submission to Hughes's authority did not indicate any tacit acceptance of his fate at the hands of school administrators. In fact, Woodward remained as antiauthoritarian and individualistic as ever. In March, about a month later, Woodward's class read Ray Bradbury's *Fahrenheit 451*, which described a loss of freedom and civil rights under a tyrannical government. In discussion, the students requested outside reading on the topic of student and individual rights, freedom, and liberty. Woodward obtained and delivered to a male student the *Handbook of Student Rights* published by the ACLU. This delivery once again occurred between classes during a passing period. Woodward had submitted to authority, but he clearly believed that his own rights had been violated. He continued to do what he believed was right.[37]

Woodward thus clearly read between the lines to determine that his impending firing stemmed entirely from his membership in the ACLU. His superiors at the school (as well as the Hereford public) would later claim that outward engagement in politics was unsavory for a public servant like a schoolteacher, but immediate evidence actually proved contradictory. The promotion of politicized groups or even, by implication, the political perspectives of certain organizations had previously required no special approval from the principal's office. Loudspeaker announcements at the beginning of each day—a common occurrence at any public school in the United States—were, of course, commonplace at La Plata. In fact, announcements had been made in classes about almost every organization related to the community, none of which had to be cleared through the principal's office first. Youth organizations such as the Bluebirds, the DeMolays, and the Rainbow Girls received support through announcements at the school. Tellingly, so did the Young Democrats. Support for the Young Democrats would seem innocuous, especially given that (as shown previously in chapter 1) much of the party's base at the regional and state levels remained thoroughly conservative.[38] One can clearly deduce that the ACLU, then, represented the perception of some kind of serious threat at the local level.

Woodward's newly probationary status only seemed to grow increasingly more confusing as the spring semester unfolded. A few weeks after giving Woodward his letter, Hughes rated the teacher as "outstanding" in his presentation planning, communication with students, correct usage of the English language, and personal growth. In his teaching evaluation, Hughes rated Woodward's performance as "needs improvement" in the following areas: handling behavioral problems; complying with school policies and procedures; willingness to cooperate with the administration, co-workers, and parents; accepting constructive criticism from his supervisors; "loyalty," or showing a supportive attitude for school programs and pedagogical philosophies; and personal grooming and dressing in an appropriate manner for a schoolteacher. Woodward signed the document, but on the bottom he wrote that "I am signing this with the understanding that I disagree with some of the above statements."[39] Woodward received another letter from Hughes on April 1; this time, Hughes informed Woodward that, in his view, the teacher had improved in two areas: "professional effectiveness" and "personal qualities." Where Woodward still needed improvement, according to Hughes, was in the realms of "professional attitude and competence," which included such metrics as "procedures," "cooperation," "criticisms," and "loyalty." Woodward agreed to continue to work on these areas, about which he and Hughes would confer sometime after May 1.[40] After being given only three instances of written communication, Woodward made repeated requests that he be given specific statements about deficiencies in his conduct. Hughes could later only remember two acts that he considered specific misconduct on Woodward's part: making a student write sentences on the chalkboard for punishment, which was against school policy, and not following the proper procedure for giving passes to students to leave another teacher's class. Otherwise, there was no specific instance that Hughes could point to for not recommending Woodward's rehiring.[41]

The administrators would later make an additional argument against Woodward that they had not made clearly during the spring semester of 1975: Woodward, they believed, had violated school policy by not gaining Hughes's approval to pass out certain materials in class, *not* because the materials were controversial, but because the action had caused a change in the class curriculum. Furthermore, material was supposed to be submitted to the principal if there was any doubt as to whether or not it was above the students' maturity level. If the ACLU was, in fact, the problem, the administration avoided corroborating that through any kind of circumstantial evidence. Hughes and Hartman later said that they could neither admit nor deny that announcements about other political groups were made before classes as there was essentially no way to collect that kind of data. Hughes also later seemed to indicate on several occasions that Woodward had been propagandizing for the ACLU at the school, although such claims could never be proven. Ultimately, Hughes's story became that his coming failure to rehire Woodward did not stem from any one specific act, but rather from a series of acts of misconduct that took place over time. When his decision went to the school board later that spring, not a single board member challenged Hughes's motivations. In fact, the school board—which later did defend Hughes against charges that he had violated Woodward's right to free speech—acted as more of a rubber-stamp body for the larger community than anything else. None of the school board members admitted voting against Woodward's rehiring, and several of them claimed not to have even known about his allegation that his freedom of speech may have been violated.[42]

Ultimately, the justification from the Hughes and Hartman camp for Woodward's impending firing—or, perhaps more accurately, the "non-renewal" of his contract—rang hollow for Woodward. The school's argument is worth quoting at length, given its importance in the ensuing drama between the two sides and what that drama reveals:

> The [administration] would point "out that all teachers in the Hereford Independent School District are relied upon to judge the maturity level of their students, when selecting materials to be passed out in the classroom, and the Defendants contend that there is a written policy, in a general sense, which is contained in the teacher's manuel [sic] which is in the custody of each teacher in the Hereford Independent School District, and in said manuel [sic] under the sub-title of Duties and Responsibilities of Teachers, number 4 reads as follows, 'Any change in curriculum should be done only upon approval of the principal,' and the Defendants say that although they are not certain when said policy was established, it has been in effect for many years and was in effect during the time relevant to the issues discussed in the law suit [sic]; further, the Defendants contend that it is impossible for the Defendants to know whether or not the teacher is meeting the level of judgment required of them concerning their students and their students [sic] levels of maturity as far as handing out material in the classroom is concerned, unless these Defendants have complaints from the parents of students."[43]

In other words, the administration stuck by Hughes's initial contention—Woodward had passed out supposedly "controversial" material in class that required Hughes's approval, which he had not sought. As such, he had violated school policy. Furthermore, by implication, Woodward was out of touch with the maturity level of his students.

Woodward understood that if his impending hearing before the school board did not work in his favor, he might have grounds for legal action against the school district. If, in fact, a court of law could prove that Woodward's "non-renewal" was based on his membership in the ACLU, a case could be made that his right to free speech as well as his right to equal protection of the law under the Fourteenth Amendment to the U.S. Constitution had been violated. Woodward believed that none of the activities he had engaged in had warranted any disciplinary action on the part of the school, meaning that his membership in the ACLU had done nothing to disrupt the educational process. Additionally, given the circumstances, Woodward believed that he had been denied the minimal due process rights required by the school district as a state agency. Furthermore, the administration would thus be liable, in Woodward's view, to pay him damages as well as award him reinstatement to his old job *if* he was indeed fired. Similarly, Woodward's quick retention of an attorney after his receipt of the February 7 letter from Hughes—Robin Green, who was a young, inexperienced, up-and-coming civil rights lawyer whom Woodward had met at a recent ACLU meeting in nearby Amarillo—was completely in keeping with his constitutional rights. The administration had alluded to his retaining of counsel as one of the problems that had snowballed during the early part of the spring 1975 semester. Hughes had contended that Woodward's directive at that point to send all communication to him through his attorney had caused the lines of communication, and thus the supervisory relationship at the workplace, to break down.[44] Perhaps most unfortunately for Hughes and Hartman, even given the magnitude of taking on the administration, Woodward simply did not have the personality to back down.

To Hughes's credit, he did seem to be at least nominally reaching out to Woodward regarding his job performance. Although his motivations in doing so as well as his reasoning behind seeing Woodward's job performance as having improved are now lost, Hughes delivered a note to Woodward in April in which he "itemize[d] the points which, in my opinion, you have improved since the evaluation sheet was filled out by the undersigned." These items, in Hughes's view, included handling behavioral problems, adhering to dress and personal appearance that was appropriate for a schoolteacher, and helping "students acquire the values realized as ideals of democracy."

Hughes, though, still believed that Woodward was lacking in the already discussed areas of loyalty to the administration, accepting constructive criticism in a positive manner, cooperating with administrators, and knowing and complying with school policies and procedures. Hughes ended by noting that the two would "confer about this matter again on or about May 1, 1975."[45] Given the ensuing events, the possibility remains that Hughes simply sought to cover his tracks. The above-mentioned conferring, though, never seems to have taken place.

Finally, on May 1, 1975, Woodward received the following letter from Hughes:

Dear Mr. Woodward,

It will be my recommendation to the Board of Trustees that you not be offered a contract for the 1975–1976 school year.

This recommendation is based upon facts and circumstances which we have discussed on many occasions and of which you are aware.

Generally, the principals' recommendations are discussed and determined by the Board of Trustees, and it is expected that this recommendation will be discussed at the meeting on Tuesday, May 13, 1975.

In accordance with established school board policy, you have the right to a hearing before the Board of Trustees who eventually make the final decision. Should you wish to exercise this prerogative and participate in the discussion, and present any evidence or show cause that you believe will assist the board in arriving at a proper conclusion, please notify the superintendent's office in order to be placed on the agenda.

Sincerely,
Pat Hughes[46]

Woodward, a young man who had never belonged in a world filled with insiders, was finally thrown out on his own.

It was time to go to war.

Hereford, Texas, circa 1909. Early-twentieth-century Hereford exemplified an uneasy mixture of an older frontier and a modern future, as evidenced by the mixture of horse riding, automobiles, and electricity on its city streets.
Courtesy of DeGolyer Library, Southern Methodist University, Dallas, Texas.

Roy Hartman, superintendent of the Hereford Independent School District, receiving the "Administrator of the Year" award from the Deaf Smith County Classroom Teachers Association in October 1975. This was a few months after Woodward's firing at the end of the spring semester.
Amarillo Globe-News Collection, Panhandle-Plains Historical Museum, Canyon, Texas.

Kindergartner Leticia González, learning English through a nursery rhyme in a Hereford elementary school, 1969. González was one of many students from the Hereford migrant labor camp who, like Woodward's older students, spoke Spanish at home.
Courtesy of Wayne Woodward. Amarillo Globe News Collection, Punhandle-Plains Historical Museum, Canyon, Texas.

Construction of La Plata Junior High School in Hereford, 1965. Woodward would gain employment at the school a few years later, before his legal troubles with the school board commenced.
Amarillo Globe-News Collection, Panhandle-Plains Historical Museum, Canyon, Texas.

Wayne Woodward as a young student at West Texas State University, 1968. Woodward would go on to teach in California for the next year, before his return to Hereford in 1969.
From the University Archives in the Cornette Library at West Texas A&M University.

CHAPTER 4

BUILDING A CIVIL RIGHTS CASE IN THE TEXAS PANHANDLE

Woodward's lawyer, Robin Green, was finally able to secure a hearing before the school board on Monday, June 2, 1975. Green was an interesting man in his own right—he was, by all accounts, the only civil rights lawyer in Amarillo at the time, thus making him the only local attorney who would even have agreed to take Woodward's case. Green had previously worked as an assistant district attorney in the Potter County District Attorney's office in 1970. A colleague once mentioned to Green that there had never been a prosecution for a white-on-Black murder in Potter County or nearby Randall County because no jury would convict an accused white person.[1] Woodward's case was not necessarily about race, but such realities showed the long odds of *any* local civil rights case resulting in a victory for an allegedly oppressed person. Woodward and Green clearly faced an uphill battle.

The meeting began at La Plata Junior High School at 5:30 P.M. Present were Woodward, Green, and school board members Jim Conkwright (presiding), James Gentry, Danny Martin, Ron Zimmerman, Jim Arney, Lynton Allred, Clark Andrews, and the school district's attorney, Earnest Langley. The board members gave Woodward the option of a closed meeting if that would be better for him, but Green, speaking for Woodward, declined. Langley said that the board would not make any accusations against him, to which Green replied that he just wanted clarification as to the charges against his client. Additionally, Green went on to say that damage had already been done to Woodward since he was already put on probation, and roughly half of the applications for new teaching positions to which he had applied had inquired about that, so the possibility of anything that was potentially derogatory coming up at that point was essentially immaterial. Langley, of course, immediately defended the board when the hearing commenced, saying that Woodward had "neither required of the administration [n]or requested of it any particular substantiation or allegations of misconduct, inefficiency or otherwise of the administration." Perhaps most importantly, whether or not Woodward would receive a new contract was "an open question in the minds of the board. . . . I have not discussed it with them, any decision they have made, and I have told them specifically that they should have an open mind and be prepared to hear what Mr. Woodward has to say." In other words, the board, via its legal counsel, had clearly denied any wrongdoing and was ready for a fight.²

Making a Case

The hearing was big news in Hereford. Over one hundred people from the town attended the session, animated by one of two impulses—either support for the idealistic young English teacher or condemnation for his championing of seemingly out-of-step liberal values. The board did not anticipate such a large crowd, so it moved the meeting from its private board room into the school's cafeteria. The meeting proceeded after the board had met behind closed doors for slightly over thirty minutes.³

Green was aghast after Langley informed him at the outset that he would not be allowed to question Hughes or Hartman. "I just was brought here today with the understanding we were going to have a hearing and now," Green announced, asking the board to "pardon me if I seem abrasive because I would never have dreamed of coming to a hearing where I would not be allowed to talk to or to question the people who are the main parties that are the reason for the hearing."⁴ Either way, the school board clearly had little intention of cooperating with the upstart lawyer-client duo. Green nonetheless continued, announcing that he had spoken to forty-one teachers, none of whom spoke against Woodward but instead gave the clear impression that "Mr. Wayne Woodward is a teacher who is not guilty of any misconduct, but is a teacher who has conducted himself many times in an exemplary manner over the past two or three years, the last six years." Indeed, Green had "found out that none of those people, at least they didn't tell me, and I asked them as sincerely as I could . . . were in a position or willing to tell me any[thing] bad or to the contrary and spent a great deal of time elaborating on the virtues of this man."⁵ The school board, of course, could produce no evidence to counter such claims relating to Woodward's ability to do his job nor could it denigrate his rapport with his students or colleagues.

In fact, the limited responses that Green received at the hearing as justifications for Woodward's firing only seemed to further indicate that the teacher had been attacked for his political leanings. Hartman, prior to the meeting, had responded to Green that he did not know what the "hostile attitudes" were that Hughes had alluded to in his original letter on February 12. Apparently, neither did Hughes. When pressed on this in a previous phone conversation, Hughes had responded to Green's inquiry by saying that he "'had already told Mr. Woodward [about his hostile attitude]," and that "he didn't need to tell me.'" Woodward reconfirmed in various meetings with his attorney that he did not "know what [Hughes] is talking about. I don't know which of the things that we have talked about over the years that he is basing this on."[6]

Two other problems persisted that made it look like the administration was hiding something. The first one was Hughes's contention that controversial materials used by teachers had to first get the principal's approval before teachers could pass them out to students. Green noted a vague reference to a similar idea in a previous faculty handbook, though Woodward maintained that such practice was never common at the school.[7] Nonetheless, the charge was moot: the only possible sticking point for Woodward was his previously mentioned handing of the ACLU literature to Pam Whitley and Cindy Ford during a passing period. But, as already demonstrated, Woodward had apologized for the incident and already confirmed with Hughes that he would not do it again.

Corroborating evidence indicated that the school board had behaved inappropriately. In fact, an incident had recently come to light in which Hughes and Hartman appeared to have mistreated a student in their efforts to damage Woodward's credibility. Mike Hull was a young man who had lived in Hereford for about seven years. His family had relocated there from rural Colorado City, Texas. Hull was a seventeen-year-old high school student in the spring of 1975 when Woodward's employment was in jeopardy; he had taken classes with Woodward previously and, like so many other students, liked and respected his former English teacher. Hull had blossomed into an outstanding student at Hereford High School. He was a member of several student organizations, perhaps most notably the school's chapter of the Young Democrats, for which he served as president. When Hull caught wind of Woodward's predicament, he decided to act. At a Young Democrats meeting, Hull introduced the idea of starting a student petition to save Woodward's job. According to Hull, a draft version of that petition read: "We the undersigned organizations or individuals do hereby support Wayne Woodward in his stand for civil rights as—and there was one word I don't remember—a teacher and as an American citizen."⁸ Clearly, a number of the students felt the same way Woodward did—that his rights as an American citizen had been violated by the administration.

The petition was Hull's idea, and the other students in the organization supported it, but the group never actually circulated the document. The Young Democrats, in fact, eventually decided to back off entirely. On March 24, 1975, the principal of Hereford High School, Jerry Don George, unexpectedly called Hull into his office. Hull did not initially know what the meeting was about. Upon arriving at the office, George brought up the petition; Hull did not know how George had learned of its existence, but nonetheless, Hull spoke in support of the petition and of Woodward more generally. George immediately responded that he wished that the Young Democrats would not push forward with the petition. George went on to say that he believed that Hull had "inadequate knowledge" of the true situation surrounding Woodward and that he wanted the young man to go to the middle school and speak to Principal Hughes. Next, George did something that can only be described as strange—he immediately excused Hull from his classes, lent him the keys to his own car, and instructed him to drive over to La Plata Junior High School to have a conversation with Hughes. George then made phone calls to Hull's parents regarding the petition.⁹

The oddity of this situation—as well as George's and Hughes's true intentions—later became clear when Woodward's attorney, Robin Green, deposed Hull as a witness in the upcoming court case:

> GREEN: Did he [George] in fact tell you that if you continued in your effort to circulate this petition in favor of Mr. Woodward that you would be subject to losing his recommendations for you to receive scholarships and that the scholarships you were interested in required his recommendation as your principal?
> HULL: Yes sir.
> GREEN: Did he make reference to your position in the Key Club?
> HULL: Yes sir.
> GREEN: What did he say?
> HULL: In that organization the principal has to approve the membership list and he would remove his approval of me.¹⁰

In other words, Hull—who was clearly a talented and bright student—accused his own principal of abusing his authority and committing an act of intimidation against a minor. Hull was Lieutenant Governor of the Key Club, which was a nationwide community-service organization for high school students, so losing his principal's approval could be particularly disastrous for his future. Furthermore, George had previously asked Hull as well as another student to serve on the bicentennial committee for a local organization called Gopro. According to Hull, George flatly stated that he would remove Hull from the organization if he continued in his support for Woodward. Hull went on to discuss his in-person conversation with Hughes during the deposition, saying that it was shorter than his discussion with George, more polite, and that Hughes did not attempt to apply any pressure on him.[11]

After Hull returned to the school, George called him back to the office for another meeting to hear what Hughes had told him. Hughes, in Hull's own words, had reassured the young man that "he would not hold this terrible deed against me." That evening, Hughes telephoned Hull's mother at home and told her that her son needed to "stay away from the American Civil Liberties Union."[12]

Later that evening, the Young Democrats held a meeting at the Deaf Smith Rural Electrical Cooperative. Hull's father was present. The subject under discussion was the petition as well as Hull's meetings with Hughes and George. At first the group voted to change the wording of the petition to make it clear that it was not acting on an impulse to defend the ACLU, but eventually the students decided to abandon the petition altogether. Their primary reason for doing so was the nature of the threats levied against Hull by George in particular, but the other club members also worried that they, too, might receive some negative ramifications from other teachers, coaches, administrators, or even their own parents. One of the other members of the group, a student named Marshall Formby, later recalled Hull telling the group that he or anybody who would go through with this petition would "get no further recommendations from that office at the high school . . . [for] college and future plans after high school." When asked later by Green whether or not he believed that George meant that anyone who signed or circulated the petition could expect negative repercussions, Formby replied, "That is exactly how I took it personally."[13] Another member of the group, John Dirk Vander Zee, agreed, later saying that "if we did go ahead with the petition, we could be subject to similar circumstances that Mike was, shall we say, threatened with."[14] The students thus felt intimidated into silence by a cabal of school administrators. The next day, when George called Hull into his office for yet another meeting, Hull informed him that they had decided to drop the petition. According to Hull, upon hearing this news, George "suddenly became much more polite." Formby later reiterated that had the conversation between Hull and George not taken place, the petition would likely have gone forward.[15]

Importantly, other sources corroborate Hull's testimony. Hull reported the incident to Woodward, which occurred in the days and weeks following Hughes's February 12 letter to Woodward, who in turn immediately wrote of it to another acquaintance. Hull said flatly at the time that George told him in no uncertain terms that he would be kicked out of the Key Club as well as banned from any and all bicentennial activities. Furthermore, Hull told Woodward that George said any action in the form of a petition would not save Woodward's job. The principal also said that by signing a petition, "'that would be showing support for the A.C.L.U.,'" which "scared all the students and [then] there [would] be no petition." Woodward also said at this time that it seemed as if the school system had it out for the ACLU in particular, and that "their feeling must be to make an example of me and therefore run A.C.L.U. out." Also, around this time, a local Catholic priest named Father José Gilligan, who had worked with Woodward to form the Hereford ACLU chapter, called Superintendent Hartman about a writing contest at the school that was to be sponsored by local civic organizations, but Hartman replied that "the A.C.L.U. had caused such an uproar in Hereford that he [had] better ask the [school] board about the writing contest," which Woodward and the priest interpreted as a "no." The Hereford Chamber of Commerce, the Daughters of the American Revolution, and the Lions Club all had already gotten permission to sponsor students in the writing contest. To Woodward, this equated targeting the ACLU in particular on the part of the administrators.[16]

Getting back to the June 2 meeting, the growing evidence against Hughes and now George appeared damning. Green, naturally, was aggressive in his citation of the Hull incident:

> I don't know whether you want to call it a petition or letter or what, but I have some pretty good evidence and, again, here we are not testifying because, evidently, that is not the way we are going to conduct this hearing, but we have evidence that indicates to us that somebody is lying, and that somebody is either some school administrators or it's some people that we believe have good credibility.
>
> We have evidence that indicates to us that not only was a little pressure applied, but that a student, a high school student was called into a principal's office; that the high school student was told by the principal that he would

not—and I am making a quote there—be recommended for a scholarship if he went ahead with this petition.

I have evidence to indicate that he was put into his car by the principal; that he was sent over for a lengthy conversation with Mr. Hughes concerning that petition and that, as a result of these conversation with Mr. Hughes and Mr. George, and as a result of the conversation with this boy's father, by Mr. Hartman, the petition was not ever circulated.[17]

Green went on to make further accusations: "I can show you that somebody is lying. Somebody is not only lying, but somebody told a child, who they have authority over, authority granted to them by you by the power that is given to you by the people that vote for you and the State of Texas," that he could not make statements in favor of his teacher. Green continued by saying that "maybe Wayne Woodward has got some problems, but I don't think you have got problems with him to the extent that you do if you have administrators in your school who will use these kinds of tactics." Green was ready to levy accusations of complete incompetence: "I think you ought to quit worrying about what they are going to make on the . . . SAT or ACT and start worrying about what they are going to do when they get out in life after having been given [these] kind of people for examples."[18] These were obviously damning accusations to make. Green indicated that a protracted fight was brewing.

Finally, toward the end of his speech, Green approached the fundamental legal issue that was at hand in Woodward's case—his free speech rights had been violated due to locals' hatred of the ACLU. "When you link some of this stuff together," he said, "we have got enough to hold ourselves in Federal Court . . . when you link these things to the hostile attitude, to material in the classroom, which allegedly was American Civil Liberties Union material, you [get] into a free speech area. We have got evidence to indicate that Mr. Hughes, your agent and employee, has dismissed Mr. Woodward for things that relate to freedom of speech."[19] In other words, the fundamental issue at hand was establishing whether Woodward's constitutional rights had been violated. The irony in this claim is that Woodward's rights—if they had, in fact, been violated—had been trampled upon by people who truly believed that ACLU membership constituted a fundamental threat to being a good American in Hereford, Texas.

Green's words fell on deaf ears. Conkwright as well as the rest of the board failed to understand why any of Woodward's claims were even legitimate. After asking Green what actions he and Woodward wanted the board to take, Green noted simply that they wanted Woodward reinstated because he had been fired for reasons that were illegitimate. Conkwright closed out the meeting by asking the board members if anyone present wished to make a motion for Woodward's reinstatement. No one did.[20] At this point, the meeting was over, but the fight had just begun.

Defending Civil Rights in the Texas Panhandle

Woodward could have chosen to drop the whole matter after the school board hearing. He was still a young man (thirty years old), and although he enjoyed teaching, he was also intelligent, resourceful, and well educated. Naturally, though, his most immediate concerns were of a material nature. Could he get another teaching job? Should he go back to college to train for a different profession? Did he really want to push hard to get his job back at La Plata, in a place where he was neither wanted nor welcomed? These questions were all important, but undergirding all of this was Woodward's simple sense of right and wrong. Woodward truly believed that not only had he been persecuted because of people's perceptions of his political leanings, but it seemed quite clear to him that the administration had violated his rights as an American citizen. Moreover, his rights had been violated because of locals' perceptions of him as simply not belonging in Hereford. As the drama continued to unfold over the course of the remaining part of the year, one thing became certain: Woodward had *not* been fired simply because he was disliked or because he had failed to follow school regulations—rather, Woodward *had* been fired because he represented a perceived threat to the fundamental well-being of the political and social order in Hereford, Texas.

The only option left was for Green and Woodward to take the school district to court. The lawsuit, *Woodward v. Hereford Independent School District*, which Green filed in the District Court for the Northern District of Texas in Amarillo, laid out their claims. Woodward argued that he had performed all his duties faithfully before receiving the infamous February 12 letter, but he was unable to get any clear information from the administration (namely Hughes) regarding his firing. Their legal argument was a straightforward one: the reason for his termination was because of the exercise of his free speech and because of allegations made by school officials about his exercise of free speech. Such reasoning for his termination violated his rights, as protected under the First and Fourteenth Amendments to the U.S. Constitution. Furthermore, Woodward possessed what is known in legal terminology as a "property interest" in his right to continued employment, which was deprived of him due to his rights of due process (under the Fourteenth

Amendment) being violated; he also possessed an interest in his name and reputation as a teacher, which fell under the category of a "liberty interest" that was also denied to him when the school violated his due process rights. Finally, the initial filing noted that Woodward and Green had exhausted all potential remedies made available to them by state statute as well as the Hereford Independent School District after the unsuccessful conclusion of the June 2 school board hearing.[21]

Woodward sought numerous legal judgments. First and foremost, he wanted a declaration from the court that his employment was terminated for constitutionally impermissible reasons; second, he sought an injunction ordering the school district to reinstate him to his teaching position; third, he sought to be reinstated with no reduction in pay from his previous salary during his early years along with no reduction in previous benefits;[22] fourth, he sought $40,000 in punitive damages and $40,000 in compensatory damages against Hughes as well as the school board; fifth, in the event that the court decided against his reinstatement at the school, Woodward sought $360,000 in compensatory damages and $40,000 in punitive damages; and finally, sixth, Woodward sought to have all attorney's fees and court costs reimbursed to him as the court saw fit.[23] The clear message that Woodward and Green had hoped to send was that not only had his rights been abridged by the school administrators, but his material interests for his teaching career had been undeniably damaged along with his constitutional rights. The costs of the culture wars in rural America, in this case at least, were undeniably steep.

Establishing the mindset of the soon-to-be defendants is difficult. Nonetheless, one can read between the lines by looking at their initial responses to the filing of the lawsuit. First, the defendants challenged the very jurisdiction of the court. Langley, as counsel for the school district, argued to the court that the issue at hand was "a simple controversy involving whether or not the Defendant School District is required to employ the Plaintiff as a teacher, and the Plaintiff has attempted to elevate the controversy to the stature of a civil rights suit by various allegations which are in their face inadequate to do so." In other words, to the school district, the case was about job performance (or the implied lack thereof) as opposed to the abridgment of the plaintiff's rights as an American citizen. As such, the case should immediately be dismissed. Furthermore, Langley also offered that the nonrenewal of Woodward's contract was completely permissible by law in the state of Texas, as it constituted a simple matter of an employer being unhappy with an employee's performance, which is why the latter was on a yearly renewable contract in the first place. Furthermore, Langley argued, the purpose of annual renewable contracts was to ensure the satisfaction of the school district, which reserved the right to avoid the renewal of any teacher who failed to meet the obligations of his or her duties to the school. Woodward had also claimed in his original filing that he had been rehired previously "without difficulty"; the defendants took this as a subjective term, instead arguing that Woodward remained employed entirely at the administration's discretion. Similarly, they denied Woodward and Green's allegation in the original filing that Woodward had "performed all of his duties admirably," noting that this was a subjective assessment on Woodward's own part that was obviously at odds with the administration's judgment.[24]

Langley also countered that Woodward knew full well the reasons for his dismissal. Hughes noted certain alleged deficiencies in Woodward's performance more than a year prior to his most recent troubles at the school. The principal also, as already demonstrated, had given Woodward a handwritten copy of a report detailing areas for needed improvements in his job performance. Of course, the defendants also countered that Woodward's discussions with Hughes in the spring of 1975 as well as the documentation provided him made clear the areas where the principal believed Woodward could improve his job performance. Most notably, the administration bemoaned his retaining of Green as his legal counsel early during the previous spring semester. Langley argued that "[Woodward] considered the efforts of the administration to promote higher quality performance on the part of said Plaintiff to be a challenge to his own determination of standards to suit himself, rather than an opportunity to meet the standards established by the official policies and procedures." Not long after, Green "wrote to the school administration on at least two occasions ... [and] demanded that all communications to the Plaintiff Woodward be communicated to such Plaintiff through said attorney." Specifically, on February 20, 1975, Green communicated that "it is necessary that I ask that all future correspondence and communication be through me." Eight days later, Green repeated that "we want to assure you that we have no objection to your communicating with Mr. Woodward directly concerning any problems that arise in the ordinary course of school operation ... [but that] it will be necessary [that] all [other] communications ... [come] through me." Green specifically wanted all communication related to deficiencies in Woodward's performance to come through his office. The administration had thus concluded that if there was no direct communication to Woodward by the administration or school district that it was actually Woodward's fault, as the above is what he and his lawyer had laid out. Because of all this, they denied that Woodward had in good faith tried to conform to what the school district set as standards for teachers. The defendants also claimed that Woodward had received two hearings, noting one prior to the June 2 meeting that he apparently did not show up for, as well as complaining that Woodward had Green do all his speaking for him at the hearing in the school cafeteria. Finally, Langley argued that the administrators had followed all procedures properly and that none of Woodward's rights had been violated.[25]

The timeline of events that Green submitted to the court on Woodward's behalf obviously favored the plaintiff. By any objective measure, something strange had occurred. Entered into the court record was the following timeline of events, according to Woodward himself:

Feb. 4—Mr. Hughes called me into office and asked me what our A.C.L.U. meeting was to be about. I told him and said he was free to come. He said, "No I better not do that, I would have more people mad at me than I do now." He asked me to name the members of the A.C.L.U. (here) and I did.

Feb. 12—Mr. Hughes sent me a note to see him at 2:30 P.M.; I finally got to see him at 3:45 P.M. He handed me the letter and asked me to read it; I did. He asked me if I had anything to say, and I said, "I'll hand this over to my lawyer," and left.

Feb. 17—An announcement was made for the "Rainbow Girls" meeting.

Feb. 20—An announcement was made for the "Young Dems" meeting. This was made at High School and was told to me by Mike Hull.

Feb. 24—Mike Hull told me he was asked by Mr. George not to start my petition.

Feb. 25—Mr. Hughes stopped in my 3rd period and stood in the door for about three minutes.

March 12—I asked Mr. Hughes for a copy of my contract; he said he would get it for me. Mr. Hughes came down to my class about 8 A.M. and told me that the radio had announced my name over the air concerning the non-renewal of my contract. He said he had nothing to do with it. I asked him how he found out, and he said someone had called him. I asked him to tell me who called, and he refused to do so.

March 14—There was another "Young Dems" announcement made at high school. Mike Hull informed me of the announcement.

March 19—I went to the main office and asked the sect. for a copy of my contract. I was told that since Mr. Hartman was out of town that she did not have the authority to give it to me.

March 20—Mr. Hughes said at (8:30 A.M.) that Mr. Hartman was out of town and I would have to wait untill [sic] he was in town befor [sic] I could get a copy of my contract and "then maybe I could have it."

April 13—I talked to Mr. Huber about the A.C.L.U. writing contest. Mr. Hughes was out of town. Mr. Huber said he would talk to Mr. Farr (history teacher) later in the day. On the way back to my room I stopped in Mr. Farr['s] room and asked him if he knew the details of the contest. He said that he did not and asked me to give them to him, which I did. Mr. Huber walked in during this and asked me if he minded if I did that. I said I didn't and left. Later in the day (2:30 P.M.), I went to see Mr. Huber and explained that I didn't mean to go over his head. He said he may have been a little rude and it was nothing.

April 4—Mr. Hughes called me in at 8:15 A.M. and asked me if I thought there was a problem with the writing contest. I said I had thought of splitting the prize money into three places instead of one. He said that was not what he meant. He said I should have talked to Mr. Farr about the contest. I explained that was one of the unwritten rules and I had no idea I was doing wrong. He said he believed I knew I was wrong. I disagreed and said I was sorry I had broken any rules.

April 7—I sent a student to Mr. Hughes to find out if he met the dress code. Mr. Hughes said he did not and sent him back.

April 15—After school I went to see the counselor (Mrs. Mary Duvall). She said she was not the one who had complained and asked me about my whole situation. She agreed with Mr. Hughes on everything. She said that all members of the A.C.L.U. were radicals. I asked her if she thought Mrs. Birdsong was a radical because she was an A.C.L.U. member, she stopped talking about the A.C.L.U. She told me that if I worked for someone[,] I should follow all their rules. I said that I would as long as those rules were within the law. She warned me that if I when [sic] ahead with this[,] I would ruin a lot of lives. I said I would still continue on the same course (talked 1½ hours).[26]

New details thus emerged that clearly favored Woodward. If, as the administration would later claim, the school district restricted so-called controversial speech on campus, why would campus-wide announcements for the Young Democrats still be allowed? One can assume that the reason is because the still largely conservative Texas Democratic Party remained firmly in line with the political culture of Hereford as well as the larger Texas Panhandle. Hughes had also appeared to be targeting Woodward over a student's fairly innocuous violation of the school's dress code after the issue of Woodward's ACLU membership had already risen to the fore. Hughes clearly did not like Woodward's engagement of the students in an ACLU writing contest, even though inaugurating the contest would perhaps demonstrate that the organization was well intentioned. Perhaps most telling was the entry for April 15. This exchange with Mary Duvall is revealing; her response that Woodward's attempt to protect his own rights as a member of the "radical" ACLU was wrong because it would "ruin a lot of lives" clearly demonstrates the functionality of the school's political culture—superiors were meant to be obeyed, and rules were meant to be followed, even when those rules and ideas about certain people or groups (in this case, any ACLU members) resulted in an individual's rights and liberties being restricted.

By Woodward's own recollection, things had only continued to deteriorate from that point forward until the June 2 hearing. In April, Woodward noted a church group selling popcorn for a fund-raiser at the school. Naturally, this begged the question of why a simple discussion of the ACLU brought down the administration's wrath upon him (obviously, a church group raising money was more socially acceptable). Woodward had also attempted during the latter part of the spring semester to prove himself as more of a disciplinarian, perhaps in an attempt to save his job; that same month, he sent multiple students to the principal's office for minor infractions, such as dress-code violations or tardiness. Five students sent to the office for tardiness drew a classroom visit from Hughes on May 5, during which he came back with them and explained to Woodward in a loud voice next to the classroom door that they did not need a pass. "When I walked into class, everyone laughed at me," Woodward later recalled. That same day, Woodward "also received my letter (fired). He said it was nothing personal, I said I thought it was." Three days later, in another seemingly odd exchange, Hughes "asked me to write outlines for 'Shakespeare' and 'Short Story' courses. This was really strange because he had them in a folder in his hand (I had already done them about a week ago). I suggested that maybe he should see Miss Sheffy about those outlines since I had heard she would be taking my place next year. He said that was not true."[27]

Approaching the impending lawsuit was a rather large undertaking that Woodward and Green—the latter also a young man in his early thirties only then embarking on his legal career—needed to do cautiously. To that end, the two sought outside assistance. The Texas Classroom Teachers Association (TCTA) offered financial support as well as legal advice. The first idea that the TCTA proposed was for Woodward and Green to push for a trial without a jury, given that Hereford school board members could potentially influence the average small-town juror, especially if the teacher "flouts unpopular views." There was also good reason to suspect that the typical jury in the Texas Panhandle would not make any findings in favor of a civil rights claim; thus, a so-called bench trial had the best chance for a successful outcome. Additionally, in order to show that Woodward's constitutional rights had been violated, the TCTA set forth the following questions for Green that would shape his interrogation of all the school administrators:

> What is your political party, persuasion, or direction and degree from center? What is Mr. Woodward's political party to the best of your knowledge? How do you know or what specifically gives you that impression? Would you want Mr. Woodward to teach your children? (If not), [is it] because of his tendency to speak of his political beliefs? Do you govern your school district with the same care as you do your own family? Did you fire Mr. Woodward so as to protect the children in your district from Mr. Woodward as you would protect your own child? You fired Mr. Woodward so as to isolate the school children from his influence? Because he chose to speak out?

Clearly, Woodward and Green knew that the entire set of issues stemmed from Hereford's prevailing conservative political culture. This line of questioning might potentially demonstrate that the board's primary motivation for dismissing Woodward was his ACLU participation, which, if true, violated federal law. As time would show, Green employed all the above-mentioned advice during the upcoming case.[28]

One of the other things that the plaintiffs had to prepare for was potential charges that Woodward's teaching was overtly political, thus meaning that he had broken the restrictions against teaching controversial material without any prior approval. Woodward and Green discussed his teaching philosophies and approaches to several texts. For example, George Orwell's classic, *Animal Farm*, was a satirical take on big government in the United States and Soviet Russia that Woodward discussed within the context of the recent Watergate scandal. Woodward drew certain parallels for the book's characters: Farmer Jones was Tsar Nicholas II; Napoleon was Stalin; Snowball was Trotsky; Old Major was Karl Marx; the dogs were the secret police; Mr. Pilkington was the western allies; Mr. Frederick was Germany; and the sheep, of course, were the mindless masses who followed their leaders unquestioningly. In a similar vein, Orwell's other classic text, *1984*, was a satire on big government—"Big Brother" in the story had taken the place of individual liberty and religion in particular. Clearly, in conservative Hereford, Texas, such a message would be far from controversial. Other works that Woodward used in the classroom, though, may have come across as slightly more controversial. *Romeo and Juliet* was about the dangers of too much parental control—clearly this message might have symbolized to the students the strict control of the administration's role in Woodward's own life. Other classics included Homer's *The Odyssey*, which displayed a time of belief in many gods as opposed to a monotheistic culture, which also undoubtedly had the potential to shock students who had been raised in conservative households.[29]

Woodward also prepared statements about a series of what he considered to be harassments at the hands of Hughes and others. These ranged from the obnoxious to the downright frightening. Regarding the latter, Woodward believed that the Hereford school board hired private detectives to follow him. On numerous occasions, Woodward noted a black Chevy sitting outside his mother's house for about a month. Woodward also had a friend who liked to smoke marijuana, but Woodward would not let him smoke any in his car in case any of the seeds fell off. Even more threatening than being followed, Woodward once received an anonymous phone call to his house during which the caller threatened to shoot him. Naturally, Woodward reported the incident to the sheriff's office, although officials seemed unimpressed with the threat and did little to investigate the incident.[30] Clearly, many people in Hereford had little sympathy for a young man who stood in such stark contrast to what locals perceived to be acceptable points of view, let alone proper public decorum.

Most of the threats and offenses against Woodward were less direct, though they still infringed upon his rights or his simple sensibilities as a grown adult. Previously mentioned is the issue of Hughes believing that Woodward needed to cut his hair to fit in better with local society. Woodward distinctly remembered Hughes speaking loudly to a group of students in a room next to his about their teacher needing to get a haircut. Furthermore, in 1974, on Hughes's first day as principal, he informed Woodward that he had been displeased with him for years and that he should do the following: get a haircut (allegedly emphasized with a finger in Woodward's face) and change his attitude and start acting like a teacher. In yet another incident, Hughes dressed Woodward down after a pep rally in front of a group of students for not informing him of an upcoming field trip (Woodward claimed that he *had* informed the then assistant principal, however). Other incidents, such as being informed not to discuss a controversial new horror movie called *The Exorcist* in passing with students, were somewhat less egregious.[31]

Two elements become increasingly clear. First, plenty of evidence suggested that the administration had gone out of its way to restrict Woodward. Second, and perhaps most important, it is evident that Woodward did not take well to what could be interpreted as the arbitrary exercise of authority. In short, Woodward was an outspoken person who plainly, in the eyes of many, did not fit in with the local community. This list of conflicts, compiled by Woodward himself, was substantial: he was told not to say that he didn't go to church when students asked him about it; he was told by school administrators not to wear his hair over his ears, even on the weekends (the insinuation being that he was some kind of social misfit); he was told to stand up for all decisions of the school board, whether he agreed with them or not; he was told not to stand up for students' rights, "because students had no rights . . . [and] had not earned them"; he was called into the office for polling students on the dress code; Hughes told him that he was in the "Bible Belt" and that joining a church would allow him to "become part of the community"; Hughes called him into the office because he was apparently worried that Woodward was an atheist; Hughes told him that he was never to have an opinion on anything in the classroom, this despite the fact that Hughes evaluated his teaching without ever having visited his classroom; once, while standing up for a Mexican American student who had long hair, he was told that "Mexicans can't have long hair because they won't keep it clean"; and, finally, Hughes told Woodward that he "didn't need to be in Hereford, [but that] I needed to be in N.Y. or Calif.," where, presumably, someone with such an allegedly "liberal" mindset would fit in much better.[32]

Woodward's problems thus did not seem to consist of violations of school policy; rather, his superiors deemed Woodward a problem because he was in a position of authority yet at the same time he bucked the school's chain of command. Not going to church was threatening; wearing his hair over his ears was threatening; challenging the school board's authority was intolerable;

and supporting the dress code as well as the school board was required. These issues aside, perhaps most telling were the comments that Woodward needed to understand that he was in the Bible Belt and that joining a church would make him "part of the community," as well as the statement that he would be better served teaching in California or New York. To the community members, then, Woodward was a threat—a threat not only because he did not fit in, but also because, as a teacher, he stood to shape the minds of the young in a way that would cause them to fall out from the local sociopolitical order. Simply put, according to the locals, Woodward could never be one of them—he was a problem whose only solution was to be banished from society.

Naturally, the defense conducted further research to ascertain the specifics of the case. Green retained cocounsel for the case in January of 1976 with a well-known Lubbock civil rights attorney named Thomas Jefferson Griffith, who worked for the National Education Association (NEA), a teachers' advocacy group meant to assist those who had legal needs.[33] Support from the NEA was important, as it was an organization whose mission was to defend the rights and liberties of teachers. The NEA also had a history of working with the ACLU in many cases related to education, so the alliance was clearly a natural one.[34]

Bringing in Griffith also served another important end that should not be overlooked. As stated earlier, Woodward and Green were both young men in their early thirties at the time of the case. Taking on the entrenched power structure in Hereford was certainly a daunting task. Green, in particular, as a young lawyer, only served to benefit from the larger legal as well as financial help. The NEA was a national organization based out of Washington, DC, that had extensive experience in cases like Woodward's. This kind of help could make all the difference in Hereford, especially given that no such action as the impending lawsuit had ever occurred in the town, and the entrenched power structure that Woodward and Green were taking on had never dealt with such forceful opposition. Indeed, as early as March 1975, Woodward hoped that the addition of NEA support meant that he and Green could in fact go on the offensive against the school district. Adding Griffith and the NEA was a strategic move legally as well as financially.[35] The backing of the larger organization, along with Griffith's experience in civil rights cases, could prove essential to any legal success.

Griffith conducted his own interviews with Hartman, Langley, Conkwright, and Hughes, further revealing the defendants' mindsets. Langley contested early on that teachers in the district had no right to continued employment and that the school district could terminate anyone without any specific justification (this would become a central argument for the district). Conkwright, in backing Hughes, believed that if a teacher did not work to a certain standard set by the administration, such a shortcoming was enough for the nonrenewal of any annual employment contract. Neither of them, however, gave any specific reasoning for Woodward's termination. Hartman in particular was rather general in his discussion with Griffith, perhaps naturally echoing some of the sentiments provided by Langley. He believed that loyalty was the most desirable characteristic of any school district employee, essentially arguing that Woodward was disloyal. Hartman, however, did enumerate specific instances of Woodward's allegedly unsatisfactory performance during his conversation with Griffith: he was supposed to teach English, but he allegedly strayed from the curriculum; he failed to support school policies and programs; his judgment in response to questions from students was poor; he had allegedly received numerous complaints from parents (this point would later be debated); one of those complaints was that a child had inquired, "What do you think about God?" to which Woodward had replied, "Well, I think he would make a good second baseman"; he apparently made disparaging remarks about the school's dress code; three different sets of parents apparently complained that Woodward's class discussions had disturbed their children to the point that the kids could not eat or sleep; and finally, although the repeated writing of sentences as punishment had been prohibited, Woodward required that of one student. The joking line in which Woodward stated that "Jesus would be a good second baseman" (because his arm was too weak to play centerfield, as the rest of the joke went) was Woodward wanting to say something so shocking because he was tired of the students badgering him about where or whether or not he went to church.[36] Obviously, such a statement, when it came out, was a shock to many in the school as well as the larger community. Hartman concluded by saying that Woodward was highly qualified and that his students performed well, but he attributed that more to their attending an economically advantaged school than any characteristic of Woodward's performance as a teacher.[37]

Bizarrely, Hartman as well as Hughes both denied to Griffith that the ACLU literature was even part of the problem. In fact, both men went to great lengths to explain their own personal positions as being *supportive* of the ACLU. Griffith found this claim incredible, not to mention the above-mentioned circumstantial evidence belying any sense that most Panhandle Texans would find the ACLU anything short of repugnant. Hughes went on to relate to Griffith his chief concern that Woodward had strayed into the realm of politics in his classroom as opposed to just teaching English. Hughes also said that his own claim that Woodward had violated school policy by not clearing controversial material disseminated to students related to a handbook of student rights as opposed to any incident with a particular student. "I knew this was wrong," Hughes claimed Woodward had told him at one point, and "I asked the student not to tell anybody." Finally, Woodward's so-called hostile attitude arose from his failure to heed Hughes's warning not to stray from English into the realms of religion and politics in the classroom.[38]

Griffith's opinion on the matter as a somewhat independent arbiter supported the plaintiff's contention that Woodward's nonrenewal constituted a violation of protected freedom of speech. Previous court cases also set a precedent that made clear Woodward's case would have legal standing in court. Griffith further "noted that the persons interviewed were unwilling to identify the persons making the complaint. They seemed almost unanimously to be parents whose information could be barred as hearsay." Finally, Griffith arrived at the heart of the whole matter:

> Of course, it is reasonable to anticipate that some students and citizens may testify to some violent departure from normal standards of classroom conduct. This may be done through some misapprehension of the actual facts, or even through desire to curry favor with the school administration or with the prevailing political and social climate in Hereford, Texas. *I do not think it an exaggeration to say that Hereford is a tightly structured community with an extremely limited view of permissible expressions and opinions.*[39]

The nature of Hereford and life in the Texas Panhandle during the middle of the twentieth century thus mattered more than anything else. The town's political culture did not allow for anything that stood as a threat to the perceived sanctity of society, which was rooted in mid-twentieth-century conservative ideals. Woodward was not one of them, despite being a native Texan himself. As such, the knee-jerk reactions to Woodward's natural tendency toward dissent from the social order as well as his clear aversion to abject authority marked him as someone who could potentially bring the whole project of protecting the town from outside influences crashing down. The reactions against Woodward made little sense on the surface; upon peeling them back, though, we begin to see the underlying factors at play in the administration targeting Woodward for dismissal.

Griffith and Green assembled a strong case that Woodward's rights had been violated for no reason other than the fact that he was an outsider in a world governed by a domineering sociopolitical consensus. They henceforth set out to press the issue in court. Both lawyers came to the ready conclusion that Woodward had a strong case for wrongful termination. Direct evidence from Hughes and Hartman, they believed, supported the contention that Woodward had suffered through all of this simply because he had made the mistake of joining the ACLU. Depositions had already proven this before the case even went to trial; corroborating evidence included the support Logan received for his resignation from the organization and his subsequent re-employment by the administrators, coupled with Hughes's clear preoccupation with the teachers' ACLU presence during the winter of 1974–75 and the following spring semester. Finally, Griffith and Green believed that the administrators' admission of motivation for placing Woodward on probation due to a parent's allegation that Woodward had passed out ACLU materials in class was, put simply, a lie used as a justification for getting rid of him. Even if Woodward's termination was only partially motivated by a dislike of ACLU activity, Woodward was entitled to relief, they believed, based on legal precedent. Nevertheless, the soon-to-be prosecuting attorneys believed that the pretrial evidence gathered offered no rational conclusion other than the simple fact that Woodward was terminated because of his association with the ACLU. "Speech" statements, they believed, regarding or even criticizing the school's dress code as well as allegations of private communication with students (again, even though proven false by the testimony of affected students) pertaining to school regulations and practices all fell within the ambit of constitutional protection and even statutory protection of the Texas education code.[40] Put simply, there were no clear, justifiable, or even legal reasons why Woodward should have been denied a contract renewal for the 1975–76 school year.

Further, it seemed plainly obvious that the administration had denied Woodward his due process rights, hence the prosecution included the Fourteenth Amendment—which encompasses due process rights—along with the free speech clause of the First Amendment as having been abridged in Woodward's case. Green and Griffith decided to argue in court that all charges against Woodward were hearsay and never communicated to him in any understandable form. Along with the denial of due process was the fact, they believed, that Woodward had neither been allowed to confront his detractors nor gotten any kind of tribunal with "apparent impartiality," which, again, was part of his due process rights as a U.S. citizen. The school board's acceptance of Hughes's recommendations against Woodward displayed an apparent attitude that they were not required to be fair on behalf of a school employee. Finally, the burden of proof in Woodward's case was so slanted that he had to prove his employability to his superiors by demonstrating qualities that were not necessary to the successful performance of his job, nor were they proper metrics against which any teacher or even an employee of the state could or should be measured.[41]

Griffith and Green also made a new case for damages to be collected. The evidence that they presented, argued the two lawyers, authorized damages in the amount of $170,000; what they truly desired, however, was Woodward's reinstatement to the school along with his lost salary plus interest. Such a settlement was justified in their view because of Woodward's unsuccessful attempts to gain employment as a teacher elsewhere in the months since his dismissal from La Plata. His inability to procure employment in his primary field could be proven in court by Woodward's recent pursuit of a secondary career in the field of nursing. An argument could be made that since the board's decision cost him the entirety of the remainder of his teaching career, $170,000 would cover all his lost future earnings. Clearly, reinstatement with back pay plus interest was a smaller number—the prosecutors simply sought to build the strongest case possible against the defense.[42]

Teachers' Rights and Legal Precedent

The above arguments would be presented as oral evidence during the opening stages of the upcoming trial. Finally, along with the preliminary evidence pointing toward Woodward's rights having been violated, his legal team also believed that legal precedent was on its side. Even a simple cursory glance at some recent circuit and district court decisions appeared to confirm that Woodward had a legitimate case. Most notable among these was the 1968 decision in *Pickering v. Board of Education*, which stated that a teacher's employment could not be conditioned upon surrender of his or her constitutional rights. Building on that decision, another court ruled three years later in *Fluker v. Alabama* that if a teacher's contract is terminated or not renewed because of their First Amendment activities, then the Constitution has been violated. Also, in a decision made by the Fifth Circuit Court of Appeals—the same court that would hear the later appeal in Woodward's case—a judge ruled that interference with a teacher's constitutional rights by school authorities is only permissible "if the exercise of these rights materially and substantially impedes the teacher's proper performance of his daily duties in the classroom or disrupts the regular operation of the school."[43] Woodward and Green believed that they could prove that such was not the case.

Perhaps most damning for the Hereford administrators was the 1971 case of *Mailloux v. Kiley*, which at first glance might have appeared to lend weight to the defendants. Essentially, this case argued that teachers do not have broad authority to conduct their classes solely as they see fit. "Free speech does not grant teachers a license to say or write in a class whatever they may feel like," argued the judge, but "the propriety of regulations or sanctions must depend on such circumstances as the age and sophistication of students, the closeness of the relation between specific techniques used and some concededly valid educational objective, and the context and manner of presentation." In the *Mailloux* case, a teacher was suspended and later dismissed after a student complained to a parent that the teacher used the word "fuck" in discussing taboo words and phrases. The court noted that a secondary school acts in loco parentis with respect to minors and that academic freedom in schools below the college level is subject to restrictions, primarily because minors are involved. Although secondary schools are not rigid disciplinary institutions, neither are they open forums in which mature adults, already habituated to social restraints, exchange ideas on a level of parity. Nonetheless, the court ruled in the teacher's favor, stating that when a teacher consciously used a controversial teaching method "in good faith, the state may suspend or discharge the teacher. But, the state may not RESORT TO SUCH DRASTIC SANCTIONS UNLESS IT PROVES THAT HE WAS PUT ON NOTICE BY REGULATION OR OTHERWISE THAT HE SHOULD NOT USE THAT METHOD. In this case the state failed to meet its burden."[44] Green in particular had to be cautious in approaching this case as precedent for his client. Given the *Mailloux* case's precedent, the Hereford administrators could potentially argue that Woodward had used teaching methods that were unorthodox or not approved by the preponderance of his profession, thus necessitating the nonrenewal of his contract. But for Green, such was not the case. *Mailloux* provided that for the termination to be handled properly, clear notice of a violation of school rules had to be given to the teacher in question beforehand. Evidence from Woodward's case showed that the administration had not given clear or proper justification for his termination. The vagueness of the circumstances surrounding his firing indicated that there was no reason for his termination other than his membership in the ACLU.

Regarding communities' political economies, legal precedent had also rejected the notion that schools or communities could purge teachers for saying things contrary to popularly held political opinions at the local level. In the case of *Sterzing v. Fort Bend Independent School District,* a teacher at the beginning of the 1967–68 school year had been surprised by some complaints from parents to school officials that he had said, while teaching a civics class, that he was not opposed to interracial marriage. Administrators instructed the teacher at a board meeting to confine his teaching to the text and avoid controversial matters, which was clearly similar to Woodward's experiences in Hereford. Over the course of the next year, Sterzing, the teacher, distributed some printed materials on dissent against the Vietnam War as well as a few other "controversial matters." In February of 1968, Sterzing taught a six-day unit on race relations in the United States, which one parent complained to school administrators as being "propagandistic." On February 28, without giving the teacher any kind of hearing, administrators voted to discharge Sterzing. His lawyers noted that the school principal had never visited Sterzing's class, and no administrators had any sense of the effectiveness of his teaching methods. In the end, the court declared that Sterzing's free speech activities had been violated due to the administration's arbitrary actions. The judge in the case did note that "it is the duty of the teacher to be cognizant of and sensitive to the feelings of his students, their parents and their community," but the judge also found insufficient evidence to suggest that Sterzing's teaching methods were not in keeping with professional standards.[45] Therefore, Woodward could not be fired for the simple fact of his not fitting in to popular notions of political ideology within the school or larger community.

Hughes and Hartman's contention that Woodward did not have the right to engage in political activities or be critical of the school board in his spare time also did not fit within the realm of legal precedent. In the aforementioned *Pickering* case, the courts established the right of a teacher to speak freely outside of the classroom by engaging in political activity, even when such activities were critical of school board members or other people in supervisory positions relative to the teacher. This case involved the dismissal of a teacher who wrote a letter to a newspaper attacking the school board's handling of revenue raising and spending. The court stated that when comments on matters of public concern are substantially correct—as seemed to be the case in this instance—they may not be grounds for dismissal. If the statements were directed toward persons with whom the teacher was in daily contact, making it important to maintain discipline by immediate supervisors or even harmony among coworkers within the school, then obviously a different or more pragmatic question regarding the teacher's employment could be posed. The court concluded that the dismissal was a violation of Pickering's First Amendment rights, as he did not have a close enough working relationship with the board or school superintendent to justify dismissal by virtue of challenging workplace authority or damaging a positive workplace environment in his school. A more recent case from Dallas, Texas, just two years prior to Woodward's own troubles—*Lusk v. Estes*—cited *Pickering* when a school board dismissed a teacher for making comments critical of the administration to the local news media.[46]

If Woodward's failure to be reemployed was the result of distribution of ACLU material to one student, then the *Mailloux* case clearly stated that termination in such an instance could be valid only if the school board could show that the teacher was on notice that such activity was prohibited. There was no documentary evidence to suggest that this had occurred. If his termination resulted from his ACLU membership, then *Fluker* showed that this was not legal, either, as membership in organizations like the ACLU was protected for American citizens under the First Amendment to the U.S. Constitution. Finally, the Sterzing case showed that Woodward's dismissal could not have been because of statements made in the classroom, since Hughes had visited Woodward's classroom and gained a favorable impression of his teaching.[47] What the upcoming case really boiled down to was, of course, the apparently threatening nature of the ACLU's arrival in Hereford.

CHAPTER 5

MEXICAN MIGRANT LABOR, THE AMERICAN CIVIL LIBERTIES UNION, AND COMMUNITY GUARDIANISM IN HEREFORD, TEXAS

The Hereford School Board was clearly willing to go to great lengths to purge the ACLU from town in 1975. Like the rest of the Texas Panhandle, the town had grown and matured in an isolated geographical space and maintained a relatively homogeneous local culture, where people's adherence to community values had been reinforced during the trying times of the Great Depression and, more recently, where those same values had been challenged by the development of national liberalism during the post–World War II era. When Wayne Woodward brought the ACLU to town in January of 1975, he unknowingly threatened the perceived sanctity of this rural farming and ranching community in the Texas Panhandle.

Clearly, as shown in the previous chapter, Woodward and his legal team had built a strong case that school administrators in Hereford had violated his civil liberties. It is important to take seriously the people of Hereford on their own terms, though, before unpacking the drama of Woodward's court case against his former employers. Why did they *really* fire him? Moreover, why did people at the local level clearly consider the ACLU such a grave threat? This chapter reconstructs the voice of the people in Hereford who did not like the ACLU and what it allegedly stood for. Although explicit empirical evidence as to the nature of a material threat to the town's well-being remains somewhat elusive, when the ACLU's arrival in Hereford in 1975 is placed in the larger context of the town's immediate history after World War II, the worldview of Hereford's dominant Anglo-American population comes into sharper relief. For some, the ACLU no doubt existed largely as an abstract threat in the realm of the larger nation's deepening political divides; fear of the ACLU for others, though, was in fact a surprisingly reasonable response on another level, even though such fear potentially led to the trampling of a young, well-intentioned teacher's constitutional rights. Arguably, the threats embodied by Woodward's actions existed on multiple planes—on the one hand, the town's social culture could become upended, but on the other, if the new chapter of the ACLU had proven successful in the long term, then it might have actually threatened the town's economic interests, as well. To fully appreciate Hereford's prevailing conservative political culture, those economic interests must be taken seriously and placed alongside the perceived cultural threats of the ACLU and post–World War II liberalism. Hereford during Woodward's time was a town that relied heavily on Mexican and Mexican American migrant agricultural labor; those same workers, as this chapter will show, proved to be the catalyst for Woodward to bring the ACLU to town in the first place. In certain respects, Mexican and Mexican American migrant workers played a central role in the unrest surrounding Wayne Woodward, his firing from his teaching position, and his subsequent court case.

The ACLU Threat

Earlier evidence from the 1950s suggests that locals' hatred of the ACLU cannot solely be cast as a knee-jerk reaction against liberal political trends. Recent history prior to Woodward's case suggests that the people of Hereford truly believed that the ACLU was an actual, substantive threat to the well-being of their town.

The civil rights movement initially seemed to garner little attention in Hereford. The landmark Supreme Court decision of *Brown v. Board of Education of Topeka* (1954), which began the process of school desegregation throughout the country, triggered little public reaction in the school system. This is unsurprising, given that Hereford's African American population was small during the 1950s and thus posed no threat to the town's white racial hegemony.[1] In fact, the *Brown* case was of such little consequence that it garnered no significant discussion at any of the Hereford School Board meetings during the second half of the 1950s. The first mention of desegregation at the board meetings does not appear in its minutes until May 15, 1956, exactly two years after the *Brown* case. At the meeting, "a delegation from the Negro population met with the Board" and presented itself to request that segregation actually be *continued* for children in the first through sixth grades.² Although it is not recorded why the parents made this request, one can assume that African American parents sought to protect their young children from whatever racist treatment or backlash from white students might have come through school integration. Otherwise, the town's Black population was so small that, presumably, the presence of African Americans in the middle school or high school among the large majority of Anglo students meant that desegregation intimidated few whites.³ The protests and clashes seen throughout the U.S. South over integration represented no threat to the isolated and then mostly Anglo population in Hereford.

None of this is to say that the people of Hereford exhibited widespread racial tolerance. Speculation suggests that the relatively small African American population meant that the school district could potentially integrate at the middle school and high school levels simply to be in compliance with federal law. Few in the town seemed bothered by such prospects. Nonetheless, in September of 1958, the local newspaper, the *Hereford Brand,* published a story that demonstrated the local population's still deep commitment to racial segregation and intolerance. A group of parents who had students enrolled at the above-mentioned African American elementary school presented a list of demands for improvements at the facility; the paper, however, published an article entirely sympathetic to the school board, decrying "the use of 'pressure tactics' and affirming the administration's efforts to do all possible for the school." At face value, however, the petition seemed relatively innocuous; its points included: "(1) [an] improved road to the school; (2) restrooms in the barracks building which is one of the two buildings comprising the school; (3) clean and level grounds and landscape; (4) install[ation of] a drinking fountain in the barracks building; and (5) hire a janitor to maintain the building and grounds."⁴

Such requests would seem reasonable to make for a school that had apparently endeavored to be in compliance with federal law. Nonetheless, the school board balked. Earnest Langley—the same lawyer who would later represent the district against Woodward—argued that restrooms had been installed, weeds had been cut on the campus, drinking fountains had been ordered for months, and that it was not economically feasible to hire a janitor for a school with such relatively low attendance, where so little routine cleaning needed to be done. Furthermore, "Langley explained to the four delegates from the Parkview PTA that 'the school board (legally) cannot do anything about paving.' He pointed out that the road which approaches the school is owned by two individuals and a cooperative business and that they would have to pay the paving costs." The lawyer "also pointed out that the city commission would have to be consulted in any paving matter."[5]

But the board, as well as the newspaper, felt that it had not gone far enough to oppose this apparent attack on its good name. Bert Boomer, the school board's president, made the seemingly bizarre accusation that the original petition had not only *not* been presented by any of the children's parents, but that it was "actually signed by several persons who have no children subject to school enrollment." Furthermore, speaking for the board, Boomer stated that "we deplore the use by this group of persons of pressure tactics." Additionally, "we do not feel that a Board of Trustees elected by all the taxpayers and patrons of the District should ever bend to the will of any pressure group." Excusing the district from perpetuating the clearly "separate but unequal" status of the schools, Boomer stated that there were "many variations in facilities of different kinds within the District—our school buildings are of different designs, different ages, and different stages of suitability for the educational needs of our children. Naturally," he continued, "not all of our students can be placed in exactly the same type of new and modern classrooms with the newest and best equipment." Other excuses abounded. The board expected Parkview's teachers to do their own janitorial work since the school, in their view, was not large enough to warrant employing a full-time custodian. The superintendent of schools, Fred Cunningham, went even further in trying to silence the parents of Parkview students: he pointed out the minimum state requirements included one toilet for every twenty girls and one for every forty boys. He said that there were two for girls and two for boys at Parkview, even though during the previous year the school had an average daily attendance of fifteen girls and sixteen boys. "You have, certainly, more drinking fountains per number of students than any of our other schools," he added. The message was clear: parents needed to be grateful, in his view, for what they already had at the school. In other words, they needed to sit down and shut up.[6]

The fact that Hereford remained deeply conservative in its racial and social outlooks during the 1950s and '60s still does little to explain the overwhelming backlash that Woodward faced two decades later when he began an ACLU chapter in the town. Woodward himself clearly had ideas that did not fit with Hereford's political culture; nonetheless, even though people looked askance at him, as previously stated, a certain level of tolerance existed for the idealistic young teacher during the early 1970s. Understanding the perception of liberalism as an abstract threat only goes so far—what, instead, caused locals to believe that the ACLU's presence in the town crossed the line into the realm of an *actual* threat?

The answer to this question can only be fully revealed by placing the specific history of Hereford in a larger context. Many Texans during the preceding decades since World War II recognized the Texas Panhandle as having one of the highest per capita incomes in the state. As explored in chapter 1, a strong contingent of what might be called "far-right" politics did exist in the region, although even groups like the John Birch Society (JBS), despite their popularity, held limited appeal for many. Local political candidates during the 1960s who were known JBS members drew the support of the region's populace, even though many conservatives declined membership in the organization. Key to such developments was the relative isolation of Panhandle cities and towns, like Hereford and nearby Amarillo. These areas, only settled during the early twentieth century, by the middle of the century had failed to bring in large numbers of diverse people with new ideas. The isolation of the early twentieth century, in essence, had remained a fact of life in Hereford over the course of the intervening decades.[7]

Stasis, then, was the defining factor in the history of Hereford through the middle of the twentieth century. Even World War II, which produced disjuncture and dislocation in many U.S. cities, did little to change Hereford. Many people on local farms who could avoid the draft and get deferments did so because the country needed food to be produced. Things like meat and gas, of course, were rationed, but there was no shortage of the latter in Hereford because farm tractors needed gas to run. Few would have thought to have accused local men who worked on farms of cowardice or a lack of patriotism, as they were doing their duty and contributing to the war effort through their labor. The only local men who went off to fight, according to one observer, were those who specifically wanted to volunteer. The only measurable change that took place on the local landscape was the establishment of a camp during the war for four thousand Italian prisoners of war in the town to provide the necessary labor to keep the town's growing agricultural sector economically viable. The founding of the Italian POW camp would have interesting if indirect ramifications for the story of Wayne Woodward a few decades later.[8]

Incremental changes began taking place in Hereford after World War II. Jim Witherspoon, a former judge and then a regent for Texas A&M University, wanted to make changes to boost Hereford economically now that the international conflict had come to a close. Now an influential Hereford attorney (Witherspoon's powerful law firm included a young Earnest Langley), Witherspoon organized a diverse group of people into farmers' cooperatives to plant a large amount of acreage in the area to vegetables. Witherspoon considered this a good usage of local resources that would help Hereford take advantage of the then booming national economy. About 2,200 acres were eventually planted to potatoes, onions, and lettuce. Witherspoon helped the farmers gain access to refrigerated cars to ship the produce nationwide. Like much of the rest of the agricultural Southwest, workers came in from Texas's Lower Rio Grande Valley as well as from Mexico as immigrants under the Bracero Program, a guest worker initiative begun in 1942. By 1946, the prisoner-of-war camp had been closed; Witherspoon as well as a few other influential men involved in the commercial farming boom successfully negotiated moving some of the camp's barracks to the southern end of Hereford, where it would now be used to house Mexican and Mexican American migrant workers who picked the town's crops. In keeping with the traditions of mid-twentieth-century migrant labor in the United States, the camps soon turned into a segregated slum.[9]

Hereford transformed rapidly because of these post–World War II changes. Just two decades previously, demographics in the town had overwhelmingly favored Anglos—by 1962 they still maintained a tight grip on power, but the town's Anglo population had for the first time become a slight minority, at 48 percent of the local population. Most of the remaining 52 percent were ethnic Mexicans, the vast majority of whom worked as crop pickers and lived in the migrant-labor camp. As stated previously, there was little outward tension between Anglos and African Americans up to this point in the town's history, in large part because of the small demographic makeup of the latter. Not only did the isolated nature of the town provide fertile ground for the flowering conservative movement, however, but the new shift in the local economy toward agriculture had thus added a new element to the town's social makeup. The booming local economy of the early 1960s had fast become heavily dependent on the presence of an impoverished ethnic Mexican underclass.

Reams have been written about the flowering of the farmworkers' movement in California, which quickly spread throughout the U.S. Southwest around the same time that Hereford became dependent on commercial agriculture. Fruit and vegetable growers everywhere feared the name of César Chávez, founder of the National Farm Workers Association and icon of the soon-to-be widespread Chicano movement. According to Joe Whitley, a dentist who had relocated to

Hereford in 1962, the very mention of Chávez's name struck fear in the minds of many Herefordites. The powerful and well connected in Hereford could not afford a labor strike.[10]

The ACLU's threat itself was both historical and very real—none of this existed within the realm of the abstract. The organization first came to Texas in 1938 to protect workers in San Antonio's pecan-shelling industry who had gone on strike under the leadership of a young communist organizer and Mexican American named Emma Tenayuca. Many of these desperately impoverished workers displayed the subversive threats of communism among the ranks of poor nonwhites, at least in the eyes of many conservative Anglo Texans. All of this occurred under the watchful eye of a liberal and pro-labor president, Franklin Delano Roosevelt. By 1975, then, conservative Texans engaged in commercial agriculture thus had good reason to fear the ACLU's arrival anywhere in the state, much less in their own isolated small towns.[11]

Anxiety thus crept into Hereford. As explored in chapters 1 and 2 of this book, locals had been nervous about big government since the New Deal state had stuck around after the Great Depression; they had been nervous about national politics and the people of the larger United States telling them that their rural agricultural community was out of step with the rest of the country; and they had been nervous that their values and ethics no longer garnered the respect from other Americans that the people of Hereford felt they deserved. The gathering storm of liberalism now threatened to blow over the skies of Hereford—the catalyst for all this at the local level might come in the form of a civil rights movement in which workers asserted themselves against the political and moral authority of the town's leaders.

Witherspoon and his cadre also raised twenty million dollars to bring in a sugar mill after local growers added sugar beets to the bevy of crops grown and shipped out of Hereford. Unionized steelworkers and carpenters built the mill in 1963 and 1964, which Holly Sugar, a national corporation that also consisted of unionized workers, operated. Locals continued to worry what the presence of unionized workers might bring. Despite some brief unrest at the mill in 1972 and 1973, however, Holly remained free of any full-blown strikes or pro-labor demonstrations.[12]

Intolerance for anything resembling liberal ideas grew apace over the course of the 1960s along with fears of the bevy of ideas regarding workers' or liberals' self-perceptions of their rights, which, if pushed, might hold real-world consequences in the town. By the late 1960s and early 1970s, Hereford had also become a stopping point for young hippies from the East making the trek across the country westward to California. Mother's Park in downtown Hereford was where many of these young people congregated. Local police routinely arrested hippies on the charge of vagrancy; it was common practice for the authorities to shave their heads before turning them loose and encouraging them to move on from town. Lawyers and police in the downtown Hereford court building laughingly claimed they were "doing it because of lice." Similarly, students at La Plata Junior High School where Woodward taught also had their heads shaved if they got into trouble. Several locals remembered that this punishment was almost always meted out to Mexican and Mexican American students from the migrant labor camp.[13]

Such practices can only be described as local powerbrokers attempting to maintain some semblance of order in a world that was rapidly changing around them. Given that Hereford had developed in relative isolation even among most of the rest of the far-flung Texas Panhandle, it makes sense that a uniform outlook would take shape. To make matters worse, in 1969 when he first arrived in Hereford, Woodward—again, an Amarillo local—had the misfortune of driving into town with a California license plate on his car, having taught in the Golden State during the 1968-69 school year. What is more, as mentioned earlier, Woodward wore his hair slightly longer than the tops of his ears. As a result, he had the appearance of someone who was an outsider. His actions after moving to Hereford only made the problem worse. The young outsider, who had few friends in the town, quickly became friends with the aforementioned Father José Gilligan, a Catholic priest stationed at the migrant labor camp who ministered almost exclusively to Mexican and Mexican American parishioners. The two men were friends who developed the habit of having a drink together once a week on Thursday evenings. Woodward and Gilligan clearly had certain views in common that led them to becoming friends—thus, it comes as little surprise that Gilligan worked with Woodward in forming the Hereford chapter of the ACLU in early 1975.[14]

Hanging out with Father José in his small apartment made a deep impact on Woodward. Workers toiled and lived in squalid conditions at the camp. Both men wanted to make positive changes for the Mexican and Mexican American workers living in Hereford. Starting an ACLU chapter, which was originally the priest's idea, was only a small step toward advocating for local people's rights. Neither Woodward nor Gilligan necessarily sought to bring labor strikes or radical change to Hereford. Father José simply wanted to protect his flock; Woodward, a teacher, of course wanted to help his students and their families. Many of his students lived in the camp. He would later recall that his students from the migrant labor camp and their families were the nicest, most polite group of people one could hope to find. Unfortunately, the school's attitude toward the migrant students was far less sympathetic. Woodward recalled a conversation in which Principal Hughes told him that "they're just Mexicans, they're never gonna amount to anything. Just pass them and get them out of here." So, to make a small impact, Woodward and Gilligan started a branch of the ACLU. They held their first meeting, and ten people showed up. The naïve young Woodward called the *Hereford Brand* and informed them of the new chapter. Again, he thought that the news—locals advocating for the civil rights of all Americans—would be welcomed by the Hereford public. He never could have guessed how wrong this would turn out to be.[15]

The fact that locals reacted so negatively to this new ACLU chapter cannot be adequately explained by citing a simple distaste for liberalism or the ACLU's radical roots, both of which have been discussed previously. There are several possible more precise explanations. First, few locals would have had any experience with the ACLU; those familiar with the organization might have resented its propensity for protecting the civil liberties, even, as mentioned previously, of questionable figures like convicted murderers. Second, it is quite possible that the perceived threat was whether the ACLU would push local workers' rights to the point of unionization. According to Joe Whitley, many people in Hereford likely mistook the word "union" in the organization's name to mean that Gilligan and Woodward plotted to organize the migrant workers against their employers.[16]

Fears that the ACLU was a radical, far-left-leaning labor union were in fact grounded in historical reality. Examples, even in recent Texas history, are not difficult to find. The above-mentioned Pecan Shellers Strike in San Antonio, during which thousands of mostly ethnic Mexican women walked off their jobs in protest, is a case in point. Young communist firebrands Emma Tenayuca and George Lambert led the strike, which drew resounding support from the Texas Civil Liberties Union as well as the national ACLU. During the summer of 1938, Lambert wrote a long article, published by the ACLU, which detailed police brutality, unfair arrests, and the stifling of free speech in San Antonio. The organization slammed San Antonio as one of the most oppressive municipalities in the nation.[17]

Hereford's powerbrokers could ill afford a similar kind of attack on their town, which, like San Antonio, now boasted an indispensable working-class ethnic

Mexican majority. Nevertheless, even greater than its perceived threat to bring union activism to Hereford, the last reason why locals despised the ACLU was the precedent that the organization's presence could set at the local level: the potential unionism or even just the organization's presence could act as a gateway to workers' rights cases in Hereford or for the assertion of individual rights above the body politic. Indeed, in 1972, one Hereford school board member bemoaned that the top challenge that the district would soon face would be students' rights cases, which had become a central component of the counterculture during the 1960s. Clearly, Woodward, in the eyes of locals, served as a stand-in for either students' rights cases, workers' rights cases, or perhaps even both.

This is the immediate reason why Woodward became a viable threat to the culture and economy of Hereford only in 1975, nearly six years after his initial employment and when he had a clear link to establishing the ACLU at the local level. Before this, his presence with his seemingly out-of-place ideas was relatively tolerable. Either way, the young idealistic English teacher could not have fully comprehended any of this, let alone the enormity of the trouble that would soon encircle him because of his involvement with the ACLU. Coincidentally (and unfortunately), the nature of the ACLU literature that Woodward had handed to young Pam Whitley and Cindy Ford on that winter day in early 1975 did not help things—it was a handbook of students' rights.[18] Would things stop with labor unionism disrupting the town's economy or students potentially disrespecting authority? Other things, such as the right to purchase alcohol (Deaf Smith County, where Hereford is located, was a "dry county" during the 1960s and '70s) might follow. Hereford, to many, thus faced complete social, economic, and moral decay. The ACLU's arrival augured the very collapse of a deeply conservative local society.

The fact that people who subscribed to the emerging conservative politics in the Texas Panhandle believed that the ACLU was an *actual* threat to the economic and social well-being of the town is of critical importance to understanding Woodward's case. Herefordites believed that they were protecting their town from a threat that stemmed from larger left-leaning political trends at the national as well as even the global levels, which they first noticed under the auspices of the New Deal and which seemed to be growing with the *Brown v. Board* case and the larger civil rights movement of the 1950s and '60s.[19] Hereford's isolated nature made it less susceptible to national political trends while at the same time more susceptible to suspicion of outsiders as well as larger phenomena that could infiltrate the town. Prior to January 1975, all this existed within the realm of the abstract. Perceptions of liberalism as aggressive and resting on political or cultural trends sweeping the nation all but shoved the town's political culture to the emerging right, which stood for—among other things—the primary goal of local government. The people of Hereford felt that the larger country did not understand them. Maybe they were right. Their politics rested entirely on perceptions of their town's place in the larger world. Hereford had to be protected, now forcefully if necessary.

Hereford conservatives were not necessarily culturally intolerant. Woodward's case shows that powerbrokers in the town primarily ascribed to a previously mentioned sense of guardianism, protecting the town from perceived threats to its general well-being. Conservatives indeed tolerated some liberalism in their midst—Woodward was a misfit during most of his time in Hereford—in as much as liberalism did not stand as a threat to the vitality of life in this rural, isolated space. The administrators in Hereford, then, would never have stopped to consider that they were trampling on Wayne Woodward's constitutional rights when they dismissed him for promoting the ACLU locally; indeed, they believed that they were protecting the actual well-being of their town against an actual threat. It was only when the ACLU appeared to be emerging in their midst, along with the dreaded specter of labor unionism, that locals finally had to purge an allegedly communistic and anti-American threat from their town. The ACLU, many in Hereford believed, was poised to attack. The townspeople had thus moved forward aggressively in the Texas Panhandle while young liberals like Woodward attempted to change things in rural America during the civil rights era.

Clearly, then, something else had gone into Woodward's firing other than being an allegedly bad teacher who broke rules at the school. The dreaded ACLU threatened to bring massive changes to their little town, which thus far had remained undisturbed during a time when the larger country was experiencing unsettling social unrest. All of this centered around the necessity of migrant agricultural workers to Hereford's economy. According to the local historian Joe Rogers, conditions at the migrant labor camp deteriorated badly over time and occasionally became the point of "considerable controversy." Furthermore, he argued that there was no doubt that the Italian prisoners of war "lived in better surroundings than the poor farm laborers."[20] The people of Hereford in Wayne Woodward's time had good reason to fear that this population might be susceptible to labor organizing. Moreover, publicity about the poor living conditions that migrant workers endured could undoubtedly have been embarrassing for the town. All of this is to say that racial liberalism as well as the wave of migrant-labor unionism that had taken over the country in recent years had finally become very real to Hereford's white population. Nonetheless, conditions in the labor camp probably seemed natural to them, as they no doubt had to agricultural communities across the U.S. West that relied so heavily on Mexican and Mexican American migrant workers.

The looming specter of labor unionism and social unrest, then, is ultimately a reasonable explanation as to why the Hereford School Board felt compelled to go on the offensive against Wayne Woodward in 1975. The ACLU wasn't just an abstract threat; it threatened to upend the entire social and economic order of the town. As shown in chapter 4, Woodward's legal team had constructed a promising case that local officials had violated his constitutional rights specifically because his presence in town had suddenly become threatening due to his new association with the ACLU in 1975. Now it was time for the case to go to court. The ensuing drama would further reveal the rifts that the new liberalism, the new conservatism, and the arrival of the culture wars had brought to this town in rural America.

CHAPTER 6

THERE WILL BE NO WINNERS DOWN THE LINE

Prosecuting a Civil Rights Case in the Texas Panhandle

Robin Green's actual words, uttered to the local news media when he stormed out of the June 2 hearing with the Hereford school board, were "There will be not winners down the line." Little could he have known how prophetic such words would turn out to be; although there *would* be a clear winner in the upcoming courtroom drama, the case's significance reached far beyond the abridgment of Woodward's rights as an American citizen. In fact, Woodward's case was evidence of the growing malady of American political culture as the twentieth century raced to a close.[1]

Green also announced to the press later that evening that he would soon file a case in the district court with the backing of the ACLU and the NEA.[2] The fight would soon be on, with the entire town of Hereford watching the drama unfold.

Preparing for the Courtroom

Green deposed about a dozen witnesses prior to the trial in federal district court in Amarillo. The young attorney considered these to be "prophylactic depositions," meaning that they were important in staving off the defendants potentially making up charges against Woodward during the trial phase. He went on the offensive against the school administrators almost immediately. Some handled it better than others, although the depositions and later courtroom testimonies revealed more about their motives than any of them had intended. One of the first to be deposed was Clark Andrews, a school board member. What became clear from the beginning was that all members of the board were pillars of the local community: all were white, Protestant, business-owning, farm- or ranch-owning men. Green intentionally highlighted political as well as religious views in order to emphasize the wider context for Woodward's alleged persecution. Andrews was forty-three years old and lived six miles south of Hereford. He was a military veteran as well as a farmer, and he had three children, ages sixteen, eighteen, and twenty. Andrews only knew Woodward from the June 2 hearing, thus implying that he could not be considered to have held any kind of personal animosity toward the young teacher. Hartman had mentioned Woodward a handful of times to Andrews as well as other board members prior to the La Plata hearing, particularly with regard to the possibility of a lawsuit.[3]

Andrews was not a man to mince words. Likewise, he was also the first school board member to demonstrate what was clearly a coached position in terms of his support for Hughes in not rehiring Woodward. As he told Green: "I based my decision on the fact that there is not a teacher in our school system or outside of our school system that I would vote to give a contract without a principal recommending that teacher, thereby saying to me, 'I want this teacher to work with me in the school where I am the principal.'"

> GREEN: In other words, the principal is God as far as you're concerned?
> ANDREWS: That don't sound like God to me. If I am working in your law firm and you had a partner, I mean it doesn't make any difference to you who he hires, whether he cannot get along with him or not. Business—any business—whoever is going to be the manager in any business, doesn't he have to get along with who he's working for?[4]

But Green did not have to dig deeply to uncover an antagonistic bent on Andrews's part toward Woodward. Andrews testified regarding a class that his daughter, Lynette, had once taken with Woodward, as well as her student-teacher relationship with him, saying: "I felt at the time on one occasion, at least, that she felt like in class that she was being sort of ridiculed for some of her beliefs. Other than that, I don't know. That's all I know. I don't know anything else better."[5] Andrews may have been trying to avoid complicating the administration's defense, but one thing is clear—he resented Woodward. His temper came out when Green pressed him on Woodward's political views:

> GREEN: Do you belong to a political party?
> ANDREWS: I don't think so.
> GREEN: In other words, it would be an informal joining of a political party, like in order to vote in a primary?

ANDREWS: Yes, sir.
GREEN: You're pretty much of an independent?
ANDREWS: I classify myself as an independent.
GREEN: Do you belong to a church?
ANDREWS: Yes, sir.
GREEN: What church do you belong to?
ANDREWS: Narrow-minded Baptists.
GREEN: You have been a Baptist all your life?
ANDREWS: Yes, sir.
GREEN: Do you go to a particular church?
ANDREWS: Frio Baptist church, six miles south of Hereford.[6]

Andrews's defensiveness—particularly his sarcastic quip about being a "narrow-minded Baptist"—indicates that he was fully cognizant of the conservative-liberal battle lines that Green clearly hoped to draw out in the courtroom. One could also conclude that Andrews did in fact have a sense of Woodward being treated as a misfit due to his cultural or religious differences with the rest of the community. Andrews closed his testimony by castigating Woodward for his attitude, saying that he believed Hughes when the principal said that Woodward's attitude was poor and that said poor attitude had been on display during the earlier public hearing.[7]

Next to be deposed was Mike Hull. Earnest Langley, attorney for the school district, questioned Hull first and also revealed that Hull had actually sought him out when the case became local news to ask him to investigate the "ramifications of a 17-year-old becoming involved in matters of community concern" (Langley, at that point, was essentially acting as an independent arbiter for Hull and had not yet officially been retained as counsel for the school district).[8] The questions next took a turn that can only be described as strange:

LANGLEY: All right, Mike, I noticed just now you turned around and talked to your mother and father who are here with you. Do you feel that your mother and father have been people who have pressured you into positions that you have taken during your time growing and maturing here?
HULL: In some ways, yes.
LANGLEY: Have they ever attempted to pressure you into being an upstanding person morally? Have they attempted to persuade you by the force of their example as well as admonition and encouragement to be a good Christian young man?
HULL: Yes sir.[9]

Langley then let the matter drop, never indicating why Hull's relationship to his parents or his qualities as a "good Christian young man" mattered with regard to his status as a witness in the case. Hull clearly did not necessarily always agree with his parents on the definitions of right and wrong; Langley questioned Hull as to whether or not his parents had ever pressured him to do anything wrong: "Well I don't know what you mean by wrong. What is right for them . . . you know . . ."[10] Even at seventeen, Hull was his own person who could formulate his own opinions.

Those opinions were still decidedly pro-Woodward. Hull reiterated during his deposition that his support for his teacher had not changed. Langley pressed him to see whether Principals Hughes or George had changed his mind on Woodward, to which he replied they had not. Hull stated that George had not directly threatened him—the truth of which statement may have hinged on specific legal technicalities—but he did confirm that George indicated that things could potentially get embarrassing for any student who chose to support Woodward over the school district. Hull also stated that he subsequently had some troubles with George over the remaining year and a half of his high school career, finding himself called into the office on multiple occasions, though these incidents never resulted in any disciplinary action. Hull concluded his testimony by confirming that he had experienced some social retribution on the local level due to his friendship with Woodward, although he did not indicate to Langley that any of it involved any persons related to the school board or the defense.[11]

Green next took over questioning Hull. Instantly things went poorly for the defense. Hull testified to Green that threats to his well-being or attempts to intimidate him into silence had abounded throughout the spring of 1975. Hull mentioned getting strange phone calls on an almost daily basis whereby people would simply say nothing and then hang up on him. In March of 1975, he received threatening anonymous notes in his locker at school, several of which were profane. Things even turned violent. While driving in town one night, Hull alleged that another driver forced him off the road in what he determined to be an intentional effort to scare him. One night he received a threatening phone call that his dog had been killed; when he walked out the front door of his house, he found a stuffed toy dog that had been ripped to shreds on his porch. Although he never had any direct evidence that any of this activity stemmed from his support for Woodward, the potential petition, or his conversations with Hughes and George, he concluded that of course all of it was related. Hull finished his testimony by saying that he was happy that he could avoid openly testifying in the case until after he graduated from high school out of fears of the retribution that could take place at the school (the trial phase would not take place until the fall of 1976).[12]

Even a casual observer could only conclude that Hull's deposition constituted a major victory for Woodward. What might have shocked so many in the court were the lengths to which anonymous individuals attempted to intimidate a young boy with such overt threats of violence. Tactics such as those employed against Hull augured the Ku Klux Klan or other groups who throughout the history of rural America have attempted to use intimidation to silence people or threaten them away from bringing about any social change. Hull's testimony thus made clear to the court that something larger than a teacher having a "bad attitude" was probably at play in Woodward's case. Larger, more sinister forces were at work.

Green continued to collect depositions throughout the fall of 1975. Up next was school board member Ronald Zimmerman. Zimmerman was a local dentist who had graduated from West Texas State University in 1965, meaning that he was roughly the same age as Woodward (in his early thirties). He had been on the school board for three years; one of his three children, fourteen-year-old Zan, had been a student of Woodward's.[13] Zimmerman almost instantly reflected the defense's position that Woodward had strayed into subjects other than English (thus justifying Hughes's actions), but he also betrayed certain biases against Woodward that had already begun to become clear during Andrews's deposition:

> GREEN: Was there anything that your daughter ever said about the class that caused concern or anxiety on your part?
> ZIMMERMAN: The subject of English. I don't know—I can't—that's been a while to recall specifically what someone says about something, but, generally, I would say there was a lot of areas maybe covered that wasn't purely English. It may be that way in math or other class, but—
> GREEN: That did not involve English grammar?
> ZIMMERMAN: Yeah.
> GREEN: Can you tell me of the subjects?
> ZIMMERMAN: No. Being a while ago, it had to do with more of a teacher can express philosophy to children and their feelings are expressed to children and I would say overall—I don't know the word I'm looking for, but a philosophy more liberal than my personal views may be. Is that what you say?[14]

Zimmerman continued, mentioning that his daughter had to write a report on something that she did not feel was "morally correct." These vague memories aside, Zimmerman claimed not to have considered Woodward to be any different from many of the other teachers. He said that he did receive a few complaints from parents about Woodward straying into areas other than English in his classroom, although this was nothing out of the ordinary, given that he received calls from parents on possibly twenty to twenty-five other teachers over the course of his tenure on the board.[15]

Zimmerman perhaps unintentionally pointed out that Woodward was different from most other people in Hereford, although he continued to follow what was a clear position by the defense that Woodward's firing was justified. He also, like Andrews, gave his opinion that he had felt no compunction to question Hughes's decision-making process.[16] Zimmerman's responses to Green remained relatively benign for the next several minutes, until, unprompted by the prosecuting attorney, he spewed forth a completely unprompted diatribe, where he offered "that as a member of the Board and as you cancel patients or whatever you do to make sure that things are handled properly, I do feel that to be individually listed in this lawsuit is a form of harassment." Woodward's charges, he felt, were replete with frivolity.[17] If a job candidate "wants to sue us individually and the Board and the school, because they didn't get the job," then the school district would be in the same mess that it currently found itself in with Woodward.[18] In short, according to Zimmerman, Woodward was a troublesome liberal who sometimes strayed in his curriculum and ultimately filed a lawsuit that Zimmerman personally considered to be frivolous. Any question of Woodward's constitutional rights having been violated was the furthest consideration from Zimmerman's mind.

Green pressed Zimmerman on another issue that would turn into a major problem for the defense: the administrations' uniform attitude of following whatever recommendation Hughes or any other principal in the school district gave to the board members regarding the rehiring of teachers. Green argued in his line of questioning that it was this very attitude that fostered a climate of ideological uniformity at the school. Zimmerman did not appear to be bothered by this:

> GREEN: Are you aware of the fact that when you take the policy that the school board is a rubber stamp for the Administration, that this facilitates the rehiring of teachers who have an attitude of go-along

and get-along and means that those teachers that have different ideas, different concepts, different approaches than the administration will not be rehired?

ZIMMERMAN: If we don't like that policy, then we would change our administrators. You see, we have to function by changing our administrators, to change the superintendent, to change the principals.

GREEN: Are you aware of the danger that this attitude allows in meaning that you may have in your administration somebody who will force teachers to have the same ideological concepts, the same political and religious concepts, in order to remain a teacher in their school?

ZIMMERMAN: I think that would be less of a problem than having to depend on my judgment whether the teachers were qualified and good to be teaching in our system, because I would be a lot less qualified to say they are good teachers. It would be more on personal motivation than educational standpoint. That would be a greater problem.[19]

In short, Zimmerman basically admitted that he was aware that the board's "rubber-stamp" approach to recommendations by the school principals did, in fact, potentially foster not only a sense of ideological uniformity but that it also marginalized teachers who might have different or nontraditional ideas. By arguing that changing administrators could take place *if* the board did not like such a policy, Zimmerman tacitly implied that the board consented to this approach. Zimmerman and his colleagues were less concerned with that than they were with overriding decisions made by a qualified principal like Hughes. Zimmerman's statement thus clearly demonstrated that there was room at La Plata Junior High School for just such a political culture to exist as the one being charged by Green and Woodward.

Following Zimmerman's deposition was that of James Conkwright, another member of the school board. Conkwright was a thirty-three-year-old rancher from north of Hereford, married to a woman who stayed home with two children. Conkwright had never met Woodward, had never discussed him outside of board meetings, and had never visited his classroom.[20] Conkwright was immediately on the defensive; when Green asked him whether or not at the June 2 hearing he had felt that there was any indication that Woodward's constitutional rights had been violated, he responded by saying that he "personally didn't feel enough evidence or statements were given that today or on June 2 would merit that."[21] Much of his testimony echoed that of his colleagues in that he felt no reason to question Hughes regarding Woodward's firing, and that any literature circulated in class probably should have been cleared with the principal.

Several elements in Conkwright's testimony gave cause for concern. One concerned a past telephone call between himself and Mike Hull, which lasted for about ten to twenty minutes before Conkwright spent the next twenty to thirty minutes speaking to Hull's father. Why a member of the board who claimed not to know Woodward personally would feel the need to converse with a student who sought to make a petition on a teacher's behalf—as well as that student's parent—is mysterious, although Conkwright noted that Hull's father believed that school officials "had handled everything properly and he had no complaint about them."[22] Green next criticized Conkwright for some throwaway statements he had recently made to the local newspaper, the *Hereford Brand*:

> GREEN: My question was that you were quoted in the Hereford paper as—you specifically were quoted as saying that you were not surprised that the classroom teachers *statewide* were backing Wayne Woodward, but that you would be surprised if the *local* classroom teachers were? [emphases mine]
> CONKWRIGHT: I did make that statement.
> GREEN: Is there any particular reason that you made that statement? Had you talked to some of the local classroom teachers?
> CONKWRIGHT: No, but I feel that a majority of our local teachers are loyal. I'm not saying Mr. Woodward wasn't at this point. I'm using the terminology here. I think that most of them are supportive of the district. They like their job here and I do feel like on a State level—what I'm saying is, I think on a local level your teachers are more nearly in a school this size, probably even smaller, to be cohesive in their beliefs, but on a state level, you get more varied beliefs and thoughts coming in, the input from other areas and I think there are areas in the State that would have different beliefs than our teachers do here.
> GREEN: Did it occur to you that local teachers might in fact be afraid of reprisals for supporting Wayne in this lawsuit?
> CONKWRIGHT: No, I didn't think about it that way.
> GREEN: That wouldn't have anything to do with this statement?
> CONKWRIGHT: I don't think so.[23]

Conkwright had made what he probably had considered a safe declaration to the local press about the earlier-mentioned TCTA, characterizing the group's politics as out of step with the local town's as well as the local teachers' general views. This was a careless mistake on Conkwright's part, given that Hereford's political culture was ultimately what was under consideration in Woodward's case. Woodward, in his mind, was a singular misfit who did not cohere to the rest of the local populace, teachers included. Green's question about teachers being worried about reprisals, which in his view created the illusion of "loyalty"—itself such a seemingly important concept to the men in charge of the town—perhaps never even occurred to Conkwright as being relevant.

Green did his best to get Conkwright to reveal his own political biases. Regarding the question of whether certain "controversial" materials required proper authorization from the principal before a teacher could circulate them in class, Conkwright stated that an application for the Boy Scouts would require no approval from the principal, but an application for the ACLU would. "I further feel that a membership application to the Democratic party or the Republican party should have clearance before they're circulate[d], also," Conkwright said, as should, he claimed, even a copy of the Bible. Green responded by asking him whether the ACLU was a political party in a clear attempt to get Conkwright to reveal a personal bias against the group: "It is, in my opinion," he responded. "I have never studied it. They do have certain political beliefs depending on which group, which magazine you might read, probably varies from one part of the country to another."[24]

Conkwright had unwittingly played directly into Green's hands. His contention that the ACLU's views might gain acceptance in certain parts of the country over others was revealing. His statement clearly implied that the ACLU was not popular locally, which Woodward's legal team had already established as being the primary motive for Woodward's firing. Langley had likely coached Conkwright against saying anything negative about the ACLU, knowing this was a tactic that Green would use to make his case in court. Nonetheless, this line of questioning seemed to work perfectly for Green.

Finally, Green pressed Conkwright, as he had done Zimmerman, about procedural matters relating to the rehiring of teachers at the school. Green contextualized his questions within the June 2 hearing:

> GREEN: And I did make statements to the effect that I was concerned that Mr. Hughes, acting in a position of authority under you, was violating Mr. Woodward's constitutional rights?
> CONKWRIGHT: I think you made that statement.

GREEN: And did you think it incumbent upon you and the other Board Members then to question Mr. Hughes about these matters before finally not rehiring Mr. Woodward?
CONKWRIGHT: No, sir, I didn't. I personally didn't feel enough evidence or statements were given that today [sic] or on June 2, would merit that.
GREEN: Did you consider that you could get at the truth of the matter without hearing some of the motives of Mr. Hughes in not recommending Mr. Woodward for rehire?
CONKWRIGHT: Yes, sir, I feel that we could.
GREEN: Did you have any other reasons besides Mr. Hughes not recommending Mr. Woodward for rehire for your personally not voting to rehire him?
CONKWRIGHT: No, sir.
GREEN: Was that the total fact that you took into consideration, the fact that he was not being recommended by his principal?
CONKWRIGHT: Yes, sir.
GREEN: And that's all?
CONKWRIGHT: Yes, sir.
GREEN: Did you not then feel it incumbent upon yourself to question or to allow us to question Mr. Hughes as to whether or not that was true [that Woodward was right in believing he was fired because his ideas and concepts didn't fit with Hughes's]?
CONKWRIGHT: No.[25]

Green let the issue drop at that point, clearly satisfied that he had demonstrated the existence of a procedural culture in the school district that, again, allowed Hughes to operate in whatever manner he saw fit with regard to the political or social outlooks among the teachers and administrators at the school.

Hereford High School principal Jerry Don George naturally had a different story than Mike Hull did. George told Green that his conversation with Hull came at the behest of James Hull, Mike's father, who worried that his son was wading into the realm of school personnel business: "His dad had just asked me to visit with him . . . in a way he felt like that he could not visit with him [and] that he might listen to me in some things that I might advise him on, I guess. I don't know. I really was—I was really doing it out of a service to Mr. James Hull." When the questioning turned to the subject of his alleged threat to Hull over the issue of scholarships, George sought to bide his time by playing ignorant: "I don't recall saying anything about an honor scholarship or whatever. In a public school a youngster is not on a scholarship[,] and the way I interpreted this is that a scholarship might be taken away from him. No one in public school is under a scholarship."[26] When Green directly asked whether he had threatened Hull, George attempted to dodge the question, arguing that "as principal of the high school I am not the only one who makes recommendations for scholarships. There are a number of people, including teachers, other administrators and counselors." He continued, stating that any "organization may contact me and ask for names who they may choose for a scholarship and I will go to the teachers and to the counselors and other people and consult with them such as Boys State, American Legion. We may turn ten names, eight names to them[,] and they make the final decision."[27] The principal thus attempted to imply that nothing of the sort could even be remotely possible, without directly impugning himself by admitting to the charges or denying them.

George next tepidly engaged in a series of questions and answers with Green during which the witness grew increasingly defensive:

> GREEN: My sole question to you was did you imply, insinuate, state or tell him in so many words or any way that you would not recommend him for certain scholarships that he might be eligible for upon graduation?
> GEORGE: To my knowledge a scholarship was never mentioned.
> GREEN: He is just mistaken about this?
> GEORGE: I feel certain that he is.
> GREEN: Seems like that would be sort of something that would be hard to be mistaken about, wouldn't you say?
> GEORGE: Possibly.
> GREEN: Do you recall that you have to approve the membership list to the Key Club organization?
> GEORGE: No sir, I do not have to be the sole one who approves this.
> GREEN: Are you one of the ones who approves it?
> GEORGE: I am part of a team who may give suggestions to the faculty sponsor of the Key Club and to Mr. Owens, who is the Kiwanis Club representative. They may visit with me and usually do visit with me on recommendations[,] but to the best of my knowledge in the eight years I have been involved with this I have never asked that anyone not be given membership into our Key Club.[28]

On the question of sending Hull over to the middle school to speak with Hughes:

> GEORGE: I asked him if he would like to[,] and Mike kept referring to the things that he just was totally confused. He was totally confused about the situation.
>
> GREEN: How do you mean that, he kept saying he was totally confused?
>
> GEORGE: Yes, that he was confused about the situation and needed more information and I said he could possibly visit with Mr. Hughes and gain more information because I didn't have a lot of the information to give him.

When asked whether it was just a "nice conversation" or an attempt to dissuade the petition and Hull, George replied: "Anytime I visit with a youngster and counsel with a youngster and just visit or whatever, I think it has been a nice conversation."

> GREEN: Now, in Mike's deposition he says that part of the conversation that went on in your office was that you said something to the effect if he persisted in his efforts to circulate the petition on behalf of Wayne Woodward that you would see to it that his name was removed from that committee, Gopro Committee. Is that an accurate statement?
>
> GEORGE: That is false.
>
> GREEN: You never said anything to that effect?
>
> GEORGE: I never said anything to that effect. If I was leading in a direction in what I said, this is the interpretation that he made. I repeat that in giving his name and the other girl's name [for recommendation for the Gopro Committee]—in visiting with the teachers that they all felt like that we would try to be representative of someone that would represent the entire student body and I impressed upon him that he needed to try to do this, to represent the entire student body.²⁹

In other words, George, while clearly deflecting certain responses, contradicted Hull with many of his statements. Who was to be believed—a young student supporting a teacher, or a high school principal who was a colleague of a group in the town that had dismissed that same teacher for seemingly vague reasons?

Green re-upped the pressure on George, restating that in Hull's deposition the young man had mentioned that George had threatened to have him removed from the Key Club (a service organization for high schoolers, which looked good on college applications) as well as mentioning that George had at least insinuated that he would withdraw his recommendation of Hull to the Gopro Committee. George responded, "I don't know how that I could possibly do those things even if I had a desire to." George next went into a long dialogue of not being able to personally understand why his testimony was in direct contradiction to Hull's, although he recognized that such was the case. He did not accuse Hull of lying, but rather, to George, the issue stemmed simply from him having reached contradictory conclusions from the conversation. He ended his deposition by saying that Hull's father had called him, during which conversation George related to him that he and Hull had had a "good visit" but that he did not know if the conversation did the younger Hull any good.[30]

Was George credible? Pam Whitley certainly didn't think so. Whitley was one of the top students at La Plata—she also loved Woodward's classes. Woodward, according to Whitley, was beloved by the students. Naturally, many of the adults disliked the outspoken young teacher who was a product of the 1960s, but nonetheless, there was also, in her view, a group of adults who adored him. One was Whitley's father, Joe Whitley, a local dentist. Pam Whitley, as already stated, was one of the students involved on that fateful day when Woodward gave out an ACLU tract. Whitley had read in the local newspaper, the *Hereford Brand*, about Woodward being the founding vice president of the local chapter of the organization. Being curious about the goings-on of a teacher whom she held in the utmost respect, Whitley, as already shown, asked Woodward for more information during a passing period before class one day. Woodward obliged, handing her a pamphlet. Whitley's close friend Cindy Ford was sitting next to her and innocently asked for a pamphlet, too, which Woodward promptly gave to her. Ford's father, a conservative Christian, later discovered the pamphlet and promptly telephoned Superintendent Hartman to lodge a formal complaint against Woodward. According to Whitley, this was the final evidence that the administration had needed to get rid of Woodward—to her, they disliked him immensely, but he was a good teacher who could not be fired given his stellar classroom performance. Now, however, Hartman and Hughes believed that they finally had all the ammunition they needed to fire him.[31]

Whitley was not sure if the administrators' targeting of Woodward was long-standing but to her, an attitude of extreme prejudice permeated the ranks of the town's leading citizens. Even as late as the 1970s, local citizens would call the police if an African American happened to be traveling through Hereford and stopped at a store or a restaurant; that person would then be escorted to the edge of town and told never to return. Whitley's own father actually ran for the school board himself after the drama of Woodward's case exploded on the local scene. He lost miserably. Part of his motivation to run for the board might also have been to protect his own family. Although Whitley was a leading student and captain of the cheerleading squad, her sister Sandy was gay, thus making her something of a social misfit in the small, deeply conservative town. One day, while a student at the high school, Sandy and her mother were called into Principal George's office. Someone had found a love note that Sandy had written to George's daughter Monica, who was also a student at the school. George threatened to expel Sandy. In response and showing a strong sense of intuition, however, Sandy's mother countered by saying that she had also found a love note written by Monica to Sandy, which she had kept in a safety deposit box. George immediately dropped the threats to kick Sandy out of school, and she returned to class. The Whitleys had clearly outsmarted the administrators.[32]

Men like George, Hughes, and Hartman were thus not averse to taking a threatening posture toward people whom they did not like. In fact, according to Whitley, their behavior could turn downright shocking. Mike Hull had previously testified that a truck had run him off the road at one point after a school dance. According to Whitley, the culprits were none other than George and Hughes themselves. Whitley also had a similar experience. In August of 1975, Whitley and her family were moving out of Hereford to escape the hostility of the town's culture. Of course, this was after Woodward had already filed his lawsuit but before any testimonies had begun. One day, Whitley noticed a car containing two grown men wearing ski masks driving back and forth down her street. Whitley then left to go to a friend's house, where the same car followed her; the car next followed her back to her family's house when she went home. Of course, Whitley could never prove that it was the town's two senior-most school principals who were in the car, but her sense as well as Hull's told them that it had to be Hughes and George. That summer, also around the time of the case, a series of five bizarre fires had been set near people's homes all around town—one, in fact, was at a school board member's house. What with the fires, being followed in cars, Whitley's sister being harassed by school officials, and the case surrounding Woodward, Whitley's father felt as though he had no choice but to abandon his successful dental practice and relocate the family far away, to San Antonio, Texas. Whitley and her family never looked back, satisfied to leave Hereford and the Texas Panhandle in their rearview mirror.[33]

The next witness to be deposed was school board member James H. Gentry. Gentry's profile was similar to those of the other school board members: he was a farmer, had lived near Hereford for a number of years (in this case, since 1949), had a stay-at-home wife and three children, was a Democrat and a member of First Baptist Church in Hereford (several of the school board members attended this same church).[34]

Gentry's testimony seemed to toe the administration's line—they did not feel the need to challenge Hughes, and they did not think that Woodward had provided sufficient defense of himself at the school board hearing to merit rehiring. Gentry echoed his colleagues, saying in no uncertain terms that "it was my understanding that we were offering Mr. Woodward a chance to come before the board and give us some reason why we should offer him a contract for 1975, 1976[,] and it was my personal opinion that no substantial reason was offered in that meeting." Furthermore, "there could have been reasons Wayne provided that he be rehired," but he did not feel that Woodward gave any and he did not feel that he needed to ask Hughes about the alleged violation of free speech.[35]

Gentry's true colors, nonetheless, were soon revealed. Green pressed Gentry as to whether Woodward could obtain another teaching job after not being rehired in Hereford, after which the following exchange took place:

GENTRY: I personally felt like the Hearing, after the community talked about this thing, I personally felt like that he probably could relocate in another part of the country where maybe his philosophy, if that's the correct word, was a little more acceptable.
GREEN: Where would that be, do you have any idea?
GENTRY: No, I do not from personal experience. I have heard that some places in the East and in the North and West, almost anywhere but here.
GREEN: And so, you thought because of the philosophy that you had heard expressed that he would be better off in the East or North or West, not here?
GENTRY: Yes, I really did.
GREEN: Assuming that Mr. Woodward had not been relieved from his teaching duties here, because of this incident, would you have any personal objection to him teaching your children in the Hereford School System knowing what you know about him, now?

GENTRY: If all the hearsay that I have heard is true, I would have an objection, yes.
GREEN: Would you be willing to base an opinion on that hearsay?
GENTRY: Probably not.[36]

Put simply, Woodward did not belong in Hereford, due primarily to his "philosophy." He was a misfit and a canker who had to be expelled from town, if for no other reason than men in positions of power either believed that he did not fit in or somehow felt threatened or undermined by his views. Gentry gave his opinion on the matter with less subtlety and grace than did Conkwright, but they were clearly of like mind on Woodward, along with his views, not fitting in locally in the town.

Woodward's legal team also deposed J. Lynton Allred, who was another member of the school board. Allred had lived most of his life in Hereford, had a degree in marketing from Texas Tech University, was a Democrat but "not real solid at all," and was a member of First Baptist Church in Hereford. Allred did not know Woodward personally and had not even met him yet at the time of his deposition. Allred also said that when he saw Woodward at the June 2 hearing that this was the first time that he had knowingly even seen him. Allred also claimed that he could not recall any students or teachers complaining to him about Woodward during his tenure on the school board.[37]

Allred thus implied that he had no personal reasons for not recommending Woodward's rehiring. His primary justification, again, echoed by other members of the board, was that Woodward had not been recommended for rehire by Hughes. This, for Allred, was his practice in all cases that came before the board regarding the rehiring of teachers. Green went on to ask Allred if he would ever go against the principal's recommendation in such a situation, to which he responded that "there are no absolutes to me in a situation like that. That would definitely be a break with a policy that our system has operated under for as long as I have been aware of it and certainly since I have been on the board." Allred did not believe that he should have consulted with Hughes regarding Woodward's firing. Things were perhaps unique in Hereford: "It would be very difficult to me to insist that a teacher be hired to serve in a school that evidently the compatibility was not such that the students would be receiving the best benefit of education that we're trying to provide for him. I don't know if that makes sense," he continued, "but if someone came to me in my business and required me to hire someone that I could [not] work with for some reason, then that would not maximize the efficiency of my business. It's the same way in a school."[38] Allred further stated that he felt no need to question Hughes's original letter, which, for him, was good enough reason for Woodward's dismissal.[39] As such, Allred, like others, left the impression that the school board essentially was a rubber-stamp body for decisions made by the school principals, whom they hired and in which they maintained complete professional faith. Again, if Hughes had a reason to discriminate against Woodward, then it would be quite easy for him to get away with doing so.

Still other board members were deposed in the early part of the case. Board member Danny K. Martin accused Woodward of ridiculing the Baptist beliefs of his young sixteen-year-old daughter. After responding in the affirmative to Green's question of whether he had heard people in Hereford talk about Woodward, Martin replied: "Oh, most people, I would have to say, would probably be critical. Mr. Woodward was, I would say, thought of as being different, as kind of progressive, I think. Teachers at different times, were opposed, and some weren't. You know, saying that's kind of weird or—you know."

GREEN: Because of his progressive attitude and because of who he was?
MARTIN: Well, I would say because of the way he handled his class was different. Maybe progressive is not a good word, but it was different.[40]

Again, another high-ranking member of the local community made it clear that the popular notion about Woodward was that he simply did not belong.

Obviously, one of the trial's main events would be Hughes's deposition. Indeed, the defense's case hinged on whether Hughes could defend his actions.

Robert Patterson Hughes was forty-three years old when the deposition phase of the trial began. He had been married for twenty-three years, had a nineteen-year-old daughter and a thirteen-year-old son, and had moved to Hereford from small Hamlin, Texas (close to Abilene but still in the western part of the state), in 1968. By 1975, he was then only in his third year as principal at the school; previously, he had been assistant principal as well as a biology teacher and a football coach. Hughes had known Woodward since his tenure as assistant principal, meaning that his only dealings with Woodward were in a supervisory role. Interestingly, Woodward was the only teacher that Hughes had not recommended for rehiring during his tenure as principal at La Plata Junior High School up to this point.[41]

Hughes's deposition was replete with vagueness. Hughes claimed that he had numerous conversations with Woodward during his six years at the school, but he could not recall, while being questioned under oath, what any single one of those specific conversations was about.⁴² This might seem strange, given that Woodward clearly stood out during Hughes's time as principal. Hughes's memory lapses continued on the subject of the ACLU literature, where he stammered, "Let's see, I believe, sir, that I asked him if he was a member of the American Civil Liberties Union and at that time his answer, I think, was yes, I am." The matter seemed settled, though: "I said, have you ever been passing out materials to students in your classes and he said yes, sir, I have." Woodward then told him about giving the materials to Pam Whitley and Cindy Ford: "He said, I gave it to one girl and I didn't ask him her name. What he said, he said I gave it to one girl and I knew I was wrong when I did it and I asked her not to tell . . . He said, I won't do it again. I said, thank you, Mr. Woodward, please don't[,] and I left."⁴³ It appeared, then, that Hughes, by his own account, seemed to leave things on good terms with Woodward regarding the ACLU pamphlets. Hughes also claimed that he had talked with Woodward "about [his] action in class with his students," but that he could not remember any specifics. Green asked Hughes about an alleged parental complaint regarding Woodward not going to church, but Hughes stated that he could not remember such an incident.⁴⁴ Thus, neither the ACLU pamphlet nor any specifics about Woodward's job performance seemed to strike Hughes as having been relatively meaningful.

Green grew tired of Hughes's apparent memory lapses:

GREEN: Specifically, can you tell me any specific incident that came to your attention that caused you to believe that Mr. Woodward was not adequately helping his students acquire values realized as ideals of democracy?

HUGHES: Sir, in my estimation, a person in charge of a class of students such as ours, where they are thirteen, fourteen and fifteen-year-old students, sometimes sixteen, is a person that I feel must stand before the class and take comments from them and guide their maturity level and I think perhaps Mr. Woodward would have done well in another situation with students that age. In my estimation, I think sometimes the conversations, which he headed and related to me or gave to me that he had had with these students[,] was [sic] a little bit above their maturity level and there were times when I asked Mr. Woodward to guide the conversations as the classroom leader more toward the child that he had in his class. Now, this is not to say that he couldn't have

> done a good job elsewhere to more mature people, but in this situation I am saying that perhaps—
>
> GREEN: Are you talking about the subject matter or the subject matter that he was covering in class?
>
> HUGHES: No, not necessarily the subject matter, these are conversations which come up in the classrooms periodically and it wouldn't have to be in any specific class. There are items which come up in all classes.
>
> GREEN: You feel that Mr. Woodward then was giving information that was a little bit—was conducting conversations that were a little bit too complicated for the students to understand what was going on?
>
> HUGHES: No, I wouldn't say all students but there are—our schools today are just like our communities. There are some students of greater ability than others. We try to do an ability-grouping in our school in some areas.
>
> GREEN: In other words, what you are saying is he was catering more to the intelligent student that was doing well than he was the other students on the other end of the spectrum?
>
> HUGHES: In my estimation, sir, he was not getting to all of the students in his class.[45]

Frustratingly for Green, Hughes could also not remember the number of times he had visited Woodward's classes, simply that it had occurred more than once and that most of his observations of Woodward's teaching lasted no longer than two minutes.[46] To Green, as well as to the court, none of this could have come across as anything other than run-of-the-mill principal business in a public school.

Hughes, in fact, had positive remarks about Woodward's teaching, telling Green that he was surprised at how professional Woodward was as well as the seemingly "good rapport" he had with his students. Hughes also said that he had never received a single complaint from a parent about what was going on in Woodward's classroom.[47] Nonetheless, Hughes persisted in his claim—in a seemingly contradictory way—that Woodward was not always professional:

> GREEN: Can you think of an example?
>
> HUGHES: No, I can't right now, sir, but he would say, well, these kids stand up and they ask me a question point blank and he said, what do you want me to do, lie to them about my ideas or about anything and I would tell him, no, I certainly don't want you to lie about that situation, but

you as the educational leader in that room, I expect you to guide their conversation to a more enhancing—to a situation where it would meet the needs of the children better that he had in his room.

GREEN: Can you think of one of the subjects that you and he talked about?

HUGHES: Sure, religion, is that one?

GREEN: And what was the nature of that conversation?

HUGHES: I don't know that conversation. I would never ask him what he was—he and I wouldn't talk about what he and his students talked about necessarily and neither would he say, look, these are my views and I stand for them. I never did ask Wayne that.

GREEN: You found through talking to him that some students would ask him about his religion?

HUGHES: No, sir, that may not be so. No, but religion might come up in the class, nor necessarily, say, look what is your religion? What are your beliefs?

GREEN: In other words, they ask him something like that, what are your beliefs about a particular subject?

HUGHES: I don't know, sir, what they did ask him specifically.

GREEN: Anyway, a part, a large part of your dissatisfaction with Mr. Woodward's performance in the classroom, then, came from conversations that you had with him wherein it was related to you by him that subject matter was being discussed in the classroom that you did not feel was appropriate?

HUGHES: You said in large part. I don't feel that is it, no, sir. I feel like that is a part of it, yes, sir. And I told him you should never just come out, I would think—Wayne said, what if they ask me my views, do you want me to stand up and lie to them and I said, no, sir, don't ever want you to do that, but I think Wayne should have been mature enough and had more education than those that he taught so that he could guide that conversation in his classroom, which would be more beneficial to his students than giving them a wealth of information on the subject that might arise. My contention was that these students were maybe too young . . . Not to deal with certain subjects but to go into them intricately.

GREEN: Do you recall whether or not you received any complaints from parents regarding his conduct in the classroom?

HUGHES: Yes.

GREEN: Can you remember the nature of any of those complaints?

HUGHES: Basically just what you and I have been talking about now.

GREEN: Somebody complained that Wayne had made a statement in the classroom concerning religion or God or Christ, anti-Christ or something like that?

HUGHES: No, that wasn't it.

GREEN: Okay, can you tell me what the complaint was?

HUGHES: Mostly the complaints, again, were not that he expressed himself in class, but it was the length at which he expressed himself, the time covered on a certain subject.[48]

The confusing back-and-forth nature of Hughes's exchange continued, as Hughes seemed unable to recall any specific instances that were a direct cause for concern.[49]

What Hughes *did* seem concerned with was Woodward's alleged level of maturity in the classroom. Hughes again repeated that Woodward had the tendency to stray from topics other than English. Again, however, Hughes stammered and was unable to communicate anything more directly about Woodward's allegedly poor behavior. The information that Hughes had surmised regarding Woodward's performance stemmed not just principally but solely from the conversations that he and Hughes had shared.[50] Interestingly, as the questioning progressed, one thing became clear—part of Hughes's problem with Woodward was his seeming aversion to the principal's authority. In one issue relating to Woodward allowing retests for a specific student and Woodward's eventual relenting to one student's parents who applied pressure to allow a retest for their daughter, which Woodward had initially refused, Hughes said that "I thought Mr. Woodward acted very fair, was professional in his action with the parent and the student." He continued, though, that "after the parent left and he confronts me again and he says, look, you didn't do right by me. You didn't stand behind me and I expected you to and the tone of voice which he used and the atmosphere of his conversations seemed to me, he was not a professional person."[51] Woodward was a problem for Hughes because he did not seem to show any deference to Hughes in his role as principal.

Still, despite these statements, Hughes continuously exhibited a remarkable lack of clarity while being questioned. Observers in the courtroom where Hughes gave his deposition could only speculate as to his credibility or his competence as a professional, as evidenced by the following exchange with Green:

GREEN: Did you have complaints from parents about Mr. Woodward's teaching?
HUGHES: No, now, you said about his teaching, no.
GREEN: Did not?
HUGHES: No.
GREEN: Did you have complaints from parents about other things?
HUGHES: About perhaps what he was talking about, now, I don't think the question—I don't think Mr. Woodward's performance in the classroom—now, I am talking about the ability to perform in the classroom has ever been a question. I think sometimes it is what we say in the classroom, yes.
GREEN: And parents would complain about the subject matter, then, that he was bringing up?
HUGHES: Yes, no, no, now, that may not be so. Mr. Woodward may not have brought it up.
GREEN: The parents complained about the subject that was being discussed in his classroom?
HUGHES: I would be more inclined to agree with that than the last statement.
GREEN: Then, was religion the only thing you recall having complaints on?
HUGHES: Sir, I asked Wayne a while ago if we had discussed religion and I probably wouldn't have mentioned that had I not asked him had we discussed it first.
GREEN: Okay. Now, listen to my question. Do you personally recall any other subject that you received complaints from parents concerning Mr. Woodward's discussing in his class other than religion? You received some complaints from parents about religion, obviously. Was there anything else they complained about him talking about?
HUGHES: I don't recall at this time.[52]

Green seemed to have Hughes where he wanted him. The critical matter, for Green, was simply whether Hughes wanted a man like Woodward teaching at his school, or even living in Hereford, at all. Hughes argued that "[his] attitude was not compatible with Hereford, Texas." Hughes went on to say that "the people in Hereford are concerned about the welfare of their children and if you are not compatible with those persons here, if you don't think that you can get along here with their criticisms, then why don't you move to a place that you can do a better job and if I remember right, Mr. Woodward said, I don't care to move." Hughes almost seemed baffled by such a response: "If he was, you know, disgruntled about the situation there at La Plata or his working conditions, Mr. Woodward never came to me to speak about a transfer, going to some other school or even staying in Hereford."[53] Why such a person would want to stay in Hereford seemed beyond his understanding. Once again, evidence suggested—this time on court record—that the administrators did not believe that Woodward belonged in Hereford. Hughes, naturally, expressed as much in polite terms, but the meaning behind his words was clear—Woodward did not belong teaching in Hereford, and he was a threat because he had the power to change the children in the school. Circumstantial evidence, at this point, suggested that there was a connection between this belief on Hughes's part and the potential that Woodward's ACLU involvement was a pretext to finally get rid of him.

Hughes thus never saw anything in Woodward's classroom that was bad enough to give him any pause; in fact, the principal even admitted to having a letter on file from another teacher in defense of Woodward's performance. If Woodward was a teacher who enjoyed a fairly strong reputation not only among his peers but also, in fact, with his students, how could Hughes as well as the school board justify his firing? Necessary to this end was any kind of complaint that could be levied against Woodward in terms of either his professionalism or his ability to fulfill the wishes of the school administration. One complaint did come from Mary Duvall, the school counselor. One day, Woodward was in the administrative offices hoping to take some students out of the classroom to a track meet at the school's stadium. Hughes was out of the office at the time, but Duvall informed him that the school had not taken any steps to allow whole classes of students to attend the event. Duvall alleged—and Woodward himself denied ever having said the following—that Woodward responded by informing Duvall that "I have to do something with these little monsters this afternoon." Duvall considered the remark unprofessional due in no small part to there being a student's mother sitting in the offices at the time of the occurrence. Duvall said that this made dealing with this particular mother, who had a completely separate problem that did not involve Woodward or one of his classes, even more difficult for her, although she knew that "Wayne had already started having some problems and I know he was upset, too." Hughes could not recall any other complaints coming from staff or administrators at the school regarding Woodward's performance.[54]

Duvall, nonetheless, was unwilling to let Woodward off the hook. She later said during her own deposition that she remembered having a conversation with him about everything after the February 12 letter, during which he said, "Well, I'm glad you asked me, because no one has asked me to tell . . . my side of the story." Duvall went on to say that she was having some trouble understanding what all of this was about, because she was under the impression that Woodward had not been fired outright, and that "I felt that perhaps if Wayne had wanted to be rehired, he could have been. Now, that was my feelings." Soon thereafter, Woodward met with other teachers in the library the morning after he got his letter, which was something that the teachers often did. He told them about the letter and basically said, "I'm fired," and that a number of the other students were alarmed and upset because this kind of thing was highly unusual at the school. But Duvall chalked all of this up to a lack of personal responsibility on Woodward's part: "I think he insinuated that under no circumstances would anyone tell him what to do and that he was himself." Duvall backed up these assertions by saying that she did not understand why Woodward went to the group of teachers like he did, and that if she was in his position and she really wanted to come back, she would have kept quiet and done whatever she could have done in order to keep her job. In short, she seemed unable to wrap her brain around the matter. "I think Wayne kept saying that he couldn't act or do like he wanted to," she said. "I don't even remember if he said that . . . [but] I never could understand what the problem was."[55]

Duvall agreed with Hughes regarding Woodward's alleged lack of professionalism. Duvall argued that Woodward completely ignored Hughes during the last two or three months of his time at the school. When Woodward went to the office, he would do anything to avoid speaking to Hughes, including turning his back to him and speaking only to the office secretary. In Duvall's opinion, this was unprofessional. She did not feel that Hughes ever ignored Woodward, though, and she also commented that Woodward's behavior was mostly the simple result of "undue strain" being placed on him. But still, Woodward drew her criticism. Duvall also mentioned that Woodward had told some teachers that they might be subpoenaed or called as witnesses for the upcoming trial, which caused many of them to visit the school office and express their concerns to her or to Hughes. Duvall, in fact, had mentioned to Green something negative about Woodward previously: "It was hard for me to understand how Wayne could do the teachers that had respected him for all those years and had been good to him, how he could have made them feel as bad as he made them feel, and this I didn't appreciate." To Duvall, the other teachers simply did not appreciate being involved with the trial. When Green asked if Woodward had approached her about testifying on his behalf, she responded that "he didn't tell me, because I'm sure he didn't feel that I was anti-Hereford, you see, because he knew I respected the school system."[56]

"He didn't feel that I was anti-Hereford"—what did Duvall mean when she said that? Clearly, Woodward's case showed that some kind of battle lines had been drawn in the school; his pushback against the administration's purging of him indicated Woodward's sense of belonging—or lack thereof—in the town. From a simplified point of view, Hereford was quiet, white, rural, Christian, and deeply conservative. By implication, Woodward was everything that challenged this dominant narrative—loud, liberal, not Christian, and potentially pro-Black (as someone who came of age during the civil rights era and the 1960s). What is perhaps most interesting about Duvall's statement is that it was grounded in the politics of place. Woodward was "anti-Hereford," not even "anti-Hughes" or anti–school administration. The ACLU, to locals, was viscerally "anti-Hereford." Herefordites wanted to maintain a certain level of stasis; the changes of the time threatened the things that locals believed were right, good, and orderly in their small town. Nobody opposing Woodward seemed to care that his constitutional rights might have been violated or that he had been fired for potentially unfair reasons. He was, to them, against Hereford and everything for which the town stood. Grounding political viewpoints in the name of town and home served as a salve for locals who felt threatened (and perhaps condescended to) by the many changes that had taken place in the U.S. political arena during the previous three or four decades.

In summing up her perceptions of the case, Duvall clearly felt some unease because of Woodward's actions as things escalated at the school. "He just put the whole place in a turmoil, you see, the last two or three months," she said. When asked by Green for clarification, she continued: "He just constantly—it was just that little constant, you know, talking in the library. After about a month, I think, then he probably didn't do very much of that, but it was enough to keep everything pretty well torn up."[57] For Duvall, Woodward was a troublemaker. He could, in her view, easily have protected his job had he wanted to do so. This kind of attitude stemmed from a common belief in this former frontier area grounded in perceptions of an individual's responsibility to do what was right by one's friends or neighbors in any given situation. Like the school administrators, Duvall showed surprisingly little concern for the central issue under consideration in the case—whether or not Woodward's constitutional rights had been violated. To her, Woodward stood firmly in the way of harmony within the school itself, and by implication the community as a whole.

Teachers on Trial

The entirety of the case hinged on Woodward's own testimony, as well as that of his friend and colleague, the history teacher Bruce Logan, who, as stated earlier, was also involved with the local ACLU chapter. Was he a rabble-rouser? Was he a political activist seeking to force change upon a small community whose inhabitants simply wanted to maintain the status quo of quiet rural living and conservative small-town values? Or, was he the victim of a cabal of coconspirators who sought to run him out of town to places like California or New York, where they thought he would be a better fit?

Langley, the defense attorney for the school district, deposed Woodward first. Woodward began by stating that he had been an ACLU member for about three or four years but that he had formed the local Hereford chapter only in early 1975. The Hereford chapter would answer to the chapter in nearby Amarillo, which served as a sort of district headquarters for ACLU activity for the larger Panhandle region.[58] Still at the opening of his remarks, Langley next turned the question in an odd direction—he wanted to know, without explaining why, where the money to pay Green, the defense attorney, had come from. Green, of course, smelled a rat, and went on the attack:

> GREEN: At this time I am going to object to any further questions along these lines and I want to point out for the record that present in the room is Mr. Hartman, who is taking notes on what is going on here and who has already flown to Washington, D.C.[,] to try to block support from other organizations for us in this lawsuit[,] and I don't think it is relevant at this point for us to go into this thing. The only reason you are going into it is to try to cut off our support and bring political pressure[,] and if you want to file your motion, I would rather the judge hear it than argue it over here [during the deposition phase].
>
> LANGLEY: Then, you are instructing your witness—
>
> GREEN: I am saying—
>
> LANGLEY: You are instructing your witness not to answer any more questions along this line?
>
> GREEN: I am saying at this time I have personal knowledge from people [that] Mr. Hartman went to see in Washington, D.C.[,] to try to

dissuade at least one organization from supporting us in this lawsuit. I have information from other organizations that he has done the same with them and the only reason you are doing this is not for the prosecution of this lawsuit but to try to use it to bring political pressure to block support for us in this lawsuit. Mr. Hartman is [a] national board member of the N.E.A. and the state, T.S.T.A. As I understand it[,] I believe you are going to try to use the information to cut off our funds and I do not believe it is relevant to the prosecution or defense of this lawsuit.

LANGLEY: And you are instructing your witness not to answer any more questions?

GREEN: I am not saying any more questions but not that question about where we have asked for funds and where our funds have come from to this point because we have already been subjected to the defendants in this lawsuit using political pressure to try to stop their support of this lawsuit.

LANGLEY: And you believe that is a worse thing, if it has taken place, than the instigation of this litigation by someone like Mr. Woodward at the cost of someone else?

GREEN: I believe it's not proper or appropriate at this time.[59]

Langley's aggressive tactics seemed to backfire, as no other purpose for questioning the origins of Woodward's funding could be given. One can speculate that perhaps the purpose of such questioning was to imply that a cabal of ACLU forces sought to either change or simply interrogate life in Hereford. Nonetheless, the matter, due to Green's quick thinking, was summarily dropped.

Langley next peppered Woodward with a series of questions related to teaching that carried the implication of a liberal political agenda on Woodward's part. The deposition fell flat at this point—Langley simply seemed unprepared. A long but fruitless discussion developed over the teaching of evolution, prayer in public schools, and whether Woodward would consider it a violation of his civil liberties if his duties as a teacher forced him to do things with which he disagreed.[60] The line of questioning fell so flat that Green did not even feel compelled to cross-examine his own client when Langley had finished.

Langley needed to turn things around fast during the deposition phase if the defense was going to have any chance when the actual trial commenced. He turned to one of his bigger clients at this point: Superintendent Roy Hartman. Hartman had in fact left Hereford at this point, to become superintendent at

Grapevine Independent School District—a small community in the Dallas–Fort Worth area—in July of 1976. Langley immediately turned toward school policy regarding the hiring as well as renewal of teachers' contracts. Hartman said that he could not recall a single incident during his time on the board when it had overturned the decision or recommendation of a principal not to rehire (or hire) a teacher. Principals, in his view, were held responsible for teachers' performance at their schools. Notions of "cooperation" or "loyalty," though, seem to have come up previously, although whether or not they related to teachers' political persuasions was unclear. Hartman stated: "When a teacher had not been cooperative with a principal and they have attempted to work out their problems and have been unable to[,] then it is an unfair thing for boys and girls, students suffer and there have been those who have not been recommended on that basis."[61] Nonetheless, the defense's contention at this point in the testimony seemed to hover vaguely around two unrelated issues: whether Woodward had passed out inappropriate materials to his students and whether or not he was generally cooperative with school officials. It was still not entirely clear why he had been fired, but the haziness surrounding the issue was telling. Whether the principal himself had been cooperative in any contentious cases, however, seems to have been of no concern to Hartman, nor by implication to the rest of the board when such decisions needed to be made. None of this had changed by the time of Woodward's case.

Hartman's testimony did not seem to be improving the defense's case. Hartman identified board member Danny Martin as having been the person who had received a complaint from parents about Woodward "passing out ACLU membership forms," thus beginning the inquest.[62] Things took a turn for the worse for the defense when Green trapped Hartman regarding not questioning the principal's decision-making process. Hartman simply echoed his colleagues from the school board:

GREEN: You are now saying that there were other things that figured into your—

HARTMAN: Well, that figured into—I took Mr. Hughes's recommendation on this, Mr. Green, the same as Mr. Conkwright testified the board took the recommendation coming through the principal to me, the same way, yes. Now, you are asking with regard to our conversation in the office. Of course when you are in conference with a principal[,] all sorts of things come up.

GREEN: Actually where he talks about the prohibition is in paragraph two. Mr. Woodward had apparently used material in the classroom which has not been cleared for use through normal school channels prior to their actual use.

HARTMAN: Which would be the principal.

GREEN: Okay. Do you know what policy he was referring to or—

HARTMAN: He is not referring to policy, Mr. Green, I believe it says personnel in there.

GREEN: Did you inquire of Mr. Hughes what policies he had established over there at La Plata Junior High School for material being cleared through him?

HARTMAN: No, sir, I didn't.

GREEN: Did you feel it encumbent [sic] to do so before going along with his recommendation even though you knew about the letter and the specific material he was talking about?

HARTMAN: No, sir, I didn't.

GREEN: No further questions.[63]

The defense's case was crumbling rapidly.

Bruce Logan's deposition was perhaps more revealing than that of any of the other witnesses who had previously taken questioning. Logan was not deposed until early 1976; like the Whitley family, he and his wife had moved to San Antonio following the spring semester of 1975. Logan and Woodward were longtime friends who had attended Tascosa High School in Amarillo together. After making a statement at the outset of his testimony that Superintendent Hartman had been a positive influence on his development as a teacher, Logan informed the court that he had been asked multiple times by Hughes if he had solicited ACLU membership at the school, and that Hughes had attempted to exert a certain level of control over Woodward in particular, saying that "Hughes said that he had the right to be a member of any organization that he wanted to be but that teachers needed to fit a certain mold, that they had to—that there was certain things that teachers had to do that possibly other members of the community didn't have to do." Logan said that the word "mold" was used many times that year in reference to personal decorum. Hughes told him on numerous occasions that "if you didn't fit into this pattern[,] there really is no place for you in the Hereford Independent School District."[64] If this was true, Woodward's legal team had a real case that his rights as a private citizen had been violated.

Logan's situation was remarkably similar to Woodward's. Logan was a popular young teacher and, as stated earlier, a known member of the ACLU. Naturally, the conversation with Hughes seemed to center around the question of whether he had been recruiting students to the organization, which Logan had not done. Logan felt that the "loyalty question" was ultimately why he had been placed on probation on February 12 along with Woodward; the only problem was that Logan was not entirely sure what loyalty meant to Hughes. Although Logan felt that he *had* been a loyal teacher, Hughes still questioned him around the time that he resigned from the ACLU about whether he was "sure everything was all right, everything had been rectified but he still had the question of loyalty, loyalty . . . I never was quite positive what that meant." This amorphous notion of loyalty was, to Logan, his [Logan's] main problem. Asked by Green why he felt he was placed on probation as well as whether the subject of loyalty or fitting a certain mold continued to be raised with him, Logan responded that "it was raised all over town."[65] Again, the community's point of view came into play in terms of whether these two teachers belonged in the school district. Presumably, even though he eventually received a contract renewal after resigning from the ACLU, Logan's nearly immediate relocation to San Antonio after the spring semester of 1975 indicated that Hereford was not a place where he felt he could continue living, either on a professional or on a personal level.

Logan also revealed more regarding Duvall as well as the apparent factionalism surrounding her and the administration. Duvall could, in Logan's view, be considered something of a partisan: "Miss Mary Duvall is a counselor at La Plata, [and] on many occasions rendered advice as far as fitting the molds . . . on one occasion Mrs. Duvall stated that Hereford is a small rural community and we are not like the big city and there are certain things we have to do in Hereford that we can't do in other places." Duvall apparently related to Logan that one should not say anything negative about the school publicly out in the community, should avoid "rocking the boat," and that "on many occasions [she] would state that Hereford has always been a conservative community and that people who didn't like being conservative should move, should go someplace else."[66] Needless to say, Logan did not like Duvall, who apparently had told Logan that "Mr. Woodward was making a fool out of me, that he was saying things in the library like, you know, Mr. Logan's gone over to their side, he is kowtowing to Mr. Hughes and Mr. Hartman and the School Board." All of this came across with a clear tone of pedantry: "I felt like it was kind of like father-son talk. It was like, you know, hey, look, Mr. Logan, you need to get—you need to get away from that guy and realize that, you know, he is trying to . . . make fun of you as far as your obligation goes and so forth." Logan concluded by saying that he "felt like it was a very unprofessional conversation, the whole thing. My opinion of our counselor changed dramatically that day."[67] Although Duvall had stated in her deposition that she did not understand Woodward or his points of view, such levels of factionalism as revealed in Logan's testimony are perhaps unsurprising. Logan believed that Duvall was essentially a part of the chain of command at the school.[68] Notions of loyalty, belonging, and "fitting the molds" were clearly held more widely than just among the official administration.

What did all this talk of loyalty really mean to the administration? Words and phrases like "loyalty," "fitting the mold," and not "rocking the boat" indicated that Herefordites expected that anyone who differed from the town's mainstream somehow constituted a problem. Logan and Woodward experienced this mistreatment firsthand. The question was not one of race or racism per se; rather, Woodward's clear lack of determination to maintain the sociopolitical status quo mattered more than any direct questions of policy or personal politics. The state had been attempting to intervene in the lives of Panhandle Texans since the time of the Great Depression; now, not only was the state no longer needed, but the shifting political sands of the greater United States were threatening the perceived safety of life in Hereford. Woodward's recalcitrance, in other words, had cost him.

Green next cross-examined Logan. Logan—despite having resigned from the ACLU, receiving a new contract offer from the administration, and then *still* fleeing for San Antonio—noted that the ACLU membership was not only the crux of the drama at the school but that it also naturally detracted from his own ability to do his job, and that "all of a sudden I was having to be a broken field runner. That was interfering with my ability as a teacher[;] I felt . . . like there was too much of this fringe stuff and my students were not getting the best fair [sic] in there." Logan thus remained dedicated to his craft, keeping himself above the fray and remaining dedicated to his students. Such an environment was indeed inhibiting to a conscientious professional.[69]

Logan next went on to flat-out accuse Hughes of firing Woodward solely because he had been involved with the ACLU:

> My personal opinion is that Mr. Hughes felt like the philosophy of the American Civil Liberties Union was probably in some ways contraven-

tional [sic] to the general philosophy of the Hereford, Texas[,] community. Mr. Hughes on one occasion said I want you to know that Hereford may be a 4-A district and so forth, you know, but we are still a little rural town and so forth. I don't think that there was any doubt as to that many people think that the American Civil Liberties Union is a radical organization."[70]

Logan himself claimed that he had never been to a single ACLU meeting. Furthermore, despite all the ensuing drama surrounding the court case, Logan had only been marginally involved with the San Antonio chapter of the ACLU since moving to that city.[71] Consequently, Hughes's self-perceived stewardship of the town's political economy could be implied from Logan's testimony.

All of this was not enough, however, to fully convince the court of the school district's wrongdoing—how, in fact, did Logan *really* know that all of his troubles with the administration stemmed from his personal affiliation with the ACLU? Simple logic led him to this conclusion, which he testified to under oath. During his first two years of teaching at the school, Logan remembered having administrators visit his classroom maybe twice, but after he joined the ACLU, he "started being visited in a classroom about seven or eight-hundred percent more."[72] Logan, though, realized that the issue was larger than simply his membership in the organization; rather, the issue was the alleged "mold" to which the administration expected teachers to conform. Logan believed that this mold included "possible conservatism in one's attitudes towards his general philosophy," but also he "felt like the mold of the Hereford teacher was to be one of a fairly low profile, not any type of particular flashing neon lights of your political philosophy or maybe the amount of freedom that students were allowed to have in the classroom."[73] According to Logan, rumors abounded about him around town after the news of his ACLU membership spread. One coworker's wife called him one night because she had heard an unsubstantiated rumor that Logan had beaten his wife. Logan was in the habit of taking students with him on study abroad trips to Europe. One parent made it known that she would not stand for her child to go to Europe "with a guy that is in that organization." Finally, one student told Logan that his mother was upset because it was a well-known fact that "the American Civil Liberties Union had a bunch of undesirables in it."[74] Although clearly none of this implicated the administration in any direct wrongdoing, it did further indicate that the mood of the public was decidedly against the ACLU, especially when its members held positions of authority and influence over children.

But Logan realized that it was also about more than just the ACLU. The real issue, he believed, was one of conformity, a desirable trait that the school administrators sought to inculcate. While being questioned by Green, Logan stated that he resigned from the ACLU for the same reason that he did not have a mustache—"bread and butter." Logan did not want to lose the ability to support himself and his wife financially, nor did he want to jeopardize his ability to step into a classroom somewhere else. Logan, in fact, said under oath that he knew of only one other man in the school who had a mustache, "and I was told through the grapevine that this man was hassled in the halls and so forth because he had one."[75] Thus, Logan resigned from the ACLU to protect his well-being; as shown earlier, Logan was indeed eventually offered a new contract, while Woodward, the unrepentant one, was not.

Another part of the problem revealed during the trial's deposition phase was that few of Woodward's contemporaries agreed with the administration's line on the ACLU. A number of the other teachers believed that Woodward should be allowed to remain in the organization; one who was unfamiliar with it investigated the organization's purpose and came to the conclusion that it was, indeed, harmless. But Logan understood the problem of Woodward's misfit status as being fundamental to the case, stating that he was "kind of a cosmopolitan, I think there is definitely [more of] an orientation to large city life and so forth than an orientation to more of a bucolic or rural life. You know, I feel like, you know, that maybe some of the ideas that Wayne has might be a little different from the general philosophy of the average person living on a West Texas farm." Such was beyond condemnation, though, as he concluded—"not that one is right and one is wrong."[76] Logan, who taught world history, went on to say that he believed that "ideas are in a less waxing stage in a rural area than a metropolitan area." When asked how Woodward's ideas about education fit in with those of the typical West Texas farmer, he responded:

> Any West Texas farmer? I would say probably most of them are a little more conservative in their attitudes and would like [a] conservative type of education. I think for example . . . probably, you know, people in a big city are probably exposed to a lot more things that you are not exposed to in a rural community. On the other hand, if education transcends the school[,] that does not mean they are not being educated in some of those areas at home and so forth. It is not fair to put any type of label, I suppose,

on either one. I think our country's history proves that there have been great contributors from big cities and small rural communities.[77]

In Logan's more academic view, Woodward's ACLU membership was symptomatic of a larger problem: Woodward was the victim of social purging in rural America as opposed to breaking any clear-cut school policies. He simply had no place within the political consensus of not just Hereford, Texas, but more broadly in modern rural America.

Woodward and Logan were close friends despite not socializing much outside of work. Logan defended Woodward's appropriateness with the students, arguing that he never criticized the administration to the students despite the fact that he was vocal in his criticism of the administration to his colleagues. Woodward had several administrators who were friends; this, in Logan's view, belied Mary Duvall's claim in her testimony that there was a "Woodward vs. Administration" factionalism within the ranks of the school.[78] But Logan himself lacked Woodward's penchant for confrontation. Nonetheless, he, too, felt as though he was a misfit within the school's culture, as well as that of the larger town. On why he relocated to San Antonio, Logan responded that he "felt like larger cities fit me better than small towns. Although I think small towns are part of the United States and they definitely should go by their laws." Nonetheless, on a personal level, Logan was unwilling to argue that his own rights had been violated due to the ACLU debacle: "I think at times they were at least amended to an extent, yes. I don't think that nobody [sic] ever threatened me physically[,] but I felt like there was a bit of difference of opinion between me and the community, not to say that I don't have a lot of good friends in Hereford, Texas." Finally, the administration's alleged propensity for intimidation seemed to have more of a detrimental effect on Logan's desire to fight back than it had on Woodward. "I was scared," he testified under examination by Langley. He continued: "I was afraid I would end up having to go out in the community and make a lot of money and never teach again. I wanted to be a teacher. I was scared to death that there was a possibility I couldn't. And certainly I talked to a lot of people."[79]

Logan further elaborated on his fear after Green reexamined him. The greatest interference to his ability to properly conduct his job was the "psychological interference" of the resulting drama on Logan, which clearly meant that he suffered from anxiety due to the situation, as well as, quite possibly, some depression. The buildup of such pressure led Logan to resign from the local ACLU chapter, which he informed Hughes about in a letter during the middle of the spring 1975 semester. For Logan, the issue was again one of "bread and butter . . . I felt like in my opinion that was hampering my employment possibilities for next year." Put simply, Logan had been bullied into submission: "I felt like it would help clear the air if I was not a member and I felt like it would be more wise at that time to exclude myself from the goings-on inside the organization . . . I felt like it had possibilities of easing tension a little bit."[80] The administration, in his view, acted as an agent on behalf of the wishes of the local population:

> Well, the agent—I felt like once the fact that I was involved in the Civil Liberties Union[,] I felt once that was known to the community[,] I felt like that the community, per se, you know, may have acted as a mold-forming imposer. I would say as a representative of that community I feel that probably the school district and its officials probably, you know, hastened that along. They communicated to me that, you know, that the mold—that I needed to [con]form [to] the mold. The man that talked to me about the mold more than anybody was Mr. Hughes.[81]

There was no doubt in Logan's mind that Hughes acted as a stand-in for the larger community. In other words, it was the community consensus that Logan and Woodward be pushed out of employment at the school. Hughes merely delivered on the wishes of the apparent community consensus.[82]

The depositions concluded with Logan's remarks. Green and Woodward had reason to feel confident, perhaps even before all the witnesses had been deposed prior to the actual trial. "The testimony of the School Board members and Superintendent Hartman," noted Green in a private conversation with a colleague, "could be summed up by saying that they laid all the blame for the dismissal of Mr. Woodward at the doorstep of Mr. Hughes." He continued, noting that "they said that they had never attended one of Mr. Woodward's classes, had not heard bad reports on Mr. Woodward, nor had other personal problems with him, but had relied solely on the judgment of principal Hughes in deciding not to rehire him." Hughes, for Green, had been vague in terms of his reasoning behind Woodward's firing—in fact, he had noted that Woodward was "a good teacher." Furthermore, Hughes, for Green, had "failed to adequately explain why he had written the now famous letter, placing Mr. Woodward on probation because of Woodward's determination to express a hostile attitude and," Green concluded, "because he had apparently used material in the classroom which had not been cleared through normal channels."[83]

Other elements from the depositions seemed to further bolster Woodward's legal team's confidence. Green had also taken the deposition of Dr. Ruby Gartrell, a professor of counseling at Southwestern Oklahoma State University in Weatherford, Oklahoma, where Woodward had signed up for some classes in the wake of his firing from Hereford. Hughes had telephoned Gartrell—the reasoning behind this call is unknown but can be surmised—and informed her that he was concerned that Woodward had been propagandizing for the ACLU in the classroom in Hereford as opposed to teaching English. Hughes asked Gartrell whether Woodward "had had such problems at Southwestern State," to which Gartrell responded that he had not. She was, in fact, "very complimentary of Woodward as a student." Hughes never accused Woodward of actually passing out ACLU materials in class during the conversation, but he did report that Woodward had misused school time. Hughes also allegedly told Gartrell that he was really trying to help Woodward; he never mentioned precisely how the telephone call would help the now fired teacher, but it was presumably under the auspices of helping him correct his allegedly bad behavior and saving his future career.[84] Similarly, Hartman had also telephoned Audie Woodward (no relation) of the Weatherford, Oklahoma, School District, which had employed Woodward on a part-time basis while the latter had begun taking courses toward a master's degree under Gartrell. Hartman informed Audie Woodward that "the Weatherford School System should not have employed Mr. Woodward on a part-time basis for the reason that he had long hair and had been a member of the ACLU while teaching in Hereford and had not been rehired."[85] The superintendent later told Wayne Woodward that he did not care if he was a member of the ACLU.[86]

There is little doubt that Hughes and Hartman actually believed they were doing the right thing in telephoning Gartrell and Audie Woodward. Nonetheless, in a court of law, placing such telephone conversations could appear to have been character assassination on the part of the defense. Still other elements from the depositions seemed to bolster the plaintiff's case. Chief among these, for Green, was Logan's deposition, wherein he had revealed that Hughes had called him in for a discussion about his ACLU membership as well as that he had resigned from the organization subsequent to his receiving a new contract from the school system. What is more, after receiving his new contract, according to Logan (via Green), "thereafter things got better with Hughes." Finally, one last element, Green believed, was worthy of confidence in the outcome of the trial and the strength of his evidence—he had tape-recorded conversations with nine different teachers employed in the district to prevent any false statements against

Woodward. Green felt confident largely because "none of these teachers would say anything bad about Wayne Woodward . . . some of them had positive things to say, others were very noncommittal, obviously very fearful of their positions."[87] Thus, the taped conversations, which could be used on an as-needed basis, would only further strengthen Woodward's case after the courtroom trial had begun.

Everything would be out in the open and decided soon.

CHAPTER 7

RIGHTING WRONGS AND WRONGING RIGHTS

The Culture Wars on Trial in the Texas Panhandle

Woodward worked hard to prepare for the trial after the depositions were complete. Part of his preparation involved attacking the school administrators' credibility. Hartman himself was naturally one of Woodward's main targets. An external academic review (at Woodward's request) revealed some alleged problems with Hartman's dissertation, which he had written in completion for a doctorate in the field of education in 1976, one year after he signed off on Woodward's dismissal. Woodward requested the review to challenge Hartman's professional credibility, which he believed was worth questioning due to Hartman's actions regarding the nonrenewal of his contract. Hartman had written the dissertation to complete his degree at a little-known school called Western State College. The head of the English Department at Southwestern Oklahoma State University reported that Hartman's dissertation was "so sloppy and incorrect that [it] would not be accepted in a [freshman] English class at Southwestern." Furthermore, Hartman allegedly left out page numbers for books that he had cited, provided no footnotes, committed about four or five acts of plagiarism, and cited an article from a magazine that apparently did not exist. The professor described the work as "scandalous." Woodward also had the head librarian as well as a professor in the reading department concur that Hartman's dissertation was insufficient.[1]

Furthermore, other elements leading up to the trial seemed problematic. Woodward and Green noted that membership in the TCTA had declined in Hereford due in part to the intrigue generated by the lawsuit.[2] Although the larger organization supported Woodward in his case, support was weaker at the local level. A separate organization, the local chapter of the Texas State Teachers' Association (TSTA), decided not to support Woodward at all. Although the politics behind this decision are not known, the president of the Hereford chapter of the organization, Eugene Barkowsky, enumerated the reasons for the organization's nonsupport. Part of their reasoning was that Woodward had sought outside legal help before speaking to the local organization; likewise, the organization's executive committee requested a formal presentation from Woodward about his grievances, which he had allegedly declined to give. "The Executive Committee," noted Barkowsky, "feels that all local avenues of assistance should have been exhausted prior to seeking outside assistance." Finally, the group believed that Woodward and Green had not adhered to certain professional ethics, although it did not state in what ways they had failed in that regard.[3]

Only time would tell what would happen during the actual trial. What was already evident, though, was that Woodward had a strong case that his constitutional rights had been violated. Perhaps less dramatically, however, a case could be made that Woodward had also been targeted for removal. Either way, something unfair had taken place—Woodward had been targeted as an enemy seemingly because he rebelled against the larger social order in the school, which reflected in microcosm Hereford's deeply conservative sociopolitical climate as a town. The significance of this turn of events would soon come to light as the battle found itself being waged on the courtroom floor in front of Judge Halbert O. Woodward (no relation to Wayne Woodward)—a well-known conservative, "no-nonsense" judge, according to Robin Green—in the district court in Amarillo.[4] Politics, belonging, and the culture wars would soon be litigated in federal court.

One problem, though, was that a number of the teachers in Hereford seemed too intimidated to outwardly support Woodward in the case. When the 1975–76 school year began, Hartman made the clearly suspicious decision to have teachers vote on whether or not they supported Woodward (it is unclear how many teachers had been involved in the vote or whether this was simply at La Plata Junior High School or district-wide). Although Woodward did not learn the vote's outcome, he believed that it went against him, due in large part to the fact that first-year teachers had been involved who would have been too scared to do anything to jeopardize their employment. Hartman, Woodward believed, had clearly pressed for the vote to keep the district aligned under the administration as well as to stifle any opposition.[5] Similarly, although the TCTA supported

Woodward, support for this decision was polarized at the local level, with several people taking the time to telephone the organization's legal team to denounce its support. Clearly, reaction to the case by local teachers was mixed at best, due at least in part to the fear of losing employment or to intimidation tactics taken by the administration against its own faculty.[6]

Perhaps unsurprisingly, then, Woodward believed that only some of the teachers might be inclined to support him in his case. Woodward thought that about ten of them at the school who openly disliked Hughes or Hartman (or both) would stand up for him. A larger group—more than twenty—according to Woodward, would support him were it not for their feeling intimidated by the administration. Woodward knew that he had some enemies at the school among the faculty, but he believed they were few. One, only remembered as a "Mrs. Brock," once lectured Woodward on the evils of "being your own man" or of not fitting in properly with the social order or respecting authority. Brock's husband gave a speech denouncing Woodward at a school board meeting in July of 1975. Woodward knew that he had no friends among the athletics coaching staff, all of whom supported Hughes. Finally, another teacher—remembered only as Mr. Brown—seemed "two-faced" to Woodward, perhaps due in no small part to his ambition to become vice principal.[7]

Green himself worried about the administrators using political persuasion to work against Woodward during the run-up to the trial. The lawyer noted that he found it strange that Langley went to great lengths to get Woodward to expose the sources of his legal funding during the deposition phase. Green may have been correct: he and Woodward learned through an anonymous source that the local TCTA had begun a telephone campaign to pressure teachers who had publicly supported Woodward to back down. "Of course Roy Hartman thinks that these political tactics will work in blocking support for Wayne's case," Green remarked in a private conversation with a colleague, "and more importantly he knows that such political activities will leave the impression with other teachers in the region that administrations can and will block support of teachers by their own organizations."[8]

If Green was correct, the administration saw an opportunity in Woodward's case to enhance its general power at the local level. What was at stake for Woodward and Green, however, was something of arguably greater importance—protecting the civil liberties of Americans in an area where conformity to the local sociopolitical order was a general expectation. During the summer of 1975, Green had been involved with a lawsuit against the city of Amarillo, whose jail facilities he argued were not in compliance with state and federal laws. The Texas Civil Liberties Union had undertaken still other cases in Hereford and Dumas, Texas, and in Springer, New Mexico. Furthermore, the organization hoped that a cultural shift had begun to take shape in the region. Pam Whitley had submitted an essay in the previously discussed writing contest at La Plata sponsored by the ACLU, in which she argued that "a person who is afraid to talk has a noose around his neck and a silencing gag in his mouth." Indeed, the larger organization, Woodward, and his legal team clearly hoped that the people in Hereford—many of whom they believed were "afraid to talk"—would begin speaking out in defense of their own civil liberties, despite any potential intimidation or blowback at the local level.[9]

The Trial

More details came to light when the trial began and Woodward finally took the stand at 10 A.M. on the morning of September 21, 1976. Woodward testified that his problems at the school started as soon as the first year of his employment, but they accelerated when his name appeared in the *Hereford Brand* associating him with the ACLU chapter in early 1975. Hughes called Woodward into his office about a week before delivering him his probationary letter to ascertain the truth of his ACLU membership. As has already been stated, Woodward confirmed his membership in the group. He even extended an invitation to Hughes to join the group, to which Hughes replied that he "was already in enough hot water as it was." Woodward also recalled Hughes saying that he "needed to realize that [he] was in the Bible Belt," thus directly indicating to Woodward that ACLU membership was unacceptable not just at the school but in the culture of the town.[10] Woodward was doing something that residents of the community would neither understand nor appreciate.

Whatever problems Woodward had before all of this were, in his view, of the ordinary sort that any teacher could run into over the course of his or her employment at a school. Of course, Woodward's testimony differed markedly from Hughes's deposition. Woodward claimed that he never received any specific response from Hughes as to what materials he had passed out during class that were allegedly so offensive; in fact, Woodward claimed—again under oath—that the first time that Hughes made clear that it was the ACLU materials was only during Hughes's own deposition. Hughes, as already stated, would have countered that he failed to bring this up because Woodward had retained counsel and thus had stifled communication. Woodward, in truth, did not help his standing with the administration after the February 12 letter—in fact, his aversion to seemingly arbitrary authority likely made his tenuous situation worse. The following month, his classes read Ray Bradbury's classic, *Fahrenheit 451*, a story about how a nation lost its freedoms due to censorship. In the course of class discussions, students asked Woodward about their own civil rights. He later produced a students' rights handbook published by the ACLU. Regarding the students' rights handbook, Woodward went on to testify that he frequently sent off for books for students; it was a common thing and there were never any rules that he knew about regarding having to get prior approval to do something like that with or for his students. "Whatever we felt like we could do to help the student learn the material, feel free to do it," he claimed was the administration's attitude, saying that restrictions about passing out materials in the classroom had never existed. Woodward claimed that he had always used outside magazines, newspapers, and films, and never once had Hughes expressed to him any prohibitions on using outside materials before the matter of ACLU literature had come to the principal's attention.[11]

Woodward next proceeded to relate his conversations with Hughes over the ACLU materials. He told the story of Hughes asking that he not pass out ACLU literature to students, to which Woodward, again, assented. He seemed to initially agree with Hughes that it was not the right thing to do, given the general "mood of the community. Later on in the day," though, Woodward changed his mind: "I got to thinking about it and I went down to his office and I explained to him that I felt like that I might have had the right to do that legally ... so I was right in [the] end that I should have passed it out."[12] Woodward further elaborated from the witness stand while under questioning by Green:

GREEN: Did you ask Mr. Hughes what specific policy and procedures you needed to comply with or did you ask him what the problem was?
WOODWARD: Yes, I did.
GREEN: What did he tell you?
WOODWARD: Nothing at all. His—I recall at this meeting saying well, what is it that I am doing wrong and he didn't say what it was at all, there was just a silence and the silence went on for several seconds so I assumed, you know, from that that he was not going to tell me.
GREEN: He would not give you any specific concrete incidents? Did you ask him in terms of specific things that you had done to breach procedures?

WOODWARD: Yes, I did. I said was it, you know, because of handing out, you know, materials, was it because you feel I need a haircut, was it—what was it—and he would just stare off into space and not answer.
GREEN: He would not say anything?
WOODWARD: That's right.[13]

Assuming that Woodward was correct, this statement against Hughes was incriminating.

Woodward also testified that Hughes later asked him, "Well, just what do you hope to accomplish? And I said, I don't have anything to accomplish at all."[14] It was almost as if these two men were speaking different languages; Woodward, on the one hand, was an ideological person who clearly believed in what he was doing and that he had a right to do it—although he knew it would be looked at askance by the community—whereas Hughes seems to have considered Woodward a subversive threat. These two men clearly subscribed to two incompatible sets of beliefs that could not coexist within the same institutional or physical setting. Put simply, if Woodward was to be believed, then his testimony displayed just how easy it was for someone in the structured, ordered, and isolated setting of Hereford to stick out from the rest of the community based simply on that person's belief system being misaligned with the dominant culture.

The communication breakdown between Woodward and Hughes became a fact that the defense hoped to use to stifle the entire case. Woodward argued that Hughes simply would not direct any communication to him at all regarding how he could improve on his job performance. Langley responded on behalf of the defense that Hughes's lack of communication stemmed from Woodward retaining counsel, an argument that Hughes himself had made during his deposition.[15] Either way, whether or not Hughes was being recalcitrant or whether he felt he had an actual legal obligation not to implicate himself or the school in any wrongdoing, Hughes's previous failure to address any of the issues relating to Woodward's job performance—Woodward also argued that he could not get a straight answer from Hughes on how to fix some alleged minor deficiencies in one of his teaching evaluations—or Hughes's failure to submit any communication through Woodward's legal counsel did little to help the defense's case against Woodward's rights having been infringed. Furthermore, the fact that Bruce Logan received a new teaching contract shortly after announcing his resignation from the ACLU also made the administration look worse than it otherwise should have.[16]

Some of the things that Woodward testified to on the stand occurred later on during the spring semester and blurred the case's details. Oddly, the same ACLU chapter that Woodward helped start approached the administrators about an essay-writing contest for the school, which, as already stated, did in fact happen. This could mean two things: first, it could mean that Woodward was wrong in the administrators' purported hatred of the ACLU; or second, it could also have been a ploy by the administrators to make it look as though they had no qualms about the organization in general. Given the hostility shown toward Woodward as well as the district's about-face on Logan's employment, signs point to the latter. Woodward, given his then status with the school district, was not allowed to participate. At one point, Woodward went to speak to a colleague of his in the history department who was helping put on the contest. The school's vice principal intruded on the conversation, questioning Woodward as to why he was speaking to his fellow teacher, "why [he had] the right" since he was not involved, and eventually ordered Woodward to go back to his room.[17] No other issues related to the essay-writing contest came up.

The second witness called to the stand was the already-mentioned young Pam Whitley, who restated the story of her request to Woodward that he provide her with printed materials on the ACLU as well as her friend Cindy Ford receiving a pamphlet. But her time on the witness stand was cut short. As the proceedings neared lunchtime, Langley went aggressively on the offensive. Langley, during a back-and-forth with Judge Woodward, argued that the district had not deprived Woodward of any ability to continue his career as a teacher—one of the claims that Woodward and Green made in the original lawsuit—due to the fact that Woodward had wanted the June 2 hearing to be public, thus implying that any problems related to his employability were his own fault and that no one associated with the district talked to anyone about Woodward or did anything at all to challenge his good name publicly. He went on to say that it was not the school district's fault that Woodward did not get any subsequent interviews for teaching positions, as he had applied, by his own testimony, for around four hundred of them and that the only person he had ever run into outside of Hereford who knew about the case was a school superintendent in Weatherford, Oklahoma. Woodward had also, as mentioned earlier, gone to the local Hereford radio station to announce the new ACLU chapter of his own accord. Thus, according to the defense, he had no liberty interest at stake in the case. Before the lunch break, Judge Woodward said that he still needed to read the depositions in response to Langley's request that the case be thrown out, but that he was "still confronted with and have before me what I think is the real question in this case and that is that if the plaintiff's contract was not renewed because he was attempting to exercise some constitutionally and protected activity, he has got relief coming."[18]

The defense's weak position became increasingly clear as the day's courtroom drama unfolded after lunch. Langley called Conkwright to the stand, whose subsequent defenses against the plaintiff's charges seemed weak. Regarding the board not taking questions at the June 2 hearing, Conkwright stated that "we, as a board, felt that that was a hearing requested by Mr. Woodward for the explanation of his side. We did not feel that it was a trial situation open to cross-examination," despite the impending lawsuit with its question of Woodward's rights potentially having been violated. Conkwright also mentioned that there was a faculty handbook from 1969 that stipulated the issue of sensitive materials being approved by the principal, but nonetheless, he had only found it due to the trial's commencement just within the previous month. Bizarrely, for some reason Conkwright reported that even Hughes himself did not seem to be aware that such a policy existed before the trial. Finally, Conkwright dropped a bombshell on his own team when he said during his cross-examination by Green that he did not know from any school official that the material was actually passed out in class—this charge was only hearsay (and, as had already been established, was ultimately false). Conkwright also said that he could not provide any specifics regarding the alleged bad attitude that Woodward had, simply that "he had not been supportive of certain school policies in front of—in a school atmosphere."[19]

Langley must have felt panicked. He called Woodward back to the stand to reverse the damage that Conkwright's testimony had done. In an attempt to trap Woodward, Langley questioned him as to whether he had seen the handbook before. Naturally, he had not.[20] Any implication for this case encompassing a widely accepted school policy, given Woodward's and perhaps more importantly Hughes's own ignorance of it, could no longer have any bearing on the case. This part of the defense's case subsequently collapsed.

Somewhat paradoxically, later on Hartman attempted to downplay any perceived threat from the ACLU to local society while maintaining the notion of the town's right to community self-determination. When asked by Langley while he was on the witness stand if he was familiar with the ACLU, he responded, "Well, not a great deal, but I do know that they are concerned about people's civil rights and liberties the same as I would be or you would be and I am not—I am not sure that maybe I hadn't ought to be a member myself." Hartman followed this by offering that Randy Vaughn, who was the band director at Hereford, was an ACLU "member and just for the record, I visited with Mr. Vaughn last Friday night and offered him a job in Grapevine."²¹ Nonetheless, a seemingly innocuous exchange followed between Langley and Hartman during which Hartman, surprisingly, seemed to conclude that people in positions of authority maintained the right to protect certain practices, even when potentially out of step with federal law. For example, regarding school prayer:

> LANGLEY: What criteria do you use, community standards or local customs and so forth, what are the things that enter into the determination of how any controversial subject, unquote, is handled?
>
> HARTMAN: Well, I think you have mentioned some of them there [in] the community in which you live, what is accepted and what isn't, if you are—of course, I guess if you are speaking with regard to prayer, I suppose they will continue to do that until they are challenged and someone tells them they can't.²²

Hartman practically contradicted himself. On the one hand, perhaps the ACLU was not a bad organization, to him; on the other, community members would continue to support prayer in public schools without any challenge that doing so at a public institution violated the law. Hartman was either an incompetent witness or he was simply attempting to distance himself from any moral wrongdoing in the case with regard to Woodward's firing for being a member of the ACLU.

Green pounced on this seeming contradiction during his cross-examination of Hartman. The defense's general ineptitude once again became apparent. At the beginning of Green's cross-examination, Hartman made a stunning revelation: he did not know that the ACLU materials had been passed out during a passing period. One of the defense's contentions had been that Woodward had failed to follow school policy by passing out materials that had not been preapproved by Hughes, but the point was moot, given that it did not take place during an actual class period. "I learned that today," Hartman said regarding the materials having not been passed out during a class period. Nonetheless, Hartman seemed to take it upon himself to change the defense's strategy: "The boys and girls that we are entrusted with are ours from the time they leave home in the morning until they get home in the afternoon[,] and if it is at school, it is at school regardless of when it is."²³ Hartman thus implied that even administrators did not know about the policy of teachers requiring the principal's approval to pass out sensitive materials until the time of Woodward's dismissal, and that the specifics of the policy were more encompassing than anyone—even the defense lawyer—had known. Hartman was changing the defense's position in real time from the witness stand. How this reflected badly on Woodward—who by his own later admission had once had his students read John Howard Griffin's controversial commentary on race, *Black Like Me*, though telling the students to keep their copies of the book when Hughes forced Woodward to cancel the remainder of the assignment upon learning about it—remained unclear.[24]

Hartman, though, supported Hughes in his somewhat vague contention about Woodward having an allegedly hostile attitude toward the administration. Woodward had on several occasions protested what he believed to be a restrictive dress code for faculty that the administrators had enforced, due in part to Woodward's hair being too long, but the administrators had since abandoned that policy. Hartman also noted while under oath that to his knowledge Woodward's long hair was not the reason he had been fired.[25] When pressed on the issue, Hartman became evasive:

> GREEN: Then specifically, what was it that he was not to be rehired for?
> HARTMAN: Here again these are—when you get into the area of attitudes there were reports of conversations with regard to students. I am in a very precarious position because I did have a daughter in his class.
> GREEN: I believe you told me specifically on deposition that there was nothing that your daughter ever told you that made any difference is that correct?
> HARTMAN: I don't recall that, Mr. Green.
> GREEN: You don't recall telling me something like that?
> HARTMAN: No.
> GREEN: Do you recall telling me in your deposition that you relied solely on Mr. Hughes's judgment?
> HARTMAN: Yes, I did, and here again you are asking me questions probably Mr. Hughes needs to be answering.[26]

The entire case thus hinged on the testimony of Hughes, who took the stand next.

Hughes was first questioned by the defense. Langley began his questioning by starting with the letter of February 12, which Hughes admitted was written entirely in his hand. Hughes also noted that Woodward stated verbally that any further communication must be done through his lawyer, meaning that "any later interview that we had between each other I felt I was with his consent."[27] With this remark, any claim by the defense that Woodward's retaining of counsel stifled communication was no longer admissible. Regarding Woodward's alleged lack of professionalism and poor attitude, Hughes responded with a relatively vague assertion, again, surprisingly, to his own lawyer:

> HUGHES: Okay. Sir, now I don't feel like that Mr. Woodward, after six years, had any great confrontations going, I just felt like at this time that Mr. Woodward felt like I was picking on him for some reasons and for me to show him that he was not doing in the building what I thought was conducive to a good atmosphere in the building by way of policies and procedures, then I felt like I needed to say that he needed improvement in those areas. I went over that with him.
>
> LANGLEY: Did you get any more specific than you just stated, or did you just tell him that generally?
>
> HUGHES: I feel like it was probably more of a general statement made.[28]

In other words, for Hughes, Woodward's claim that the principal was bullying him was nonsense. Hughes went on to mention a handful of incidents regarding Woodward's performance that he deemed to be detrimental: one was Woodward's apparent habit of handing out tardy slips (a hall pass that allowed students out of certain classes) without the students having to report back to his room, instead allowing them to roam freely in the hallways. Another incident in which Hughes found fault with Woodward was his apparent support of a planned pep rally skit put on by the cheerleaders in which a group of teachers were targets for some light teasing (the nature of the skit was not made public at the trial). The students eventually caved to Hughes's pressure not to perform the skit, but Woodward had allegedly told one student, Patty Hendon, that they should not have gone along with the administration's wishes. This, to Hughes, was an example of the disloyalty that administrators had already mentioned at numerous times. Hughes, though, reiterated during the questioning that Woodward was not fired because he was an ACLU member, but rather it was a culmination of these kinds of smaller problems.

The defense's testimonies were going so poorly at this point that Green needed little time with Hughes on the witness stand. Green noted that Hughes had indicated on Woodward's teaching evaluation sheet from the spring semester of 1975 that Woodward "needs improvement" in carrying out decisions made by his superiors, which Hughes did not dispute stemmed at least in part from his passing out of ACLU literature to students. When pressed further by Judge Woodward—who supported Green's line of questioning on the matter as valid— Hughes admitted that the issue related to the ACLU literature was the reason that he had rated Woodward as being deficient in that area. Hughes's own paper trail thus seemed to point toward the issue of the ACLU as being not just the primary reason, but perhaps the only reason that Woodward had been placed on probation and later fired.

Upon cross-examination by Langley, Hughes claimed that he had never told Woodward to avoid distributing ACLU material before the initial parental complaint had reached Hartman. Hughes claimed that he did not know that Woodward was an ACLU member before, but he had known that other teachers had been involved in the organization and that it had never bothered him. Langley seemed to lead Hughes in the direction of disproving the ACLU problem; he again brought up Bruce Logan. Logan had quickly informed him of his resignation from the organization after receiving his "probationary" letter of February 12, which Hughes claimed he told Logan he did not have to do, at which point, in turn, Logan responded that he simply had wanted to resign from the group. Importantly, Logan did not dispute Hughes's claim during the trial's deposition phase:

> Mr. Hughes didn't tell me, you know, that I could not be a member of the American Civil Liberties Union. In fact when I submitted that paper to him, when I gave him a copy of the letter he said, "you don't have to do this you know." And I kind of feel the philosophy of the deal was more or less kind of my association there. Their attitude that I was associating with Wayne, supporting Wayne and it was very convenient with us teaching next to each other and I felt like the picture was drawn that I was down there with a cheerleading uniform on with a big W on it running up and down the field saying go Wayne, you know. I feel like that was something that I felt—I felt like that is what bothered them if anything bothered them.[29]

Hughes admitted that he subsequently rehired Logan "but that didn't have anything to do with the fact that he resigned."[30]

Things only got worse for Hughes. After a heated exchange with Green, who kept pressing him on why Hughes had terminated Woodward as well as whether his ACLU involvement had been one of the reasons, Hughes responded that Woodward's nonrenewal was not based *solely* on the issue of his having passed out some ACLU literature. Hughes had appeared, finally, to let slip from his own mouth—while under oath—that the ACLU had been one of the reasons he had turned against Woodward. Judge Woodward was flabbergasted. The principal had stalled, given incomplete answers, and seemed to be providing no clear reasoning behind his dismissal of Woodward. The judge pushed him and asked him point blank: "Did you fire him because he was in the ACLU?" Hughes crumbled under the judge's pressure. Hughes responded that he did not mean to use the word "solely" and reaffirmed that his only consideration was the attitude that Woodward displayed and that he did not follow instructions.

At this moment, the principal was unable to convince the judge that he had not terminated Woodward's contract because of his involvement with the organization. How could people in positions of authority have handled their defense in a court of law so incompetently? According to Woodward's longtime friend Don Cooney, the Hughes-Hartman camp had simply never had its authority challenged by any teachers or by anyone else in the town. Woodward's pressing of his case against the ruling cabal in Hereford had simply caught them off guard. In a sense, the outside world had *actually* come crashing in on rural, isolated Hereford, Texas.[31]

On October 6, the closing arguments began, which lasted for about ninety minutes. Langley did not deviate from the defense's original claims: a buildup of various grievances had led to Woodward's dismissal. Green also stayed the course, believing that he and Woodward had proven over the course of the trial that Woodward's constitutional rights had been violated.[32]

Green, in his statement, referred to several of the other court cases involving teachers to conclude that teachers had certain free speech rights that deserved to be protected. Green also concluded that speech resulting in disorder in the classroom could be used as grounds for dismissal, but no such disorder had occurred based on Woodward's exercise of his own speech to students. Langley objected to this claim, arguing that certain actions Woodward engaged in prior to the school board not renewing his contract—namely, his allegedly freewheeling tendency to hand out student passes in the hallways during the spring semester of 1975—had caused a disruptive situation in the school's hallways. Langley reiterated that certain other acts had also led to the board's decision, such as the defense's contention that Woodward had not received proper authorization to use controversial materials in the classroom; that he had given out excess academic work as punishment to some students; that he had deviated too widely from his curriculum as an English teacher; that he had vocally opposed the school dress code; and that on numerous occasions he had purposefully avoided meetings with Hughes by leaving work early.[33]

Langley also argued that Green had been overly involved in the case, due to Woodward's insistence that all communication from the administration to him be done through his lawyer. Green himself later dismissed this as a "flight of fancy" during his closing argument. Woodward's alleged stonewalling, according to Langley, had made it impossible for Hughes to work with the teacher while he was on probationary status that spring. Langley claimed that Hughes had "gone out of his way" to try to work with Woodward, referring back to the February 12 letter as evidence to back up this claim. Green retorted that the administrators gave Woodward no reasons for his dismissal even though he had asked for them on multiple occasions.[34]

With the closing arguments complete, Judge Woodward put the court into recess, retiring to his chambers to weigh the depositions, testimonies, evidence, and closing arguments before issuing his decision.

He finally reemerged on October 12 to deliver his ruling.

The Verdict and Its Aftermath

For the judge, the defense had contended that firing Woodward was not just the result of his unauthorized use of ACLU material; rather it reflected an accumulation of many factors. Judge Woodward, though, had no clear understanding as to the nature of those other factors. Furthermore, Logan's deposition appears to have been particularly damning for the defense. The fact that his contract had been renewed only after he resigned from the ACLU was, for Judge Woodward, too compelling to ignore.[35]

Woodward and Green waited with bated breath as Judge Woodward handed down his ruling. The judge found that Woodward had not disrupted the orderly operation of the school, had done nothing to corrupt the minds of his students, nor had he even violated orders from Hughes or any of his superiors in the district, as the defense had contended. In fact, in the judge's own words, "nothing unusual occurred because of Mr. Woodward's activities with the ACLU and his school function, except his contract was not renewed." Judge Woodward concluded that Woodward's contract "was not renewed because of his association with, his activities in, and his expressions concerning the American Civil Liberties Union." Evidence also showed a number of other things that could not be ignored: after Woodward's election as an ACLU officer had received local publicity, one of his students (again, Pam Whitley) requested an ACLU membership form between classes, which Woodward provided; and Woodward had discussed the history and purposes of ACLU during classroom sessions. Again, Judge Woodward ruled that there was no evidence that any of Woodward's actions were disruptive of school processes. What this meant, in the judge's legal opinion, was that the administration's actions had violated Woodward's rights under Amendments One and Fourteen to the U.S. Constitution.[36] The court issued a memorandum of opinion on October 12; its judgment appeared in written form a few weeks later:

> On the 21st day of September, 1976, this action came on for trial before the Court without a jury. The evidence having been heard and the Court having heretofore, on October 12, 1976, filed a memorandum opinion which incorporated findings of fact and conclusions of law, the following orders are made in conformity with the Court's findings and conclusions.
>
> IT IS ORDERED AND ADJUDGED that the Plaintiff Wayne Woodward is to be reinstated in his position as a teacher of English in the seventh and ninth grades of the Hereford Independent School District, or some similar position, within thirty days after this judgment becomes final, and that such reinstatement be effective as of the beginning of the school year 1975–76.
>
> IT IS FURTHER ORDERED that the School District pay the Plaintiff Wayne Woodward the full salary and benefits that he would have received up until the time that he is actually reinstated in his position as a teacher. It is specifically ORDERED that the Plaintiff be paid by the Hereford Independent School District $11,870.00 for the 1975–76 school year salary, and that he be paid a monthly salary for the 1976–77 school year based on an annual salary of $12,310.00, with the said monthly continuing to be paid until such time as he is actually reinstated. In the event that there are salary changes based upon experience, the Plaintiff is to receive a salary computed as if he had continued to teach from the 1974–75 school year until he is actually reinstated. The back pay is an element of the order of reinstatement.
>
> IT IS FURTHER ORDERED that none of the Plaintiff's rights or benefits will be altered but will remain the same as if his contract had been renewed at the termination of the 1974–75 school year and continued until he is actually reinstated.
>
> IT IS FURTHER ORDERED and ADJUDGED that the Plaintiff Wayne Woodward recover a reasonable attorney's fee in the sum of six thousand dollars ($6,000) to be paid by the Hereford Independent School District to the Attorneys for the Plaintiff, Robin M. Green and Thomas J. Griffith.
>
> All monetary damages and restitution provided herein shall bear interest from the due date until paid at the rate of nine percent (9%) per annum.

IT IS FURTHER ORDERED that all costs be taxed as against the Defendants.

ENTERED this 3rd day of November, 1976

Halbert O. Woodward
United States District Judge.[37]

Wayne Woodward had won his case.

Judge Woodward had ordered that the teacher be reinstated to his position immediately, given full back pay, and that the school district take no retribution against him. Furthermore, the judge ordered that Woodward be paid $6,000 in legal fees, since the school district had been "unreasonable and obdurately obstinate" in dismissing him.[38]

Naturally, Woodward and Green were ecstatic. "Up here in this part of the country," Green said to the press, "this is just a really important decision with special meaning in the Panhandle of Texas." Although he did not elaborate on his meaning, Green clearly indicated that not only could school administrators not get away with this kind of behavior, but his statement also implied that an individual's constitutional rights could not be infringed on simply because that person's views did not coalesce with a town's larger culture. Woodward stated to reporters that "this puts the schools on notice that they cannot fire a teacher for such frivolous reasons or they may find themselves sitting before a federal judge also." Texas ACLU director John Duncan also chimed in, saying that the judge's decision was "not a landmark ruling but it is one of those things we were fairly certain we were going to win. It has been well-established for a number of years that public schools can't fire teachers because of their basic philosophical beliefs."[39] Had Duncan taken his statement to its logical conclusion, however, he might have noted that this case indicated that legal precedent had now caught up to the small town of Hereford, cracking open the town's social hierarchy to outsiders who did not fit in.

Congratulations poured in from multiple corners. Three of Woodward's former colleagues at the school, Robbie Sheffy, Billy Jo Reiter, and John Murdock, wrote him a congratulatory note referring to themselves as "the poor slobs you left behind" while jokingly noting that "the only disadvantage [we] can see now, is that you'll have to become an Oakie [sic]," implying that he could never work in or around Hereford again despite the decision and would have to flee permanently to California.[40] Another colleague sarcastically referred to his victory as one coming at the cost of imperialistic conservative America:

Dear Comrad [sic]:

Due to the economic failings of the great foundering system of monopoly capitalism in Amerika [sic] I am unfortunately located in the Golden Spread, one of the most intensely reactionary areas in our nation. I am here to seek out employment and save some money so that I may once again head elsewhere (maybe Minnesota) to offer my humble though I hope not altogether insignificant contribution to the further demise of U.S. imperialism and repression. I am looking to find my own abode while here and you are most welcome to visit me if you so desire. I will provide good drink and excellent company.
Professor Oscar W. Outhouse.[41]

More came in. Pam Whitley, while on a study abroad trip in France, wrote her former teacher a postcard, reporting to Woodward that she "went to the ACLU meeting last month and it was really good. We've talked about your little ordeal on the trip and all the kids are behind you 100%! You're very brave."[42] Finally, another former colleague at La Plata, John Lawton, wrote to Woodward that in the days following the verdict, a despondent Hughes took his frustrations out on another teacher employed at the school, berating her for some reason that Lawton did not understand. "We are going to get him yet," Lawton said of the allegedly unpopular junior high school principal.[43]

Unfortunately for Woodward, however, he would not find himself back in the classroom anytime soon (as time would show, Woodward, in fact, would never teach again), nor would he see any money just yet. The school district's administration voted immediately to appeal Judge Woodward's decision, sending it to the U.S. Circuit Court of Appeals for the Fifth Circuit in New Orleans, Louisiana. The obstinate school board was not ready to give up the fight. Indeed, the battle over civil rights and political belonging in Hereford, Texas, would drag on into 1977.

Never was it more obvious that the purging of Wayne Woodward was an act of collusion by Hereford powerbrokers than when the school district filed its appeal in late 1976. Green feared the appeal, as now ex-president Richard M. Nixon had placed four conservative justices on the Supreme Court of the United States, meaning that legal opinion might now be firmly against civil rights claimants.[44] Langley contested several points from the district court's decision. First, he as well as the defendants believed that the court's decision that the school board had fired Woodward because of his ACLU participation was not presented by the evidence. Second, back pay, they argued, had been improperly awarded. Third, Langley argued that there were certain subjective elements in the employer-employee relationship that had not gotten adequate consideration by the judge. Fourth, the defendants believed that the court had not properly considered substantial evidence that Woodward should not have been retained by the district. Finally, Langley believed that $6,000 in attorney's fees should not have been awarded in the case.[45]

Stilted media coverage of the appeal by Bobby Templeton, editor of the *Hereford Brand*, appeared in the form of an article entitled "Woodward Suit Appealed to Circuit Court: Errors Pointed Out." Templeton noted that an appeal, prepared by school district attorneys Earnest Langley and Richard Green (no relation to Robin Green), had been placed in the U.S. mail to the Fifth Circuit appeals court, but only after "several [failed] attempts at out-of-court" settlements. The article went into explicit detail about the points that the administration took umbrage with in Judge Woodward's findings. Langley filed the appeal during the last week of December 1976, which would then be transferred to the court in New Orleans. The school district asked for either an amending or altering of the court's November 3 judgment, an amending of the court's memorandum of opinion on the case, or simply an entirely new trial.[46]

Templeton noted several elements that he referred to as "points of error," aligning with the verbiage in the school district's appeal. First, the school district believed that the court's findings that Woodward's firing stemmed from his membership in the ACLU were simply not supported by the evidence. Second, they made the strange claim that even if Woodward's constitutionally protected rights had been violated, or "if constitutionally protected conduct played a substantial part in the defendant's decision not to renew the plaintiff's employment, the judgment here cannot stand." Templeton, however, did not explain why or how, on a legal basis, such could be the case. Back pay as well as attorney's fees, argued the district, were improperly awarded. Finally, credible testimony as to Woodward's job performance as well as the subjective elements of the employer-employee relationship, according to the district, had not been given adequate consideration by the trial judge.[47]

In an article published in the newspaper a few days later, Templeton reiterated to local readers that "in the exclusive story Sunday, the *Brand* revealed these points which they are confident will validate [an eventual] reversal by the Supreme Court." Woodward was thus deserving of his fate in the eyes of the Hereford public, whereas the school board had been falsely found guilty of violating the teacher's constitutional rights.[48]

Templeton went even further in this second piece in his condemnation of the ruling. According to the defense attorneys, the decision in *Mt. Healthy City School District Board of Education v. Doyle* (1977) showed that the Supreme Court had ruled that one impermissible reason for firing a teacher (in this case, membership in the ACLU) cannot outweigh other permissible reasons for terminating a teacher's employment. Templeton wrote that "this is considered a strong point in the appeal argument since numerous reasons for Woodward's dismissal were listed originally," given that the school district argued during the trial that Hughes's recommendation for nonrenewal had nothing to do with Woodward's ACLU activities. "It is argued that even if the ACLU reason is a permissible reason," wrote Templeton, "it alone may not outweigh other reasons."[49] In other words, Templeton indicated that the school district could still refuse to renew Woodward's contract for a variety of reasons; Hughes had not refused Woodward's employment due to his ACLU activities, but Templeton seemed to indicate that Woodward still could be let go even if the administration had condemned Woodward's ACLU activities for some unknown reason. This is an especially strange claim, given that Templeton and the school district seemed to be suggesting that it almost did not matter if Woodward's constitutional rights had been violated, as long as there were other seemingly permissible reasons for firing him. What Templeton failed to consider was the judge's findings that these alleged other deficiencies in Woodward's job performance had not been adequately demonstrated by the defense, which Judge Woodward had already made clear in his decision on the case.

The article further noted that Woodward and Green had made several attempts after the October 12 decision to settle out of court but that the terms were never satisfactory to the defense. Harrell Holder, the new superintendent who replaced Hartman after he left for Grapevine, told numerous civic clubs in the area that the two had priced themselves out of the settlement: "'At one point they must have thought we were acting out of weakness (after the board agreed to an offer) and raised the price too high,' he said." Templeton further noted that another offer, which included that Woodward would never teach in Hereford again, later fell apart due to the monetary stipulations attached therein.[50]

Woodward himself had long been dissatisfied with the allegedly biased nature of local reporting against him; indeed, the day after the original ruling in the trial court, he wrote a letter to Templeton criticizing him for his previous handling of the case. He long believed that local coverage had contained certain inadequacies. An earlier article in the *Hereford Brand* had failed to mention that the now famous February 12 letter had accused Woodward of utilizing "unauthorized materials" in the classroom. Furthermore, according to Woodward, the same article in question implied that Green's letter to the administrators had affected Woodward's communication with Hughes as well as vice versa, which it had not, in the teacher's view, as communication between the two men continued through the time of his actual firing. Finally, Woodward noted that the paper had erroneously reported that he was living in Weatherford, Oklahoma, working on a second master's degree, and that he had taught eighth grade English; in fact, Woodward lived in Amarillo at the time of the story's publication, was working on a nursing degree at West Texas State University, and had never taught the eighth grade. All of these were small details, to be sure, but to Woodward they represented the larger problem of sloppy or inherently bad journalism on the part of the Hereford press.[51]

Woodward noted that along with the story on his case, there appeared in the *Brand*'s pages a story on people's basic freedoms and rights stemming from a case when a reporter's rights had been violated, but that the paper had no direct comment on his case in particular: "I find it odd that you have no comment on [my case]," noted Woodward. "Your cries are rather loud when judges limit reporters' rights; why then are you silent when an individual's rights are abused?"[52]

Woodward next lambasted the paper's editorial policies:

> I would suggest that you have fallen into delivering the straight party line dictated by the controlling interests of Hereford. Your reporting of my suit over the past year and a half has shown this. I wonder why during the trial and since the final judgment your paper has not sought my comments, while the media from throughout the state and nation has. Could it be that my comments might punch holes in the self-righteous, pompous bourgeoisie? Freedom of the press does not mean freedom to be narrow in your views, but freedom to criticize anyone, even public officials.[53]

Woodward concluded his attack by arguing that "the evidence of what happens to nations when the press follows the dictates of the powerful was clearly seen in Nazi Germany and is present today in Communist Russia." Furthermore, he hoped "that my comments are printed and your paper will not be too concerned about repercussions from the ruling class. Let the people know."[54] By this point, Woodward clearly made no differentiation between the powers that be in the school district and the conservative powerbrokers who ran the town along with its public institutions.

Naturally, the paper responded, showing that perhaps inclusion of Woodward's letter gave its staff the opportunity to weigh in on the case with the appearance of impartiality:

> Mr. Woodward: We happen to believe that Freedom of the Press carries some responsibilities, just as freedom of speech in the classroom. We have the freedom to print obscene four-letter words, but we choose not to do so. We choose not to "try" this case in our newspaper, and our editor went to great lengths to present an impartial report on the facts presented in the courtroom. I would suggest that your letter indicates some of the hostile attitudes which school officials claimed were contributing factors in not renewing your contract.—O. G. Nieman, Publisher.[55]

Woodward had once again been declared an enemy in the town, this time in print.

Woodward had a point. Coverage of the suit in the months surrounding the trial no doubt favored the administrators. For example, the *Brand* ran an article in April 1976, after Green and Woodward had filed their case but before it went to trial, entitled "Legal Suits Deter Political Potentials," lamenting the liability issues that local politicians faced because of lawsuits filed against officeholders. A number of lawsuits had been filed concurrently to Woodward's, causing the paper to note that "now each of the Hereford governing bodies, county, city and schools, are defendants in legal suits. Of course," the article continued, "the school suit for $400,000 was by far the most significant and it drew the most publicity. It was filed by Wayne Woodward, a teacher dismissed for what he thought were violations of his civil rights." The author—the paper's editor, Bobby Templeton—did not stop there:

> Already the results of these unreasonable suits has [sic] been seen in the recent local elections. Two fine school board members (Ron Zimmerman and Danny Martin) decided not to seek reelection partially if not totally because the liability of public office was not considered worth the risk. While neither admitted the suit (which they are still liable for) was the reason for not running again, it certainly entered their thinking based on comments made from time to time at school board meetings.

Templeton went on to lament that school board members were already inadequately compensated for their jobs, arguing that "society has gone off the deep end with laws and motive for suits against any public figure or for that matter any private individual." In a not-so-veiled reference to Woodward's case, he once would have applauded the "organization for protecting the rights of troddened [sic] upon individuals, but the pendulum has swung the other way. Just like the labor unions, the ACLU is paying legal fees for any little circumstance which the victim claims is unfair."[56] Clearly, the court of public opinion in Hereford had already declared Woodward guilty even before his trial had begun.

Part of the hallmark of the culture wars that this exchange, as well as the case more generally, represented in microcosm was that the two sides were clearly a part of warring camps. Woodward was in tune with the national political dialogue at the time, which lent itself well to change and considered particularly, above all, the defense of one's rights as being a primary factor in what it meant to be an American. While a trial court had found the school district guilty of restricting Woodward's constitutional rights, it is clear that in the defense's own eyes they had done nothing wrong nor had they acted out of malice. Hughes's actions, with the backing of the school board, demonstrated the decades-long flowering of an ideology meant to protect the town against the overreach of not only the federal government but now, also, cultural liberalism, which to many observers from the Texas Panhandle were hopelessly intertwined. There was simply no clear or meaningful way for the two sides to bridge the chasm of cultural as well as political differences that separated them by 1975.

Elements from the appeal itself are worth noting to show why the school board felt that it still had a case. Langley cited in the appellate brief that Woodward had quickly retained his own counsel after receiving his original probation letter, which created "an adversary-type" confrontation between himself and the administration. Second, Langley argued that the school board did grant Woodward a hearing but that they did not feel that it was appropriate to air their own views before the public in Hereford. Furthermore, in their view, the June 2 hearing "proved to be no more than a speech, or plea, from his attorney," while Woodward himself remained silent.[57] Given that the case would not make its way through the entire appeals process due to an eventual out-of-court settlement, it is relatively easy to conclude that statements such as these likely would not have been found favorable by the appellate court. Woodward, in fact, had the constitutional right to retain a lawyer—exercising such a right cannot be used as a justification for ending someone's employment. Also, Green had argued during the trial that the school board had given no clear evidence to Woodward as to why Hughes had dismissed him, meaning that the board could not reverse the burden of proof onto Woodward during the June 2 hearing.

Langley went on to argue that there was neither denial of due process nor an infringement of Woodward's liberty interests. Due process had not been denied because the administrators had allowed the June 2 hearing, which was not required by law; also, given that the administrators had not commented publicly on the case or criticized Woodward, in their view his reputation as a teacher had not been tarnished.[58] Green's contention, however, was that due process had been denied due to the fact that the reasoning for Woodward's firing was unclear, while Woodward's reputation as a teacher *had* been tarnished since the school board depicted him as rebellious as well as uncooperative. Further argumentation that Woodward's legal team would use against this claim was the fact that Woodward had applied for so many teaching jobs and gotten no interest at all, and that one school district had even cited his problems in Hereford as a reason not to interview him for a position.

In an awkwardly worded passage, Langley summed up the defense's views on the case: "In substance, the claim boiled down to this: 'Although you could have refused me a contract for no reason at all, you did in fact have a reason, and this reason was an impermissible one; therefore, your non-retention of my services has damaged me and I am entitled to reinstatement, with back pay, plus attorney's fees . . . this, in effect, was the judgment of the trial court.'"[59] Langley's irreverent and mocking tone in a legal brief aside, his missive failed to address one problem noted by Judge Woodward during the trial: the question of whether the school district had the right to fire a teacher for any *permissible* reason was never in doubt during the trial phase. What the district court had ruled, however, was that Woodward had not only *not* gotten any clear reason as to why he was not offered another contract, but that his constitutional rights—again, free speech under the First Amendment in his ability to speak in a nondisruptive way about the ACLU as well as to assemble with the organization on his own time, as well as his due process rights under the Fourteenth Amendment for not having the chance to defend himself—had been violated in the process of his nonrenewal. Ultimately, the district court had ruled that the school board had fired him for one reason alone—his participation in the ACLU. This, in Judge Woodward's view, was neither permissible nor legal.

Langley also argued that legal precedent was on the district's side. In the recently adjudicated *Mt. Healthy City School District Board of Education v. Doyle* (1977) case, the U.S. Supreme Court found that even though a school board fired a teacher for an impermissible reason that existed among other valid reasons, no judgment could be reached on the case as to whether such impermissible reason was the only or even primary reason why the teacher had been dismissed. As such, according to Langley, "the taint of an impermissible reason is no longer enough of itself alone to require judgment for the teacher in such a case."[60]

Regarding the ACLU charge, the defense contested that "the trial court's finding that the non-renewal of plaintiff's contract resulted from his 'participation in ACLU activities' is not supported by the evidence." Langley did not contest that this had been an issue for the school board. He next went on to quote Woodward's depositions to build an argument that the court's finding about ACLU membership resulting in Woodward's firing was inaccurate, since it had been established that Woodward initially consented to Hughes's request that he no longer pass out ACLU literature to students.[61] Next, Langley quoted Woodward's cross-examination, which he himself had conducted:

LANGLEY: Isn't it true, Mr. Woodward, that all that Mr. Hughes has ever said to you until today about ACLU material of handing it out in school or in classes is simply that you as a mature professional teacher should recognize that there are some subjects that some students and some parents consider controversial and that you should exercise discretion in the way you handle matters of controversy?
WOODWARD: That and [he] told me that I should realize I was in the Bible Belt.
LANGLEY: Yes, sir. And that you should reflect upon your exercise of professional, mature competent judgment with respect to materials that you were using and handing out in your classes?
WOODWARD: That's what he said basically.[62]

Langley then argued that because Woodward had noted that there was a problem with passing out certain materials to students that the court's finding that Hughes or Hartman "had some axe to grind about the organization . . . is patently not borne out by the evidence in this case."[63] If this was true, then the burden not only of proving that the ACLU had nothing to do with Woodward's firing but also of determining the true cause or causes of his firing was not left for Langley to make in his appeal to the court in New Orleans.

Langley elaborated on this problem. From the viewpoint of the defense, the problem was that Woodward had not cooperated with his superiors, thus stymying the "overall education of the children of the District that they had a right to expect from a member of the faculty." The administrators also took umbrage with

Woodward for his hiring of an attorney, arguing that "his subsequent testimony reflects that he selected litigation as his weapon, rather than communication." According to the district, asking that communication go through Green caused unnecessary problems.[64] Langley, again, did not consider whether Woodward felt that he had a good reason to take this course of action or if in fact the reasoning behind him being placed on probationary status had been communicated to him clearly (the lower court had found that it had not been).

Local officials stumped for their positions during the appeals process, again demonstrating that the issue at hand was, to them, less of a legal concern and more one of keeping the local political culture cemented. Superintendent Holder spoke at a Rotary Club luncheon in Hereford, where he emphasized that the district's position was ultimately about "preserving local control." For him, as quoted in the *Hereford Brand*, "federal and state laws are involved and the board acting independently decided to fight for what it considers local taxpayers' rights."[65] Conversely, no concern was expressed for the potential infringement on the free speech rights of a local teacher who was also a taxpaying citizen of the town.

Eventually, the school district realized that a reversal of the decision was unlikely to come from the appeals court; continued discussions of possible out-of-court settlements over the course of the spring of 1977 reached their logical conclusion. Green had initially contacted Richard Green, the school district attorney, in December of 1976, offering a settlement of $23,000 in salary for Woodward with an additional $6,000 in legal fees, which he put into writing later that month. The district, working with Woodward's legal team on behalf of the NEA, suggested to Green that he reach out to Langley with a new settlement offer of $29,000. A few weeks later, Green wrote Langley that he and Woodward would be willing to settle the case in the amount of $30,000 should an agreement be reached in the next couple of weeks. Griffith spoke to Langley on the telephone to discuss the possibility of settling for that amount; Langley informed him that the board would not agree to settle for that amount, but after Griffith reminded him of the clear legal precedent set by the recent *Mt. Healthy* case, which he believed would make it impossible to invalidate the judgment that Woodward had been fired due to his ACLU involvement, Langley relented, even though at this point the superintendent had indicated that he would not agree to settle at such a high dollar amount.[66]

By April, the school board decided that it was time to give up. Although documentation regarding Langley's or the board's exact reasoning is not available, the above discussions of the appeal's apparent lack of legal standing or credibility must have come into play. The contract settlement went before the school board at a meeting on April 25, 1977, where it was summarily approved. Woodward settled with the district for the sum of $29,000; he kept all but $6,000 of the money, which he paid to the NEA and the TCTA for the money that the two organizations advanced to him at the outset of the trial.[67] With that, the long process had come to a conclusion. Woodward, as well as the members of the school board, not to mention perhaps the community of Hereford, could now move on with their lives.

CONCLUSION

Hereford and the Two Americas

Richard Nixon's appeals to the "silent majority" during the 1968 presidential campaign season represented the shrewdness of political campaigning during one of the most turbulent times in modern American history. When Americans watched, for example, the chaos of the Vietnam War, draft riots, news coverage of assassinations (Martin Luther King Jr. and Democratic presidential candidate Robert F. Kennedy), and riots at the Democratic National Convention in Chicago, all of which took place during that tumultuous year, they saw the country standing at a crossroads. What is more, the whole thing was televised. As technology helped further collapse the distance that Americans had once held between themselves and their fellow citizens in far-flung reaches of the country, certain realizations set in. The defining tenets of what it meant to be an American—one who supported the Constitution, freedom, democracy, civil liberties, or public services—were now up for grabs. The dawn of the television age both divided as well as united people. The country would never be the same.[1]

Technology has long been the great annihilator of space; physical space, conversely, long kept Americans from getting too overly familiar with one another. Steamboats, canals, and later railroads, for example, collapsed distance in the United States during the early part of the nineteenth century. Not only could people now travel between disparate locales faster, but manufacturers could send consumer products to far-flung reaches of the United States that were once inaccessible. U.S. infrastructure thus paved the way for a nationwide consumer culture, which flattened differences between various groups of Americans. At the dawn of the twentieth century, Henry Ford's Model T further integrated people on a spatial level. Famously, the automobile flattened economic culture as well, given the car's affordability among the middle and working classes.

The Texas Panhandle's settlement around the same time as the proliferation of the first automobiles, though, hearkened back to an older era. Ranchers and cowboys during the late nineteenth and early twentieth centuries certainly lived lonely existences, a fact that undoubtedly became embellished by western lore later in the twentieth century. In reality, it was small family farmers who bought up land from the Panhandle's once-large ranches and lived on what was then arguably America's last distended frontier. Individualism and a certain community-mindedness, as this book has shown, thus became woven into the region's social fabric, which Panhandle Texans celebrated during their initial push to memorialize regional history during the 1920s and '30s.

But Panhandle residents could only stay isolated for so long. Coincidentally, as residents began celebrating older notions of pioneering and individuality with the opening of the Panhandle-Plains Historical Museum in 1933, so, too, did a new presence arrive in the region—agents of the federal government. New Deal liberalism, despite being well intentioned as well as doing a lot of good for the Texas Panhandle, augured the federal government's arrival in a region where community and self-reliance had always been the wellspring of social, moral, and economic prosperity. Moreover, to many, the government overstayed its welcome. To people in the Panhandle, this was an egregious sin; they knew best how to govern their own affairs, but local control risked being sacrificed on the altar of national liberalism (replete with coastal or urbanite condescension) from within the laudable goal of economic recovery. Of course, the politics of the New Left of the 1950s and '60s arrived in the region a few decades later. One of the things that made civil rights and college-campus organizing so successful was the television coverage of the brutality of anti–civil rights responses from people in the Deep South. Conversely, the deep social unrest that came with the new liberalism of the late 1960s further polarized the country, as people in rural spaces like Hereford, Texas, looked with shock at rioting and protesting in bigger cities. Politics itself had thus partially annihilated space; television only further heightened peoples' sense of political differences during the era in which Wayne Woodward graduated from college and began his career as an English teacher.

Woodward's story is a case study of the clashing sides in the mid-twentieth-century culture wars in rural America. Isolated living in the Texas Panhandle combined with a consistent Anglo majority (in the case of Hereford, until the early 1960s) must be considered as one of the primary factors that fed into the general mentality of the public's interpretation of Wayne Woodward serving as an outside threat to local society. Herefordites undoubtedly had watched the 1960s from afar on their televisions. Now, finally, at the tail end of the era, the new liberalism threatened to come crashing in on their seemingly self-sufficient and orderly town, along with the usurpation of an agricultural economy that, like many others in small towns in Texas and the rest of the U.S. West, relied on impoverished Mexican and Mexican American migrant workers. What similarities might this have had to the tumult taking shape across the U.S. South? Civil rights organizers had grown accustomed to the language of "outsider interference" being hurled at them as they fought for the rights of African Americans, Mexican Americans, and other minority groups organizing to effect change in far-flung parts of the country. What was at stake was one thing—power. Whites lost power to Blacks in the U.S. South. They lost power to Mexican and Mexican American agricultural workers in places like the South Texas borderlands. Now, they stood to lose power in one of the last isolated bastions of Anglo-American authority in the continental United States.

The ACLU could prove to be the final nail in the coffin of what locals believed to be a more traditional, more orderly America. The people of Hereford, Texas, knew that the larger country was changing in ways that many of them simply could not acccpt.

As Americans came into closer proximity to one another during the second half of the twentieth century, one thing had become increasingly clear: they didn't necessarily like one another. Political differences could be ignored, somewhat, during the early part of the century when the United States was less interconnected than it became with the advent of radio and later television during the early and middle parts of the century. People with seemingly foreign ideas could essentially be kept at arm's length. By the 1960s and '70s, such was no longer the case; as the foreign realm of sweeping national changes became a local reality, people confronted one another over their differences, sometimes on a near daily basis.

One would hope that problems such as those that related to Wayne Woodward's story would have been resolved in the years since his case's settlement in 1977. Woodward may have won a large settlement, but he never taught again, instead becoming a nurse practitioner for many years and later retiring. At the time of this book's writing, he lived a quiet life in Amarillo, Texas, with his wife, Linda, not far from Hereford. He only returned to Hereford once in the early 1990s, when a Democratic activist initiated a small-scale voter-registration drive among Mexican Americans in town. The town hadn't really changed, though, as this new effort at bringing in an activist bent was as limited as the ACLU presence in the town had been over fifteen years previously. In the end, despite having a good life, Woodward leaving the teaching profession was obviously an unfortunate by-product of the Hereford drama. He was a good teacher, well liked by his students and enthusiastic about his profession. Woodward lost contact with his antagonists—Roy Hartman passed away sometime after taking his new position in Grapevine, Texas, while Pat Hughes continued working and later retired in Colorado. As the decades passed, Woodward never lost sight of the fact that his constitutional rights had been violated in Hereford.[2] One cannot blame him for leaving the teaching profession. Although any legal precedent set by his case is outside the scope of this study, public schools since 1975 would become the flashpoints for many controversies, including prayer in schools, free speech controversies, school walkouts in the early twenty-first century to protest federal policies toward issues like immigration as well as gun control, and of course, school shootings, which would become shockingly commonplace across the United States in the early twenty-first century.

All the above-mentioned controversies have, of course, coincided with the modern political fracturing of the United States, which historians date as beginning around the time that Woodward's rights were violated.[3] As this book has shown, Woodward's case reveals much about the warring political cultures that clashed in Hereford during the middle of the 1970s. Political fracturing, however, arguably worsened after 1975. With the advent of social media during the early part of the twenty-first century, Americans lost whatever remaining physical space had previously kept them apart prior to the rise of the internet. In turn, the collective public mood would now shift virtually overnight: an onslaught of tweets or Facebook posts could lead the general public in a direction that democratically elected leaders might initially be unaware of or to which they might even express a certain level of opposition. "The force of [people's] discontent," according to one 2016 editorialist, "can disrupt governments and threaten the security of representatives even outside of the electoral cycle." Politicians in the United States, then, could now be held accountable outside of places where traditional democratic accountability once reigned unchallenged—the ballot box on election day. The general intensity of conversations among regular people began to have massive consequences on the national or even the world stage.[4]

And those conversations thus ran the risk of becoming even more intense than political conflicts had been during the latter few decades of the twentieth century. Politicians themselves became adept at using social media to shrink the space between themselves and the electorate. Barack Obama used Facebook extensively during his first presidential electoral victory in 2008. During the following years, national politicians used various social-media platforms, such as Snapchat, Twitter, YouTube, and Facebook. Perhaps the most adept user of social media during the early twenty-first century has been Donald Trump, whose victory in the 2016 presidential race benefited heavily from his ability to "troll" his opponents, meaning his ability to use inflammatory language at moments that would prove the most politically opportune.[5] Now, the usage of social media has become central to U.S. politics.

At first glance, social-media politics in the twenty-first century might seem to have little in common with the story related in this book. Woodward's story, though, serves as more than just an interesting tale about the origins of the culture wars in rural America. Woodward represented a threat to the people of Hereford because he embodied ideals that the people in this long-isolated conservative town had only read about in newspapers or seen on television. Their distrust for what he appeared to represent in 1975 is understandable. Finally, however, they would have to deal with that threat arriving not only in their town but in an institution in which he could change their children. As time passed since the 1970s, the alleged judgment of liberals as well as urban and coastal elites only further entrenched people in rural areas against the politics of the so-called elites from big cities. Donald Trump's election during the 2016 presidential race—Trump easily swept the Texas Panhandle that year—only proves that tough and divisive rhetoric, rather than a sense of togetherness or bipartisanship, held great appeal for millions of people in rural America.[6] Arguably, the divisions seen during Woodward's case during the 1970s only grew more pronounced over time. Woodward's case is thus significant in that it was an early public display of such tension in Hereford.

The culture wars, then, in the case of Hereford, had only first arrived on the scene during the 1970s. The so-called liberal/conservative divide continues during the age of the internet and shows no signs of slowing down during the era of Trump and beyond. What young Wayne Woodward experienced during the mid-1970s only foreshadowed the growing cultural rift that has served to separate Americans, who at the time of the writing of this book in 2020 still tend to divide themselves into one of two warring camps: the liberal camp of mostly urban America, and the conservative camp of largely rural America. Hereford, Texas, might have long been isolated before the 1970s; nonetheless, Woodward's case has shown one important truth. Hereford, Texas, was never really isolated at all—it was at the center of everything.

AFTERWORD

Wayne Woodward

My experience as a young, naïve teacher in Hereford, Texas, had a profound effect on me. I always thought all people should be treated equally. I see the similarities in my experience at that time and today. It is my hope that reinforcing the wrongs bestowed upon those who do not follow the line of those in power at the time can be brought to light so that these mistakes will not be repeated. I see that history does tend to continue to repeat itself. I contacted a young attorney named Robin Green in 1975 who was enthusiastic to take on my case.

It is for this reason that for forty-plus years I maintained a desire to tell my experience as a young teacher who was removed from teaching because I was attempting to instill in my students that there was a world beyond Hereford that they should explore and that migrant children were deserving of a good education. This always stayed with me, though I was unable to continue in the teaching profession. I went on to have a career as a nurse practitioner.

After retiring, it was always my goal to record my experience, and feeling that there was some historical significance to my story, I sought the help of Dr. Bowman to relate my experience. I am grateful that he accepted.

NOTES

Abbreviations

CLA   Cornette Library Archives, West Texas A&M University, Canyon, Texas
LEBC   Louise Evans Bruce Collection, Research Center, Panhandle Plains Historical Museum, West Texas A&M University, Canyon, Texas
JEH   J. Evetts Haley
JEHP   J. Evetts Haley Papers, Nita Stewart Haley Memorial Library, Midland, Texas
JRPC   Joe Rogers Personal Collection of Hereford ISD Desegregation Documents
WWPC   Wayne Woodward Personal Collection, Amarillo, Texas

Notes to Introduction

1. Esmerelda Perales, untitled poem, "Student Evaluations" folder, circa spring 1975, Wayne Woodward Personal Collection, Amarillo, Texas (hereafter WWPC).
2. For more, see John Henry Faulk, *Fear on Trial* (Austin: University of Texas Press, 1983); and Timothy Paul Bowman, *Blood Oranges: Colonialism and Agriculture in the South Texas Borderlands* (College Station: Texas A&M University Press, 2016), 72, 181.
3. Jeff Roche, "Cowboy Conservatism: High Plains Politics, 1933–1972" (PhD diss., University of New Mexico, 2001), 1.
4. Kim Phillips-Fein, "Conservatism: A State of the Field," *Journal of American History* 98, no. 3 (December 2011): 726.
5. Phillips-Fein, "Conservatism," 727–36.
6. Phillips-Fein, "Conservatism," 737, 739, 743.
7. John T. "Jack" Becker, "The Texas Panhandle," in *West Texas: A History of the Giant Side of the State*, ed. Paul H. Carlson and Bruce A. Glasrud (Norman: University of Oklahoma Press, 2014), 29–30.
8. Stephen Harrigan, *Big Wonderful Thing: A History of Texas* (Austin: University of Texas Press, 2019), 10.
9. This definition of the Texas Panhandle is taken from popular understandings of the region's geographical boundaries as presented in Frederick W. Rathjen, *The Texas Panhandle Frontier*, rev. ed. (Lubbock: Texas Tech University Press, 1998), 1.
10. "Southern Plains" as a region is synonymous with the Llano Estacado, which is a flat, large tableland that encompasses most of the Texas Panhandle, parts of eastern New Mexico, and western Oklahoma.

11. Quotation in Kevin M. Kruse and Julian E. Zelizer, *Fault Lines: A History of the United States since 1974* (New York: W. W. Norton, 2019), 3. For other recent studies of conservatism, see Joseph Crespino, *Strom Thurmond's America: A History* (New York: Hill and Wang, 2013); Matthew D. Lassiter, *The Silent Majority: Suburban Politics in the Sunbelt South* (Princeton, NJ: Princeton University Press, 2007).
12. Quoted in Daniel T. Rodgers, *Age of Fracture* (Cambridge, MA: Belknap/Harvard University Press, 2011), 1.
13. Quoted in Andrew Hartman, *A War for the Soul of America: A History of the Culture Wars* (Chicago: University of Chicago Press, 2015), 4.
14. David O'Donald Cullen, "From 'Turn Texas Loose' to the Tea Party: Origins of the Texas Right," in David O'Donald Cullen and Kyle G. Wilkison, eds., *The Texas Right: The Radical Roots of Lone Star Conservatism* (College Station: Texas A&M University Press, 2014), 4.
15. Rodgers, *Age of Fracture*, 4.
16. Roche, "Cowboy Conservatism," viii.
17. "Constitution and Bylaws of the Panhandle-Plains Historical Society," Constitution, 1921, Box 1, 1, Panhandle-Plains Historical Society Records, Research Center, Panhandle-Plains Historical Museum, Canyon, Texas.
18. Janet M. Neugebauer, *A Witness to History: George H. Mahon, West Texas Congressman* (Lubbock: Texas Tech University Press, 2017), 32; Clipping, "History Body Had Data from Real Pioneers," *The Canyon News*, March 20, 1928, unmarked black binder, Research Center, Panhandle-Plains Historical Museum, Canyon, Texas.
19. Clipping, "History Sprang from Soil When Plains Museum was Founded," no other information, Panhandle-Plains Historical Museum and Society Scrapbook, Building 1, Research Center, Panhandle-Plains Historical Museum, Canyon, Texas.
20. Clipping, W. U. McCoy, "Hopes High for Museum Future," May 16, 1949, no other information, Panhandle-Plains Historical Museum and Society Scrapbook, Society 1, q AM 101.P37x, Research Center, Panhandle-Plains Historical Museum, Canyon, Texas.
21. Clipping, "Historical Value of Museum Is Traced Since Opening in 1933," *The Prairie*, June 18, 1940, Panhandle-Plains Historical Society Museum #2 (1940 and 1941), untitled box, Cornette Library Archives, West Texas A&M University, Canyon, Texas.
22. For more on boosterism and land marketing in the region, see Jan Blodgett, *Land of Bright Promise: Advertising the Texas Panhandle and the South Plains, 1870–1917* (Austin: University of Texas Press, 1988); for more on the western orientation of West Texas as a region, see Glen Sample Ely, *Where the West Begins: Debating Texas Identity* (Lubbock: Texas Tech University Press, 2011).
23. For a recent look at the divide between rural and urban Americans, see Robert Wuthnow, *The Left Behind: Decline and Rage in Rural America* (Princeton, NJ: Princeton University Press, 2018).
24. Michelle Nickerson and Darren Dochuk, "Introduction," in *Sunbelt Rising: The Politics of Space, Place, and Region* (Philadelphia: University of Pennsylvania Press, 2011), 3; see also Roche, "Cowboy Conservatism," 3, 4, 11.

25. Matthew D. Lassiter, "Big Government and Family Values: Political Culture in the Metropolitan Sunbelt," in Nickerson and Dochuk, *Sunbelt Rising*, 84, 85.
26. Joseph Crespino, "Strom Thurmond's Sunbelt: Rethinking Regional Politics and the Rise of the Right," in Nickerson and Dochuk, *Sunbelt Rising*, 58–61.
27. For example, see "... Of Texas Historians," *Amarillo Sunday News-Globe*, October 22, 1995, Panhandle-Plains Historical Museum #24 (1993–), Cornette Library Archives, West Texas A&M University, Canyon, Texas (hereafter CLA).
28. Darren Dochuk, *From Bible Belt to Sunbelt: Plain-Folk Religion, Grassroots Politics, and the Rise of Evangelical Conservatism* (New York: W. W. Norton, 2012), xi–xxiv, 6–8, quotation on page xv; and Dochuk, "'They Locked God outside the Iron Curtain': The Politics of Anticommunism and the Ascendancy of Plain-Folk Evangelicalism in the Postwar West," in *The Political Culture of the New West*, ed. Jeff Roche (Lawrence: University Press of Kansas, 2008), 97–131.
29. Michelle Nickerson, *Mothers of Conservatism: Women and the Postwar Right* (Princeton, NJ: Princeton University Press, 2012), xiv–xv, xvii–xxii.
30. For more on "moral guardianism," see Nickerson, *Mothers of Conservatism*, xvi.
31. John K. Lack, "An Interview with David Danbom, Historian of Rural America," *Great Plains Quarterly* 34, no. 2 (Spring 2014): 167. For a more recent analysis of populism that debunks Hofstadter's approach, see, for example, Charles Postel, *The Populist Vision* (Oxford: Oxford University Press, 2009).
32. For more, see Robert H. Wiebe, *The Search for Order, 1877–1920* (New York: Hill and Wang, 1966).

Chapter 1. Defining Conservatism in the Texas Panhandle

1. For examples, see Walter Nugent, *Color Coded: Party Politics in the American West, 1950–2016* (Norman: University of Oklahoma Press, 2018), 308–9.
2. For more on Indian slavery, see Andrés Reséndez, *The Other Slavery: The Uncovered Story of Indian Enslavement in America* (Boston: Houghton Mifflin, 2016); for more on Cabeza de Vaca, see Andrés Reséndez, *A Land So Strange: The Epic Journey of Cabeza de Vaca* (New York: Basic Books, 2009).
3. For more on the history of the Comanches, see Pekka Hämäläinen, *The Comanche Empire* (New Haven, CT: Yale University Press, 2009); Pekka Hämäläinen, "What's in a Concept? The Kinetic Empire of the Comanches," *History and Theory* 52, no. 1 (February 2013): 81–90.
4. J. Evetts Haley, *Charles Goodnight: Cowman and Plainsman* (Boston: Houghton Mifflin Company, 1936), 276. Notably, the historian David J. Murrah argues that other important contemporary figures, such as the rancher C. C. Slaughter, have been ignored in favor of Goodnight, due in large part to the success of Haley's biography. For more, see David J. Murrah, "Caught in Goodnight's Shadow: The Un-Illuminated Legacy of C. C. Slaughter," *Panhandle-Plains Historical Review* 89 (2018): 22–32.
5. John Miller Morris, "When Corporations Ruled the Llano Estacado: The Glorious Past and Uncertain Future of the Southern High Plains Family Farm," in *The Future*

of the Southern Plains, ed. Sherry L. Smith (Norman: University of Oklahoma Press, 2003), 50, 56.

6. See, for example, Michael M. Miller, *XIT: A Story of Land, Cattle, and Capital in Texas and Montana* (Norman: University of Oklahoma Press, 2020), 1–9.
7. Timothy Egan, *The Worst Hard Time: The Untold Story of Those Who Survived the Great American Dust Bowl* (Boston: Mariner Books, 2006), 21–22; Benjamin Lee Gorman, "Fundamentalism and the Frontier: Value Clusters in the Texas Panhandle" (PhD diss., Tulane University, 1965), 33.
8. Robert Wuthnow, *Rough Country: How Texas Became America's Most Powerful Bible-Belt State* (Princeton, NJ: Princeton University Press, 2014), 1, 4.
9. Edward L. Larson, *Summer for the Gods: The Scopes Trial and America's Continuing Debate Over Science and Religion* (New York: Basic Books, 2006).
10. For more, see Joseph Locke, *Making the Bible Belt: Texas Prohibitionists and the Politicization of Southern Religion* (Oxford: Oxford University Press, 2017), 1–12.
11. For more on Zelinsky's ideas, see William B. Meyer, "First Effective Settlement: Histories of an Idea," *Journal of Historical Geography* 65 (Spring 2019): 1–8; Gorman, "Fundamentalism and the Frontier," 65–69.
12. Kyle G. Wilkison, "'The Evils of Socialism:' The Religious Right in Early Twentieth Century Texas," in Cullen and Wilkison, *The Texas Right*, 42, 46.
13. Edgar Eugene Robinson, *The Presidential Vote, 1896–1932*, 2nd ed. (Stanford, CA: Stanford University Press, 1947), 331–35; *Texas Almanac and State Industrial Guide, Supplementary Edition, 1937* (Dallas: A. H. Belo, 1937); and *Texas Almanac and State Industrial Guide, 1941–1942* (Dallas: A. H. Belo, 1942), 401.
14. Keith Volanto, "The Far Right in Texas Politics during the Roosevelt Era," in Cullen and Wilkison, *The Texas Right*, 68–86.
15. Roche, "Cowboy Conservatism," 44.
16. Clipping, *Fort Worth Star Telegram*, February 1, 1933, 2, no title, folder JEH II, A, Topical, Panhandle-Clippings, J. Evetts Haley Papers, Nita Stewart Haley Memorial Library, Midland, Texas (hereafter JEHP).
17. Joseph A. Hill, *The Panhandle-Plains Historical Society and Its Museum* (Canyon: West Texas State College Press, 1955), 83.
18. Jim Johnson, "The Rugged Texan: Recollections of J. Evetts Haley," in *J. Evetts Haley: The Legacy*, ed. J. Evetts Haley Jr. (Midland, TX: The Haley Family Trust, 1996), 64.
19. Facsimile, J. Evetts Haley, "Cow Business and Monkey Business," December 8, 1934, *Saturday Evening Post*; and clipping, J. Evetts Haley, "Cows in the Cotton Patch," October 13, 1935, *San Antonio Express*, no other information, in binder, "The Dust Bowl of 1934–35 and the Cattle Slaughter of 1935, Including the Diary and Notes of JEH, 1933–1935," Nita Stewart Haley Memorial Library, Midland, Texas.
20. Haley, "Cow Business and Monkey Business."
21. See, for example, "Student Polls Show Roosevelt Favorite; Favor Third Term," *The Prairie*, October 31, 1939.
22. Roche, "Cowboy Conservatism," 55, 56–57, 58, 59–60, 60; Hill, *The Panhandle-Plains Historical Society and Its Museum*, 83.

23. Egan, *The Worst Hard Time*, 261.
24. Marty Kuhlman, interview with the author, February 10, 2017.
25. Roche, "Cowboy Conservatism," 69, 70. For more, see James W. Loewen, *Sundown Towns: A Hidden Dimension of American Racism* (New York: Touchstone, 2006). More research is necessary to determine whether Hereford can accurately be categorized as a sundown town.
26. Volanto, "The Far Right in Texas Politics," 81; also see George Norris Green, "Establishing the Texas Far Right, 1940–1960," in Cullen and Wilkison, *The Texas Right*, 89.
27. *Members of the Texas Legislature, 1846–2004*. Vol. 2 (Austin: Secretary of the Senate, 2005), 546, 553; Bascom M. Timmons, "Panhandle Writer Praises Timmons Law-Making Record," *The Panhandle Herald*, April 28, 1950, 3.
28. For more, see George Norris Green, *The Establishment in Texas Politics: The Primitive Years, 1938–1957* (Norman: University of Oklahoma Press, 1984), 20, 44–68; "Gossett, Ed Lee," Biographical Directory of the United States Congress, 1774–Present, https://bioguideretro.congress.gov/Home/MemberDetails?memIndex=G000338 (accessed November 14, 2020).
29. Sean P. Cunningham, "The Paranoid Style and Its Limits: The Power, Influence, and Failure of the Postwar Texas Far Right," in Cullen and Wilkinson, *The Texas Right*, 102.
30. Sean P. Cunningham, *Cowboy Conservatism: Texas and the Rise of the Modern Right* (Lexington: University of Kentucky Press, 2010), 40–51. For more on the importance of Dallas to the emerging Texas conservatism, see Edward H. Miller, *Nut Country: Right-Wing Dallas and the Birth of the Southern Strategy* (Chicago: University of Chicago Press, 2015). For more on Texas politics more generally during the early part of the twentieth century, see Green, *The Establishment in Texas Politics*.
31. Bruce Alger, "Washington Report," April 6, 1963, no other information, Welfare State–I, Louise Evans Bruce Collection, Research Center, Panhandle-Plains Historical Museum, West Texas A&M University, Canyon, Texas (hereafter LEBC).
32. Clipping, "U.S. Welfare State Now Exists; How Long Before We Are Devoured?" *Amarillo Globe-News*, May 9, 1967, 18, no other information, Welfare State–II, LEBC.
33. Clipping, Leslie Carpenter, "Let's Be Friends . . . Sen. Tower Patching Up," *Amarillo Globe-News*, January 11, 1967, Politicus Columns, LEBC.
34. Green, "Establishing the Texas Far Right," 98. For more on the pivotal decade of the 1950s in Texas politics, see Ricky F. Dobbs, *Yellow Dogs and Republicans: Allan Shivers and Texas Two-Party Politics* (College Station: Texas A&M University Press, 2005).
35. Clipping, "Excerpts from Remarks of Attorney General John Ben Shepperd to a Meeting of the Civitan Clubs of Texas, Austin, February 25, 1956," LEBC; also see Marty Kuhlman, interview with the author, February 10, 2017.
36. Wuthnow, *Rough Country*, 287.
37. Dochuk, *From Bible Belt to Sunbelt*, 193. For more on the JBS, see D. J. Mulloy, *The World of the John Birch Society: Conspiracy, Conservatism, and the Cold War* (Nashville, TN: Vanderbilt University Press, 2014).
38. Mulloy, *The World of the John Birch Society*, 265.

39. Clipping, Leslie Carpenter, "Democrats Will Have Rebuttal . . . Following John Birch Radiocasts," *Amarillo Globe News*, March 13, 1966, n.p., Politicus Columns, LEBC.
40. Miller, *Nut Country*, 13; Roche, "Cowboy Conservatism," 93, 94, 143, 146–47, 148; also see "1952 Presidential General Election Results—Texas," Dave Leip's Atlas of U.S. Presidential Elections, https://uselectionatlas.org/RESULTS/state.php?fips=48&year=1952 (accessed October 2, 2020).
41. Roche, "Cowboy Conservatism," 96, 98, quote on page 98; for more, see J. Evetts Haley, *A Texan Looks at Lyndon: A Study in Illegitimate Power* (Canyon, TX: Palo Duro Press, 1964); and Roche, "Cowboy Conservatism," 170, 173; quote on page 170. Haley's was only one of a slew of right-wing publications published during the tumultuous 1960s. For more, see Barry Goldwater, *The Conscience of a Conservative* (Eastford, CT: Martino Fine Books, 2011); and Phyllis Schlafly, *A Choice Not an Echo* (Washington, D.C.: Regnery Publishing, 2014). Goldwater's pamphlet was ghost-written.
42. Nickerson, *Mothers of Conservatism*, 136.
43. Clipping, ". . . Of Texas Historians," *Amarillo Sunday News-Globe*, October 22, 1995, untitled box, Panhandle-Plains Historical Museum Collection, Cornette Library Archives, West Texas A&M University, Canyon, Texas.
44. "Haley's Up Against It," *Panhandle Herald*, April 6, 1956, 2; and "County Voters Back Winners," *Canadian Record* 67, no. 31, August 2, 1956, 1.
45. John S. Huntington, "'The Voice of Many Hatreds': J. Evetts Haley and Texas Ultraconservatism," *Western Historical Quarterly* 49, no. 1 (Spring 2018): 65–89; quote on page 65. For more on the important influences of radicalism on modern conservative thought, see Huntington, "Right-Wing Paranoid Blues: The Role of Radicalism in Modern Conservatism" (PhD diss., University of Houston, 2016).
46. Clipping, ". . . Of Texas Historians," *Amarillo Sunday News-Globe*, October 22, 1995, untitled box, Panhandle-Plains Historical Museum Collection, Cornette Library Archives, West Texas A&M University, Canyon, Texas.
47. Rick Perlstein, *Before the Storm: Barry Goldwater and the Unmaking of the American Consensus* (New York: Hill and Wang, 2001), 477–78.
48. Ibid., 89. For more on conservative pushbacks against textbooks in the Texas school system during this period, see Allan O. Kownslar, *The Great Texas Social Studies Textbook War of 1961–1962* (College Station: Texas A&M University Press, 2020).
49. "What's Tough for Tech . . . May be a Break for Texas"; "Spur of the Moment"; both in *Canadian Record* 68, no. 30 (July 25, 1957): 2; "Tempest at Tech," *Canadian Record* 68, no. 30, July 25, 1957, 6; and H. M. Baggarly, "Presbyterian Students Dub Regent's Action UnChristian, UnAmerican, Undemocratic," *Tulia Herald*, August 1, 1957, 1, 8.
50. Roche, "Cowboy Conservatism," 119–20, 122.
51. Clipping, Louise Evans Bruce, "From A to Izzard—Fancy Talk, but Faulty Logic," *Amarillo Globe News*, August 1, 1962, "Welfare State–I," LEBC.
52. Ibid.

53. Clipping, "From A to Izzard column—Crusader from South Plains," February 14, 1962, no other information, "Welfare State–I," LEBC.
54. Clipping, "'Do-Good' Moves Snubbed by Slavery," *Amarillo Globe-Times*, March 21, 1963, no other information, "Welfare State–I," LEBC.
55. Clipping, "Bruce Alger to Support Goldwater," January 3, 1964, no other information; clipping, "Barry Goldwater Campaign Tour—Amarillo, Texas, September 22, 1964"; both in "Goldwater," LEBC; Robin Green, interview with the author, August 7, 2017.
56. Roche, "Cowboy Conservatism," 163, 164, 174, 175.
57. Miller, *Nut Country*, 117–19.
58. Clipping, Leslie Carpenter, "Republican Hopefuls . . . Facing Many Problems," June 27, 1966, Politicus Columns, LEBC. Still, Tower led the party through nearly twenty-five years of struggle to wrest political control from the Democrats at the state level. For more, see John R. Knaggs, *Two-Party Texas: The John Tower Era, 1961–1984* (Woodway, TX: Eakin Press, 1986); also, for the later period, see Wayne Thorburn, *Red State: An Insider's Story of How the GOP Came to Dominate Texas Politics* (Austin: University of Texas Press, 2014).
59. Clipping, "Tower Gets Wide Margin in Panhandle," *Amarillo Globe-Times*, November 9, 1966; and clipping, "GOP Success May Restore Liberals vs. Conservatives," *Amarillo Globe-Times*, November 9, 1966, no other information, Politicus Columns, LEBC.
60. Grady Hazlewood to Ronald Reagan, March 14, 1968, Austin, Texas (Personal); Grady Hazlewood to Ronald Reagan, March 14, 1968 (Personal and Confidential); both in Correspondence, Folder—Grady Hazlewood, JEHP. All quotations from the latter.
61. Ronald Reagan to Grady Hazlewood, March 25, 1968, Sacramento, California; clipping, Jeff Searcy, "Hazlewood Rapped; Cobb Named," *Amarillo Sunday News-Globe*, August 11, 1968, 1D; both in Correspondence, Folder—Grady Hazlewood, JEHP; Green, *The Establishment in Texas Politics*, 197.
62. Cunningham, *Cowboy Conservatism*, 39.
63. Clipping, Bruce Biossat, "Wallace: Hero of Defiant Whites," *Amarillo Globe-Times*, November 2, 1966, Politicus Columns, LEBC.
64. Ibid. For more on Wallace, see Dan T. Carter, *The Politics of Rage: George Wallace, the Origins of the New Conservatism, and the Transformation of American Politics*, 2nd ed. (Baton Rouge: Louisiana State University Press, 2000).
65. Clipping, "Open Housing and Birch Society Heating Campaign in California," *Amarillo Daily News*, August 8, 1966, 14, no author given, Politicus Columns, LEBC.
66. Don Cooney, interview with the author, January 11, 2017.
67. Tom Benning, "Rep. Mac Thornberry Becomes 6th Texas Republican in House to Announce Retirement Ahead of 2020 Election," *Dallas Morning News*, September 30, 2019, https://www.dallasnews.com/news/politics/2019/09/30/rep-mac-thornberry-becomes-6th-texas-republican-in-house-to-announce-retirement-ahead-of-2020-election/ (accessed Nov. 14, 2020).
68. Clipping, Margaret Mayer, "Republicans Study Voting Trends," September 6, 1966, no other information, Politicus Columns, LEBC.

Chapter 2. Coming of Age in the Texas Panhandle

1. Hartman, *A War for the Soul of America*, 3.
2. Wayne Woodward interview with Katherine Bynum, June 9, 2016, Amarillo, Texas, The Portal to Texas History, https://texashistory.unt.edu/ark:/67531/metapth982471/?q=Wayne%20Woodward (accessed November 14, 2020).
3. Clipping, Louise Evans Bruce, "Bertrand Russell's Projected 'Trial' Violates Basic Anglo-Saxon Law," *Amarillo Daily News*, December 3, 1966, 22, Politicus Columns, 1966, LEBC.
4. Clipping, "ACLU Pushes Draft Exemptions for Nonpacifists Who Oppose Viet War," *Amarillo Globe-News*, May 18, 1966, no other information, Politicus Columns, 1966, LEBC.
5. Roche, "Cowboy Conservatism," 186–94.
6. Ibid., 194–202; Wayne Woodward, interview with the author, July 22, 2016.
7. Clipping, "'Rights' Measure Scuttled," March 24, 1965, no other information, Legislature—Panhandle Delegation, LEBC. For more on the Red Scare and Texas politics, see Don E. Carleton, *Red Scare: Right-Wing Hysteria, Fifties Fanaticism, and Their Legacy in Texas* (Austin: University of Texas Press, 2014).
8. Robin Green, interview with the author, August 7, 2017, Lubbock, Texas.
9. Clipping, Louise Evans Bruce, "'Human Relations' Cannot be Solved by Strictures of Any Government," *Amarillo Sunday News-Globe*, May 23, 1965, 16C, Human Relations, LEBC.
10. Roche, "Cowboy Conservatism," 241, 242, 243–46; also, Wayne Woodward, interview with the author, July 22, 2016.
11. Marty Kuhlman, *Always WT: West Texas A&M University Centennial History* (Stillwater, OK: New Forums Press, 2010), 338–39; quote on page 338.
12. Ibid., 333.
13. Clipping, "Student Sues WT," February 17, 1966, no other information, Welfare State–I, LEBC.
14. Ibid.; clipping, Phil Duncan, "Judge Slaps WT Policies," 2-24-66, Welfare State–I, LEBC. Perhaps tellingly, Louise Evans Bruce filed newspaper clippings related to Aldridge's case in a binder entitled "Welfare State." Although the columnist herself did not appear to provide any direct commentary on the case, her inclusion of these clippings under such a heading likely indicates a hostility to the district court's decision to challenge the decisions of local officials who—perhaps in her view—only had the best interests of the town and community in mind.
15. Roche, "Cowboy Conservatism," 247; Kuhlman, *Always WT*, 333, 339.
16. Roche, "Cowboy Conservatism," 256, 257, 258.
17. "1972 Presidential General Election Data Graphs—Texas," Dave Leip's Atlas of U.S. Presidential Elections, https://uselectionatlas.org/RESULTS/datagraph.php?year=1972&fips=48&f=0&off=0&elect=0 (accessed November 17, 2020).
18. Cunningham, *Cowboy Conservatism*, 124, 127, 153.

19. Joseph Alsop, "Conservative Speaks Out on Education . . . McCone Has Prescription for Ailments," *Amarillo Globe-Times,* 12-22-66, Politicus, November 1966–January 1967, LEBC.
20. Roche, "Cowboy Conservatism," 259, 261, 262.
21. Wayne Woodward, interview with the author, July 22, 2016.
22. Wayne Woodward, interview with the author, July 22, 2016.
23. Marty Kuhlman, interview with the author, February 10, 2017.
24. Marty Kuhlman, interview with the author, February 10, 2017.
25. Don Cooney, interview with the author, January 11, 2017.
26. Don Cooney, interview with the author, January 11, 2017; and Robin Green, interview with the author, August 7, 2017.
27. Don Cooney, interview with the author, January 11, 2017.
28. Don Cooney, interview with the author, January 11, 2017.

Chapter 3. The Teacher

1. Pamphlet, "Better Schools Make Better Communities," Hereford Public Schools, Hereford, Texas, 1959, Joe Rogers Personal Collection of Hereford ISD Desegregation Documents (hereafter JRPC); H. Allen Anderson, "Hereford, TX," in *Handbook of Texas Online,* accessed July 08, 2019, http://www.tshaonline.org/handbook/online/articles/heho2, uploaded on June 15, 2010, modified on January 15, 2018 (published by the Texas State Historical Association); and Bessie Patterson, *A History of Deaf Smith County, 1890–1964* (Hereford, TX: Pioneer, 1964), 3–33.
2. Patterson, *A History of Deaf Smith County,* 3–33.
3. "Wayne Woodward v. Hereford ISD, Request for Admissions," 1, 2, no date, U.S. District Court for the Northern District of Texas, Amarillo Division, WWPC.
4. Woodward interview with Bynum.
5. "Wayne Woodward v. Hereford ISD, Request for Admissions," 3.
6. Woodward interview with Bynum.
7. Student Evaluations, untitled, "student evaluations," WWPC.
8. Student Evaluations, untitled, "student evaluations," WWPC.
9. Wayne Woodward, interview by the author, July 22, 2016.
10. Wayne Woodward, interview by the author, July 22, 2016.
11. Wayne Woodward, interview by the author, July 22, 2016.
12. Wayne Woodward, interview by the author, July 22, 2016; John Murdock, sworn statement in front of notary public in and of Deaf Smith County, Texas, May 1975, WWPC.
13. Untitled handwritten notes, Wayne Woodward, no date, WWPC.
14. Wayne Woodward to Burt, March 1975, WWPC. Woodward was a Unitarian, not an atheist, but he believed that the students would fail to understand that Unitarianism was not an un-Christian spiritual philosophy.
15. Wayne Woodward, interview by the author, July 22, 2016; "Wayne Woodward v. Hereford ISD, Request for Admissions"; both in WWPC.

16. Richard Gid Powers, *Not Without Honor: The History of American Anticommunism* (New York: The Free Press, 1995), 34.
17. Powers, *Not Without Honor*, 35.
18. For more, see Gregg Cantrell, *The People's Revolt: Texas Populists and the Roots of American Liberalism* (New Haven: Yale University Press, 2020), 242–43.
19. For example, see Donald T. Critchlow, *Phyllis Schlafly and Grassroots Conservatism: A Woman's Crusade* (Princeton, NJ: Princeton University Press, 2005), 225.
20. Wayne Woodward, interview by the author, July 22, 2016.
21. "Wayne Woodward v. Hereford ISD, Request for Admissions," 7.
22. Untitled handwritten notes, no date, Wayne Woodward, WWPC.
23. Pat Hughes to Roy Hartman, February 12, 1975 (1), WWPC.
24. Pat Hughes to Roy Hartman, February 12, 1975 (1), WWPC.
25. "Telephone conversation on May 11, 1975, between Bruce Logan, Robin Green, and Wayne Woodward," Taped Conversations/Teacher Handbook, Woodward A-012; Woodward to Green, February 24, 1975; both in WWPC.
26. Pat Hughes to Roy Hartman, February 12, 1975 (2), WWPC.
27. "Telephone conversation on May 11, 1975, between Bruce Logan, Robin Green, and Wayne Woodward," WWPC.
28. "Telephone conversation on May 11, 1975, between Bruce Logan, Robin Green, and Wayne Woodward," WWPC.
29. "Telephone conversation on May 11, 1975, between Bruce Logan, Robin Green, and Wayne Woodward," WWPC.
30. "Telephone conversation on May 11, 1975, between Bruce Logan, Robin Green, and Wayne Woodward," WWPC.
31. "Telephone conversation on May 11, 1975, between Bruce Logan, Robin Green, and Wayne Woodward," WWPC.
32. "Wayne Woodward v. Hereford ISD, Request for Admissions," 3–4, 4.
33. "Wayne Woodward v. Hereford ISD, Request for Admissions," 4; Wayne Woodward, interview by the author, July 22, 2016; "Requested Findings of Fact and Conclusions of Law," WWPC.
34. "Wayne Woodward v. Hereford ISD, Request for Admissions," 4.
35. "Requested Findings of Fact and Conclusions of Law," WWPC.
36. "Taped Conversation with Kathy Wilson," Taped Conversations/Teacher Handbook, Woodward A-012, WWPC.
37. "Requested Findings of Fact and Conclusions of Law," WWPC.
38. "Wayne Woodward v. Hereford ISD, Request for Admissions," 4.
39. "Wayne Woodward v. Hereford ISD, Request for Admissions," 5; Wayne Woodward Teaching Evaluation, circa March 1975, WWPC.
40. Pat Hughes to Wayne Woodward, April 1, 1975, WWPC.
41. "Wayne Woodward v. Hereford ISD, Request for Admissions," 5, 5–6.
42. "Wayne Woodward v. Hereford ISD, Request for Admissions," 5, 5–6.
43. "Wayne Woodward v. Hereford ISD, Request for Admissions," 5, 5–6.

44. "Requested Findings of Fact and Conclusions of Law," WWPC; Woodward interview with Bynum.
45. Pat Hughes to Wayne Woodward, April 1, 1976, WWPC. The date on this letter is undoubtedly a misprint and should read April 1, 1975.
46. Pat Hughes to Wayne Woodward, May 1, 1975, WWPC.

Chapter 4. Building a Civil Rights Case in the Texas Panhandle

1. Robin Green, interview by the author, August 7, 2017.
2. "Proceedings of Meeting of Hereford Independent School District, Hereford, Texas, June 2, 1975," Ron Mason, Certified Court Reporter, 1, 3–4, 4–5, quote on 6–7, WWPC.
3. Clipping, "School Board Backs Principal: Teacher to File Dismissal Case in Court," Bobby Templeton, *Hereford Brand*, June 5, 1975, 1A–2A, WWPC.
4. "Proceedings of Meeting of Hereford Independent School District, Hereford, Texas, June 2, 1975," 17.
5. "Proceedings of Meeting of Hereford Independent School District, Hereford, Texas, June 2, 1975," 21–22, 24.
6. "Proceedings of Meeting of Hereford Independent School District, Hereford, Texas, June 2, 1975," 26.
7. "Proceedings of Meeting of Hereford Independent School District, Hereford, Texas, June 2, 1975," 30–31.
8. "Deposition of Michael Scott Hull," 3, 7, 8, 9–10; for more, see also the untitled handwritten notes of a conversation between Wayne Woodward and Mike Hull; both in WWPC.
9. "Deposition of Michael Scott Hull," 11, 13, 14–18; untitled handwritten notes of a conversation between Woodward and Hull, WWPC.
10. "Deposition of Michael Scott Hull," 19, 20.
11. "Deposition of Michael Scott Hull," 21–22, 23–24, 35.
12. "Deposition of Michael Scott Hull," 38–39, 39–42; untitled handwritten notes of a conversation between Woodward and Hull; both in WWPC.
13. "Wayne Woodward v. The Hereford Independent School District, No. CA-2-75-111, In the United States District Court for the Northern District of Texas, Amarillo Division, deposition of Marshall Clark Formby, June 11, 1976," 8, 9; this is also corroborated in, "Wayne Woodward v. The Hereford Independent School District, No. CA-2-75-111, in the United States District Court for the Northern District of Texas, Amarillo Division, deposition of Beverley Sue Phillips," 4, 5; both in WWPC.
14. "Wayne Woodward v. The Hereford Independent School District, No. CA-2-75-111, in the United States District Court for the Northern District of Texas, Amarillo Division, deposition of John Dirk Vander Zee," June 11, 1976, 7, WWPC.
15. "Deposition of Michael Scott Hull," 43, 44, 46, 49, 51–52, 53, quote on page 44; "Deposition of Marshall Clark Formby," 9; both in WWPC.
16. Woodward to Burt, February 25, 1975, WWPC.

17. "Deposition of Michael Scott Hull," 32–34.
18. "Deposition of Michael Scott Hull," 36.
19. "Deposition of Michael Scott Hull," 37, 38–39.
20. "Deposition of Michael Scott Hull," 50, 51, 52 and 53.
21. "'Woodward v. Hereford ISD,' in U.S. District Court for the Northern District of Texas, Amarillo Division, no. CA 2-75-111, Original Complaint," WWPC.
22. As stated earlier, Woodward, like all other teachers at the school, was employed on a yearly basis of renewable annual contracts. For example, the contract for his last year of employment was drawn up by the district on March 12, 1974, kicking in on August 14, 1974, at an annual salary of $9,070 per year. Woodward was to be paid in twelve equal monthly installments beginning on September 25, 1974. Woodward and Hartman had signed the contract on April 16, 1974.
23. "'Woodward v. Hereford ISD,' in U.S. District Court for the Northern District of Texas, Amarillo Division, no. CA 2-75-111, Original Complaint," WWPC.
24. "Original Answer of Defendant, The Hereford Independent School District," WWPC.
25. "Original Answer of Defendant, The Hereford Independent School District."
26. Untitled handwritten notes, n.d., Wayne Woodward, WWPC. The radio station was KPAN in Hereford, Texas.
27. Untitled handwritten notes, WWPC.
28. Linda Kirby to Charles F. Burns, Texas Classroom Teachers Association, August 4, 1975, WWPC; Robin Green, interview with the author, August 7, 2017.
29. Untitled handwritten notes, WWPC.
30. Wayne Woodward, interview with the author, July 22, 2016.
31. Untitled undated notes, WWPC.
32. Untitled undated notes, WWPC. Woodward believed that most of the students were opposed to the school's dress code.
33. "'Woodward v. Hereford ISD,' Entry of Appearance as Associate Counsel for Plaintiff," WWPC.
34. Wayne Woodward to Robin Green, March 7, 1975, WWPC.
35. Wayne Woodward to Robin Green, no date (circa March 1975), WWPC.
36. Wayne Woodward, interview with the author, July 22, 2016.
37. Thomas J. Griffith to Martha Ware, Teacher's Rights National Education Association, June 27, 1975, WWPC.
38. Thomas J. Griffith to Martha Ware, Teacher's Rights National Education Association, June 27, 1975, WWPC.
39. Thomas J. Griffith to Martha Ware, Teacher's Rights National Education Association, June 27, 1975, WWPC; emphasis mine.
40. "Tom Griffith to Robin Green, Woodward v. Hereford ISD et al., argument," no date, WWPC.
41. "Tom Griffith to Robin Green, Woodward v. Hereford ISD et al., argument."
42. "Tom Griffith to Robin Green, Woodward v. Hereford ISD et al., argument."
43. "Tom Griffith to Robin Green, Woodward v. Hereford ISD et al., argument"; "Re: Woodward v. Hereford Independent School District," WWPC.

44. "Tom Griffith to Robin Green, Woodward v. Hereford ISD et al., argument," no date, WWPC; emphasis in original.
45. "Tom Griffith to Robin Green, Woodward v. Hereford ISD et al., argument."
46. "Tom Griffith to Robin Green, Woodward v. Hereford ISD et al., argument."
47. "Tom Griffith to Robin Green, Woodward v. Hereford ISD et al., argument."

Chapter 5. Mexican Migrant Labor, the American Civil Liberties Union, and Community Guardianism in Hereford, Texas

1. Joe Whitley, interview with the author, July 3, 2017.
2. "Minutes of the Hereford Rural High School District Board of Trustees," May 15, 1956, JRPC.
3. Joe Whitley, interview with the author, July 3, 2017.
4. Clipping, "Answer Petitions from Parkview Negro School," September 11, 1958, no other information, JRPC.
5. Clipping, "Answer Petitions from Parkview Negro School."
6. Clipping, "Answer Petitions from Parkview Negro School."
7. Joe Whitley, interview with the author, July 3, 2017.
8. Joe Whitley, interview with the author, July 3, 2017; also see Joe D. Rogers, "The Italian POW Camp at Hereford during World War II" (Master's thesis, West Texas State University, 1987).
9. Joe Whitley, interview with the author, July 3, 2017; for a good recent study of the Bracero Program, see Deborah Cohen, *Braceros: Migrant Citizens and Transnational Subjects in the Postwar United States and Mexico* (Chapel Hill: University of North Carolina Press, 2013).
10. Joe Whitley, interview with the author, July 3, 2017; for a good recent history of the farmworkers' movement, see Matt Garcia, *From the Jaws of Victory: The Triumph and Tragedy of Cesar Chavez and the Farm Worker Movement* (Berkeley: University of California Press, 2013).
11. "May Day: Labor Lessons in a Historic Texas Tale," *Houston Chronicle*, April 28, 2017, https://www.houstonchronicle.com/opinion/editorials/article/May-Day-11107959.php (accessed May 12, 2019).
12. Joe Whitley, interview with the author, July 3, 2017.
13. Joe Whitley, interview with the author, July 3, 2017.
14. Joe Whitley, interview with the author, July 3, 2017.
15. Woodward interview with Bynum.
16. Woodward interview with Bynum.
17. Max Krochmal, *Blue Texas: The Making of a Multiracial Democratic Coalition in the Civil Rights Era* (Chapel Hill: University of North Carolina Press, 2016), 21–34.
18. Joe Whitley, interview with the author, July 3, 2017.
19. For example, see Dan T. Carter, *The Politics of Rage* (Baton Rouge: Louisiana State University Press, 2000), 12.
20. Rogers, "The Italian POW Camp at Hereford during World War II," 125.

Chapter 6. There Will Be No Winners down the Line

1. Clipping, Bobby Templeton, "School Board Backs Principal: Teacher to File Dismissal Case in Court," *Hereford Brand*, June 5, 1975, 1A–2A, WWPC.
2. Clipping, Templeton, "School Board Backs Principal."
3. "Wayne Woodward v. The Hereford Independent School District, No. CA-2-75-111, in the United States District Court for the Northern District of Texas, Amarillo Division, deposition of Clark Andrews," 3, 4, WWPC.
4. "Wayne Woodward v. The Hereford Independent School District . . . deposition of Clark Andrews," 13–14.
5. "Wayne Woodward v. The Hereford Independent School District . . . deposition of Clark Andrews," 15.
6. "Wayne Woodward v. The Hereford Independent School District . . . deposition of Clark Andrews," 22–23.
7. "Wayne Woodward v. The Hereford Independent School District . . . deposition of Clark Andrews."
8. "Wayne Woodward v. The Hereford Independent School District, No. CA-2-75-111, in the United States District Court for the Northern District of Texas, Amarillo Division, deposition of Michael Scott Hull," 55, 56, WWPC.
9. "Wayne Woodward v. The Hereford Independent School District . . . deposition of Michael Scott Hull," 58–59.
10. "Wayne Woodward v. The Hereford Independent School District . . . deposition of Michael Scott Hull," 58.
11. "Wayne Woodward v. The Hereford Independent School District . . . deposition of Michael Scott Hull," 65, 66, 67–69.
12. "Wayne Woodward v. The Hereford Independent School District . . . deposition of Michael Scott Hull," 71, 72, 73.
13. "Wayne Woodward v. The Hereford Independent School District, No. CA-2-75-111, in the United States District Court for the Northern District of Texas, Amarillo Division, deposition of Ronald Zimmerman," 1, 3, 4-5, WWPC.
14. "Wayne Woodward v. The Hereford Independent School District . . . deposition of Ronald Zimmerman," 7.
15. "Wayne Woodward v. The Hereford Independent School District . . . deposition of Ronald Zimmerman," 8–9, 9–10, 10–11.
16. "Wayne Woodward v. The Hereford Independent School District . . . deposition of Ronald Zimmerman," 21–22, 22–31.
17. "Wayne Woodward v. The Hereford Independent School District . . . deposition of Ronald Zimmerman," 38–39.
18. "Wayne Woodward v. The Hereford Independent School District . . . deposition of Ronald Zimmerman," 39.
19. "Wayne Woodward v. The Hereford Independent School District . . . deposition of Ronald Zimmerman," 40.

20. "Wayne Woodward v. The Hereford Independent School District, No. CA-2-75-111, in the United States District Court for the Northern District of Texas, Amarillo Division, deposition of James Conkwright," 1, 3, 4, 5, 6–7, WWPC.
21. "Wayne Woodward v. The Hereford Independent School District . . . deposition of James Conkwright," 9.
22. "Wayne Woodward v. The Hereford Independent School District . . . deposition of James Conkwright," 27–28; quote on page 28.
23. "Wayne Woodward v. The Hereford Independent School District . . . deposition of James Conkwright," 30.
24. "Wayne Woodward v. The Hereford Independent School District . . . deposition of James Conkwright," 16, 19, 22.
25. "Wayne Woodward v. The Hereford Independent School District . . . deposition of James Conkwright," 9, 11, 13.
26. "Wayne Woodward v. The Hereford Independent School District, No. CA-2-75-111, in the United States District Court for the Northern District of Texas, Amarillo Division, deposition of Jerry Don George," August 4, 1976, WWPC.
27. "Wayne Woodward v. The Hereford Independent School District . . . deposition of Jerry Don George," 8.
28. "Wayne Woodward v. The Hereford Independent School District . . . deposition of Jerry Don George," 9–10.
29. "Wayne Woodward v. The Hereford Independent School District . . . deposition of Jerry Don George," 11–12.
30. "Wayne Woodward v. The Hereford Independent School District . . . deposition of Jerry Don George," 17–18, 18–22.
31. Pam Whitley, telephone interview with the author, February 3, 2017.
32. Pam Whitley, telephone interview with the author, February 3, 2017.
33. It is worth noting that although Whitley believed that Hughes and George were the driver and passenger in question, there is no objective proof of such being the case, nor did this allegation ever enter into the official courtroom record during Woodward's trial.
34. "Wayne Woodward v. The Hereford Independent School District, No. CA-2-75-111, in the United States District Court for the Northern District of Texas, Amarillo Division, deposition of James H. Gentry," October 2, 1975, 1, 3, 4, 17–18, WWPC.
35. "Wayne Woodward v. The Hereford Independent School District . . . deposition of James H. Gentry," 10, 11.
36. "Wayne Woodward v. The Hereford Independent School District . . . deposition of James H. Gentry," 23–24.
37. "Wayne Woodward v. The Hereford Independent School District, No. CA-2-75-111, in the United States District Court for the Northern District of Texas, Amarillo Division, deposition of J. Lynton Allred," 4–5, 6, 7, WWPC.
38. "Wayne Woodward v. The Hereford Independent School District . . . deposition of J. Lynton Allred," 8, 10–11.

39. "Wayne Woodward v. The Hereford Independent School District . . . deposition of J. Lynton Allred," 9–10, 11–14.
40. "Wayne Woodward v. The Hereford Independent School District, No. CA-2-75-111, in the United States District Court for the Northern District of Texas, Amarillo Division, deposition of Danny K. Martin," 11–12, WWPC.
41. "Wayne Woodward v. The Hereford Independent School District, No. CA-2-75-111, in the United States District Court for the Northern District of Texas, Amarillo Division, deposition of Robert Patterson Hughes," September 12, 1975, 1, 3–6, WWPC.
42. "Wayne Woodward v. The Hereford Independent School District . . . deposition of Robert Patterson Hughes," 15–16.
43. "Wayne Woodward v. The Hereford Independent School District . . . deposition of Robert Patterson Hughes," 16–17, 17, 18.
44. "Wayne Woodward v. The Hereford Independent School District . . . deposition of Robert Patterson Hughes," 20.
45. "Wayne Woodward v. The Hereford Independent School District . . . deposition of Robert Patterson Hughes," 28–30.
46. "Wayne Woodward v. The Hereford Independent School District . . . deposition of Robert Patterson Hughes," 30.
47. "Wayne Woodward v. The Hereford Independent School District . . . deposition of Robert Patterson Hughes," 31–32.
48. "Wayne Woodward v. The Hereford Independent School District . . . deposition of Robert Patterson Hughes," 34–35, 36–37, 39–40, 40–41.
49. "Wayne Woodward v. The Hereford Independent School District . . . deposition of Robert Patterson Hughes," 41–43.
50. "Wayne Woodward v. The Hereford Independent School District . . . deposition of Robert Patterson Hughes," 32–33, 33–34, 47.
51. "Wayne Woodward v. The Hereford Independent School District . . . deposition of Robert Patterson Hughes," 48–49.
52. "Wayne Woodward v. The Hereford Independent School District . . . deposition of Robert Patterson Hughes," 43–44.
53. "Wayne Woodward v. The Hereford Independent School District . . . deposition of Robert Patterson Hughes," 111–12.
54. "Wayne Woodward v. The Hereford Independent School District . . . deposition of Robert Patterson Hughes," 50–51, 52–53, quote on page 53; "Wayne Woodward v. The Hereford Independent School District, No. CA-2-75-111, in the United States District Court for the Northern District of Texas, Amarillo Division, deposition of Mary R. Duvall," August 27, 1976, 11–12, 13, WWPC.
55. "Wayne Woodward v. The Hereford Independent School District . . . deposition of Mary R. Duvall," 15, 16, 17, 27–28, 28.
56. "Wayne Woodward v. The Hereford Independent School District . . . deposition of Mary R. Duvall," 22, 23, 29, 31–32; quotes on pages 31–32.
57. "Wayne Woodward v. The Hereford Independent School District . . . deposition of Mary R. Duvall," 32–33.

58. "Wayne Woodward v. The Hereford Independent School District, No. CA-2-75-111, in the United States District Court for the Northern District of Texas, Amarillo Division, deposition of Wayne Herbert Woodward," September 12, 1975, 6–7, WWPC.
59. "Wayne Woodward v. The Hereford Independent School District . . . deposition of Wayne Herbert Woodward," 10–15, 17–19.
60. "Wayne Woodward v. The Hereford Independent School District, No. CA-2-75-111, in the United States District Court for the Northern District of Texas, Amarillo Division, deposition of Wayne Herbert Woodward," September 12, 1975, 19–26, WWPC.
61. "Reporter's Transcript of Proceedings," Amarillo, TX, September 21, 1976, 147, 149–50, 151–52; quote on pages 151–52, WWPC.
62. "Reporter's Transcript of Proceedings," 154.
63. "Reporter's Transcript of Proceedings," 167–68, 169–70.
64. "Wayne Woodward v. The Hereford Independent School District, No. CA-2-75-111, in the United States District Court for the Northern District of Texas, Amarillo Division, oral deposition of Trenton Bruce Logan," January 3, 1976, 3, 4, 7–8, 10–11, 12; quote on page 12, WWPC.
65. "Wayne Woodward v. The Hereford Independent School District . . . oral deposition of Trenton Bruce Logan," 16, 18; quotes on page 18.
66. "Wayne Woodward v. The Hereford Independent School District . . . oral deposition of Trenton Bruce Logan," 24.
67. "Wayne Woodward v. The Hereford Independent School District . . . oral deposition of Trenton Bruce Logan," 25.
68. "Wayne Woodward v. The Hereford Independent School District . . . oral deposition of Trenton Bruce Logan, 24.
69. "Wayne Woodward v. The Hereford Independent School District . . . oral deposition of Trenton Bruce Logan," 46–47.
70. "Wayne Woodward v. The Hereford Independent School District . . . oral deposition of Trenton Bruce Logan," 52.
71. "Wayne Woodward v. The Hereford Independent School District . . . oral deposition of Trenton Bruce Logan," 52, 54.
72. "Wayne Woodward v. The Hereford Independent School District . . . oral deposition of Trenton Bruce Logan," 57.
73. "Wayne Woodward v. The Hereford Independent School District . . . oral deposition of Trenton Bruce Logan," 68–69.
74. "Wayne Woodward v. The Hereford Independent School District . . . oral deposition of Trenton Bruce Logan," 72–73; both quotes on page 73.
75. "Wayne Woodward v. The Hereford Independent School District . . . oral deposition of Trenton Bruce Logan," 57–58; quote on page 58.
76. "Wayne Woodward v. The Hereford Independent School District . . . oral deposition of Trenton Bruce Logan," 74, 75; quote on page 75.
77. "Wayne Woodward v. The Hereford Independent School District . . . oral deposition of Trenton Bruce Logan," 75–76.

78. "Wayne Woodward v. The Hereford Independent School District . . . oral deposition of Trenton Bruce Logan," 76, 78–79.
79. "Wayne Woodward v. The Hereford Independent School District . . . oral deposition of Trenton Bruce Logan"; quotes on pages 88–89, 89, and 93, respectively.
80. "Wayne Woodward v. The Hereford Independent School District . . . oral deposition of Trenton Bruce Logan," 99–100.
81. "Wayne Woodward v. The Hereford Independent School District . . . oral deposition of Trenton Bruce Logan," 101.
82. "Wayne Woodward v. The Hereford Independent School District . . . oral deposition of Trenton Bruce Logan."
83. "Robin Green to Charles Burns, June 9, 1976," WWPC.
84. "Robin Green to Charles Burns, June 9, 1976"; "Wayne Woodward v. The Hereford Independent School District, No. CA-2-75-111, in the United States District Court for the Northern District of Texas, Amarillo Division, deposition of Ruby R. Gartrell," no date, 8, 11, WWPC.
85. "Wayne Woodward v. The Hereford Independent School District . . . deposition of Ruby R. Gartrell."
86. Wayne Woodward interview by the author, July 22, 2016.
87. Wayne Woodward interview by the author, July 22, 2016.

Chapter 7. Righting Wrongs and Wronging Rights

1. Woodward to Green, January 22, 1976, WWPC. The viability of Hartman's doctoral degree would plague him for the rest of his career; for more, see Dave Seldon, "School Chief's Credentials Scrutinized," *The Oklahoman*, June 28, 1992, n.p., https://www.oklahoman.com/article/2398887/school-chiefs-credentials-scrutinized (accessed May 9, 2021).
2. Mary Jo Hamman to Jim Chandler, December 12, 1975, WWPC.
3. Eugene Barkowsky to Betty Curtis, n.d. (circa fall/winter, 1975), WWPC.
4. Robin Green, interview with the author, August 7, 2017.
5. Woodward to Green, August 1975 (date not clear), WWPC.
6. Charles F. Burns to Woodward, August 1, 1975, WWPC.
7. Woodward to Green, July 20, 1975, WWPC.
8. Green to Marilyn Johnston, September 24, 1975, WWPC.
9. "Message from the President," LINK [ACLU publication], July 4, 1975, Amarillo, Texas, no other information, WWPC.
10. "Reporter's Transcript of Proceedings," September 21, 1976, 10 A.M., Amarillo, Texas, WWPC.
11. "Reporter's Transcript of Proceedings," 16, 17, 20–21, 24, 26, 27–28; quote on page 27.
12. "Reporter's Transcript of Proceedings," 32, 34; quotes on both pages.
13. "Reporter's Transcript of Proceedings," 39.
14. "Reporter's Transcript of Proceedings," 33.

Notes to Chapter 7

15. "Reporter's Transcript of Proceedings," 39–41.
16. "Reporter's Transcript of Proceedings," 39–41, 43.
17. "Reporter's Transcript of Proceedings," 78, 79, 80.
18. "Reporter's Transcript of Proceedings," 98, 110–11, 112, 113, 115; quote on page 115.
19. "Reporter's Transcript of Proceedings," 130, 132, 133–34, 136; quotes on pages 130 and 136.
20. "Reporter's Transcript of Proceedings," 140–42.
21. "Reporter's Transcript of Proceedings"; both quotes on page 156.
22. "Reporter's Transcript of Proceedings," 159.
23. "Reporter's Transcript of Proceedings," 160; both quotes on page 160.
24. "Reporter's Transcript of Proceedings," 163–64.
25. "Reporter's Transcript of Proceedings," 166.
26. "Reporter's Transcript of Proceedings," 167–68.
27. "Reporter's Transcript of Proceedings," 177–78.
28. "Reporter's Transcript of Proceedings," 179–80.
29. "Wayne Woodward v. The Hereford Independent School District . . . oral deposition of Trenton Bruce Logan," 102–3, WWPC.
30. Reporter's Transcript of Proceedings, 189, 190–91, 204, 205, 209; quote on page 209.
31. Don Cooney, interview with the author, January 11, 2017; clipping, Bobby Templeton, "Woodward-School Trial Testimony Ends," *Hereford Brand*, September 22, 1976, 1–2, WWPC.
32. Clipping, Bobby Templeton, "Lawyers Conclude Trial on School Suit," *Hereford Brand*, October 7, 1976, 1–2, WWPC.
33. Clipping, Templeton, "Lawyers Conclude Trial on School Suit."
34. Clipping, Templeton, "Lawyers Conclude Trial on School Suit."
35. J. H., "Teacher Wins TCLU Suit," November 12, 1976, *Texas Observer*, no page number, WWPC.
36. J. H., "Teacher Wins TCLU Suit"; "ACLU Member Ordered Reinstated," *Monthly Action Report*, Texas Civil Liberties Union, 3:7 (October 1976), WWPC.
37. "In the United States District Court for the Northern District of Texas, Amarillo Division, Wayne Woodward v. The Hereford Independent School District, et al., no. CA 2-75-111, Judgment," WWPC.
38. J. H., "Teacher Wins TCLU Suit," WWPC.
39. Clipping, "Court Backs Fired Hereford Teacher," no other information, WWPC.
40. "Congratulations" card, no other information, WWPC.
41. Postcard, "Professor Oscar W. Outhouse to Rev. Mr. Wayne Woodwardsky," no other information, WWPC.
42. Postcard, Whitley to Woodward, no other information, WWPC.
43. John Lawton to Woodward, April 27, 1977, WWPC.
44. Robin Green, interview with the author, August 7, 2017.
45. Wayne Woodward v. Hereford I.S.D., et al., in the United States Court of Appeals for the Fifth Circuit, no. 77-1117, Appeal from the United States District Court of the Northern District of Texas, Brief of Appellant, WWPC.

46. Clipping, Bobby Templeton, "Woodward Suit Appealed to Circuit Court: Errors Pointed Out," *Hereford Brand*, no more information (circa April or May, 1977); Bobby Templeton, "District Offered Settlement: Schools File Appeal in Woodward Case," *Hereford Brand*, December 30, 1976; "Miscellaneous Wayne Woodward A-012"; all in WWPC.
47. Clipping, Templeton, "Woodward Suit Appealed to Circuit Court: Errors Pointed Out."
48. "Plaintiffs, to File Brief in Teacher Dismissal Suit," no author, page one, *Hereford Brand*, May 31, 1977, WWPC.
49. "Plaintiffs, to File Brief in Teacher Dismissal Suit."
50. "Plaintiffs, to File Brief in Teacher Dismissal Suit."
51. Wayne Woodward, handwritten untitled notes, WWPC.
52. Clipping, Wayne Woodward, "Letter to the Editor," *Hereford Brand*, 2, no date (circa late October, 1976), WWPC.
53. Woodward, "Letter to the Editor."
54. Woodward, "Letter to the Editor."
55. Woodward, "Letter to the Editor."
56. Bobby Templeton, "Legal Suits Deter Political Potentials," *Hereford Brand*, April 18, 1976, no other information, WWPC.
57. Templeton, "Legal Suits Deter Political Potentials."
58. Templeton, "Legal Suits Deter Political Potentials."
59. Templeton, "Legal Suits Deter Political Potentials."
60. Templeton, "Legal Suits Deter Political Potentials."
61. Templeton, "Legal Suits Deter Political Potentials."
62. Templeton, "Legal Suits Deter Political Potentials."
63. Templeton, "Legal Suits Deter Political Potentials."
64. Templeton, "Legal Suits Deter Political Potentials."
65. Clipping, "Superintendent Tells Rotary About School District Suits," WWPC.
66. Thomas Jefferson Griffith to Robin Green, February 24, 1977, WWPC.
67. Thomas Jefferson Griffith to Robin Green, January 20, 1977; Robin M. Green to Earnest Langley, February 19, 1977; Earnest Langley to Robin Green, April 21, 1977; "Appellant's Motion to Dismiss Appeal," Hereford v. Woodward, in the United States Court of Appeals for the Fifth Circuit, no. 77-1117; Robin M. Green to John E. Hill, May 27, 1977; all in WWPC.

Conclusion

1. For more on 1968, see Terry H. Anderson, *The Movement and the Sixties: Protest in America from Greensboro to Wounded Knee* (Oxford: Oxford University Press, 1995), 183–238.
2. Wayne Woodward, interview with the author, July 22, 2016; Woodward interview with Bynum.
3. For more, see Kruse and Zelizer, *Fault Lines*.

4. Vyacheslav W. Polonski, "Is Social Media Destroying Democracy," *Newsweek,* August 5, 2016, https://www.newsweek.com/social-media-destroying-democracy-487483 (accessed July 18, 9:04 P.M.).
5. Nicholas Carr, "How Social Media Is Ruining Politics," *Politico,* September 2, 2015, https://www.politico.com/magazine/story/2015/09/2016-election-social-media-ruining-politics-213104 (accessed July 19, 11:47 A.M.).
6. "2016 Texas Presidential Election Results," *Politico,* https://www.politico.com/2016-election/results/map/president/texas/ (accessed July 20, 2018, 12:17 P.M.).

BIBLIOGRAPHY

Manuscript Collections

Cornette Library Archives, West Texas A&M University, Canyon, Texas
    Panhandle-Plains Historical Museum Collection
Joe Rogers Personal Collection of Hereford ISD Desegregation Documents, Canyon, Texas
Nita Stewart Haley Memorial Library, Midland, Texas
    Correspondence Files
    The Dust Bowl of 1934–1935 and the Cattle Slaughter of 1935, Binder
    Newspaper Clippings
Research Center, Panhandle-Plains Historical Museum, Canyon, Texas
    Louise Evans Bruce Collection
    Newspaper Clippings Binders and Scrapbooks
    Panhandle-Plains Historical Society Records
Wayne Woodward Personal Collection, Amarillo, Texas

Oral Interviews

Cooney, Don, interview with the author, January 11, 2017, telephone interview.
Green, Robin, interview with the author, August 7, 2017, Lubbock, Texas
Kuhlman, Marty, interview with the author, February 10, 2017, Amarillo, Texas.
Whitley, Joe, interview with the author, July 3, 2017, Amarillo, Texas.
Whitley, Pam, interview with the author, February 3, 2017, telephone interview.
Woodward, Wayne, interview with Katherine Bynum, June 9, 2016, Amarillo, Texas, The Portal to Texas History.
Woodward, Wayne, interview with the author, July 22, 2016, Amarillo, Texas.

Government Documents

Members of the Texas Legislature, 1846–2004. Vol. 2. Austin: Secretary of the Senate, 2005.
Texas Almanac and State Industrial Guide, 1941–1942. Dallas, TX: A. H. Belo, 1942.
Texas Almanac and State Industrial Guide, Supplementary Edition, 1937. Dallas, TX: A. H. Belo, 1937.

Periodicals

Amarillo Globe-News
Amarillo Globe-Times
Canadian Record
Dallas Morning News
Hereford Brand
Houston Chronicle
Newsweek
Oklahoman
Panhandle Herald
Politico
The Prairie
Texas Observer
Tulia Herald

Books and Articles

Anderson, Terry H. *The Movement and the Sixties: Protest in America from Greensboro to Wounded Knee*. Oxford: Oxford University Press, 1995.

Becker, John T. "Jack." "The Texas Panhandle." In *West Texas: A History of the Giant Side of the State*, ed. Paul H. Carlson and Bruce A. Glasrud, 29–30. Norman: University of Oklahoma Press, 2014.

Blodgett, Jan. *Land of Bright Promise: Advertising the Texas Panhandle and South Plains, 1870–1917*. Austin: University of Texas Press, 1988.

Bowman, Timothy Paul. *Blood Oranges: Colonialism and Agriculture in the South Texas Borderlands*. College Station: Texas A&M University Press, 2016.

Cantrell, Gregg. *The People's Revolt: Texas Populists and the Roots of American Liberalism*. New Haven: Yale University, 2020.

Carleton, Don E. *Red Scare: Right-Wing Hysteria, Fifties Fanaticism, and Their Legacy in Texas*. Austin: University of Texas Press, 2014.

Carlson, Paul H., and Bruce A. Glasrud, eds. *West Texas: A History of the Giant Side of the State*. Norman: University of Oklahoma Press, 2014.

Carter, Dan T. *The Politics of Rage: George Wallace, the Origins of the New Conservatism, and the Transformation of American Politics*. 2nd LSUP ed. Baton Rouge: Louisiana State University Press, 2000.

Cohen, Deborah. *Braceros: Migrant Citizens and Transnational Subjects in the Postwar United States and Mexico*. Chapel Hill: University of North Carolina Press, 2013.

Crespino, Joseph. *Strom Thurmond's America: A History*. New York: Hill and Wang, 2013.

———. "Strom Thurmond's Sunbelt: Rethinking Regional Politics and the Rise of the Right." In *Sunbelt Rising: The Politics of Space, Place, and Region*, ed. Michelle Nickerson and Darren Dochuk, 58–61. Philadelphia: University of Pennsylvania Press, 2011.

Critchlow, Donald T. *Phyllis Schlafly and Grassroots Conservatism: A Woman's Crusade.* Princeton, NJ: Princeton University Press, 2005.

Cullen, David O'Donald. "From 'Turn Texas Loose' to the Tea Party: Origins of the Texas Right." In *The Texas Right: The Radical Roots of Lone Star Conservatism*, ed. David O'Donald Cullen and Kyle G. Wilkison, 1–9. College Station: Texas A&M University Press, 2014.

Cullen, David O'Donald, and Kyle G. Wilkison, eds. *The Texas Right: The Radical Roots of Lone Star Conservatism.* College Station: Texas A&M University Press, 2014.

Cunningham, Sean P. *Cowboy Conservatism: Texas and the Rise of the Modern Right.* Lexington: University of Kentucky Press, 2010.

———. "The Paranoid Style and Its Limits: The Power, Influence, and Failure of the Postwar Texas Far Right." In *The Texas Right: The Radical Roots of Lone Star Conservatism*, ed. David O'Donald Cullen and Kyle G. Wilkison, 101–18. College Station: Texas A&M University Press, 2014.

Dobbs, Ricky F. *Yellow Dogs and Republicans: Allan Shivers and Texas Two-Party Politics.* College Station: Texas A&M University Press, 2005.

Dochuk, Darren. *From Bible Belt to Sunbelt: Plain-Folk Religion, Grassroots Politics, and the Rise of Evangelical Conservatism.* New York: W. W. Norton, 2012.

———. "'They Locked God Outside the Iron Curtain': The Politics of Anticommunism and the Ascendancy of Plain-Folk Evangelicalism in the Postwar West." In *The Political Culture of the New West*, ed. Jeff Roche, 97–131. Lawrence: University Press of Kansas, 2008.

Egan, Timothy. *The Worst Hard Time: The Untold Story of Those Who Survived the Great American Dust Bowl.* Boston: Mariner Books, 2006.

Ely, Glenn Sample. *Where the West Begins: Debating Texas Identity.* Lubbock: Texas Tech University Press, 2011.

Faulk, John Henry. *Fear on Trial.* Austin: University of Texas Press, 1983.

Garcia, Matt. *From the Jaws of Victory: The Triumph and Tragedy of Cesar Chavez and the Farm Worker Movement.* Berkeley: University of California Press, 2013.

Goldwater, Barry. *Conscience of a Conservative.* Eastford, CT: Martino Fine Books, 2011.

Green, George Norris. "Establishing the Texas Far Right, 1940–1960." In *The Texas Right: The Radical Roots of Lone Star Conservatism*, ed. David O'Donald Cullen and Kyle G. Wilkison, 87–100. College Station: Texas A&M University Press, 2014.

———. *The Establishment in Texas Politics: The Primitive Years, 1938–1957.* Norman: University of Oklahoma Press, 1984.

Haley, J. Evetts. *Charles Goodnight: Cowman and Plainsman.* Boston: Houghton Mifflin, 1936.

———. *A Texan Looks at Lyndon: A Study in Illegitimate Power.* Canyon, TX: Palo Duro Press, 1964.

Haley, J. Evetts, Jr., ed. *J. Evetts Haley: The Legacy.* Midland, TX: The Haley Family Trust, 1996.

Hämäläinen, Pekka. *The Comanche Empire.* New Haven, CT: Yale University Press, 2009.

———. "What's in a Concept? The Kinetic Empire of the Comanches." *History and Theory* 52, no. 1 (February 2013): 81–90.

Harrigan, Stephen. *Big Wonderful Thing: A History of Texas*. Austin: University of Texas Press, 2019.

Hartman, Andrew. *A War for the Soul of America: A History of the Culture Wars*. Chicago: University of Chicago Press, 2015.

Hill, Joseph A. *The Panhandle-Plains Historical Society and Its Museum*. Canyon: West Texas State College Press, 1955.

Huntington, John S. "'The Voice of Many Hatreds:' J. Evetts Haley and Texas Ultraconservatism." *Western Historical Quarterly* 49, no. 1 (Spring 2018): 65–89.

Johnson, Jim. "The Rugged Texan: Recollections of J. Evetts Haley." In *J. Evetts Haley: The Legacy*, ed. J. Evetts Haley Jr., 64–65. Midland, TX: The Haley Family Trust, 1996.

Knaggs, John R. *Two-Party Texas: The John Tower Era, 1961–1984*. Woodway, TX: Eakin Press, 1986.

Kownslar, Allan O. *The Great Texas Social Studies Textbook War of 1961–1962*. College Station: Texas A&M University Press, 2020.

Krochmal, Max. *Blue Texas: The Making of a Multiracial Democratic Coalition in the Civil Rights Era*. Chapel Hill: University of North Carolina Press, 2016.

Kruse, Kevin M., and Julian E. Zelizer. *Fault Lines: A History of the United States since 1974*. New York: W. W. Norton, 2019.

Kuhlman, Marty. *Always WT: West Texas A&M University Centennial History*. Stillwater, OK: New Forums Press, 2010.

Larson, Edward L. *Summer for the Gods: The Scopes Trial and America's Continuing Debate Over Science and Religion*. New York: Basic Books, 2006.

Lassiter, Matthew D. "Big Government and Family Values: Political Culture in the Metropolitan Sunbelt." In *Sunbelt Rising: The Politics of Space, Place, and Region*, ed. Michelle Nickerson and Darren Dochuk, 82–109. Philadelphia: University of Pennsylvania Press, 2011.

———. *The Silent Majority: Suburban Politics in the Sunbelt South*. Princeton, NJ: Princeton University Press, 2007.

Lauck, John K. "An Interview with David Danbom, Historian of Rural America." *Great Plains Quarterly* 34. no. 2 (Spring 2014): 163–76.

Locke, Joseph L. *Making the Bible Belt: Texas Prohibitionists and the Politicization of Southern Religion*. Oxford: Oxford University Press, 2017.

Loewen, James W. *Sundown Towns: A Hidden Dimension of American Racism*. New York: Touchstone, 2006.

Meyer, William B. "First Effective Settlement: Histories of an Idea." *Journal of Historical Geography* 65 (Spring 2019): 1–8.

Miller, Edward H. *Nut Country: Right-Wing Dallas and the Birth of the Southern Strategy*. Chicago: University of Chicago Press, 2015.

Miller, Michael M. *XIT: A Story of Land, Cattle, and Capital in Texas and Montana*. Norman: University of Oklahoma Press, 2020.

Morris, John Miller. "When Corporations Rule the Llano Estacado: The Glorious Past and Uncertain Future of the Southern High Plains Family Farm." In *The Future of the Southern Plains*, ed. Sherry L. Smith, 44–94. Norman: University of Oklahoma Press, 2003.

Mulloy, D. J. *The World of the John Birch Society: Conspiracy, Conservatism, and the Cold War*. Nashville, TN: Vanderbilt University Press, 2014.

Murrah, David J. "Caught in Goodnight's Shadow: The Un-Illuminated Legacy of C.C. Slaughter." *Panhandle-Plains Historical Review*, no. 89 (2018): 22–32.

Neugebauer, Janet M. *A Witness to History: George H. Mahon, West Texas Congressman*. Lubbock: Texas Tech University Press, 2017.

Nickerson, Michelle. *Mothers of Conservatism: Women and the Postwar Right*. Princeton, NJ: Princeton University Press, 2012.

Nickerson, Michelle, and Darren Dochuk, eds. *Sunbelt Rising: The Politics of Space, Place, and Region*. Philadelphia: University of Pennsylvania Press, 2011.

Nugent, Walter. *Color Coded: Party Politics in the American West, 1950–2016*. Norman: University of Oklahoma Press, 2018.

Patterson, Bessie. *A History of Deaf Smith County, 1890–1964*. Hereford, TX: Pioneer, 1964.

Perlstein, Rick. *Before the Storm: Barry Goldwater and the Unmaking of the American Consensus*. New York: Hill and Wang, 2001.

Phillips-Fein, Kim. "Conservatism: A State of the Field." *Journal of American History* 98, no. 3 (December 2011): 723–43.

Postel, Charles. *The Populist Vision*. Oxford: Oxford University Press, 2009.

Powers, Richard Gid. *Not Without Honor: The History of American Anticommunism*. New York: The Free Press, 1995.

Rathjen, Frederick W. *The Texas Panhandle Frontier*. Rev. ed. Lubbock: Texas Tech University Press, 1998.

Reséndez, Andrés. *A Land So Strange: The Epic Journey of Cabeza de Vaca*. New York: Basic Books, 2009.

———. *The Other Slavery: The Uncovered Story of Indian Enslavement in America*. Boston: Houghton Mifflin, 2016.

Robinson, Edgar Eugene. *The Presidential Vote, 1896–1932*. 2nd ed. Stanford, CA: Stanford University Press, 1947.

Roche, Jeff, ed. *The Political Culture of the New West*. Lawrence: University Press of Kansas, 2008.

Rodgers, Daniel T. *Age of Fracture*. Cambridge, MA: Belknap/Harvard University Press, 2011.

Schlafly, Phyllis. *A Choice Not an Echo*. 4th ed. Washington, DC: Regnery, 2014.

Smith, Sherry L., ed. *The Future of the Southern Plains*. Norman: University of Oklahoma Press, 2003.

Thorburn, Wayne. *Red State: An Insider's Story of How the GOP Came to Dominate Texas Politics*. Austin: University of Texas Press, 2014.

Volanto, Keith. "The Far Right in Texas Politics during the Roosevelt Era." In *The Texas Right: The Radical Roots of Lone Star Conservatism*, ed. David O'Donald Cullen and Kyle G. Wilkison, 68–86. College Station: Texas A&M University Press, 2014.

Wiebe, Robert H. *The Search for Order, 1877–1920*. New York: Hill and Wang, 1966.
Wilkison, Kyle G. "'The Evils of Socialism': The Religious Right in Early Twentieth-Century Texas." In *The Texas Right: The Radical Roots of Lone Star Conservatism*, ed. David O'Donald Cullen and Kyle G. Wilkison, 34–50. College Station: Texas A&M University Press, 2014.
Wuthnow, Robert. *The Left Behind: Decline and Rage in Rural America*. Princeton, NJ: Princeton University Press, 2018.
———. *Rough Country: How Texas Became America's Most Powerful Bible-Belt State*. Princeton, NJ: Princeton University Press, 2014.

Theses and Dissertations

Gorman, Benjamin Lee. "Fundamentalism and the Frontier: Value Clusters in the Texas Panhandle." PhD diss., Tulane University, 1965.
Huntington, John S. "Right-Wing Paranoid Blues: The Role of Radicalism in Modern Conservatism." PhD diss., University of Houston, 2016.
Roche, Jeff. "Cowboy Conservatism: High Plains Politics, 1933–1972." PhD diss., University of New Mexico, 2001.
Rogers, Joe D. "The Italian POW Camp at Hereford during World War II." Master's thesis, West Texas State University, 1987.

Online Sources

Biographical Directory of the United States Congress, 1774–Present. https://bioguide.congress.gov/.
Dave Leip's Atlas of U.S. Presidential Elections. https://uselectionatlas.org/.
Handbook of Texas. https://www.tshaonline.org/handbook.
Politico. https://www.politico.com.
The Portal to Texas History. https://texashistory.unt.edu/.

INDEX

References to illustrations appear in italic type.

Abernethy, Byron, 32
Abilene, Tex., 132
Adair, John, 18
Addams, Jane, 62
African Americans, 3, 24, 40, 49–50, 52–53; and civil rights, 27, 38, 55, 181; in Hereford, Tex., 106, 109, 128–29; and segregation, 42, 105–7; in Texas Panhandle, 44–45, 80
Agricultural Adjustment Act (1933), 22
agriculture, 2, 12, 22–23, 67, 108–10, 181. *See also* farming; migrant workers
air-conditioning, 39
Alabama, 38–39
Aldridge, Darrell, 47–48, 194n14
Alger, Bruce, 25–26, 27, 35
Allison, Alvin R., 34
Allred, J. Lynton, 80, 131–32
Alsop, Joseph, 51
Amarillo, Tex., 4, 17–18, 35, 56; ACLU in, 141; African Americans in, 42, 45–46, 52–53; Green, Robin, in, 80; lawsuit against, 155–56; Woodward, W., in, 51, 111, 172, 182; and *Woodward v. HISD*, 87, 116, 154. *See also* Texas Panhandle
Amarillo Air Force Base, 55
Amarillo College, 33, 53
Amarillo Daily News, 39
Amarillo Globe-News, 29, 33, 38
Amarillo Globe-Times, 34–35, 38, 51
American Civil Liberties Union (ACLU): in Hereford, Tex., 2, 9, 11, 42, 67–69, 124, 146–47, 181; history of, 62–63;

opposition to, 43–44, 85, 90–91, 97, 140; publications by, 63–64, 82, 97, 128, 133, 157, 159; as threat, 6, 7, 70, 86, 103, 104–5, 108, 110, 112–15, 160; and Woods, Frederick Charles, 34–35; Woodward, W., in, 65–66, 69, 73, 92, 99, 101, 133, 141, 149, 151, 156, 161–66, 171, 176; and *Woodward v. HISD*, 116, 175–76
American Legion, 126
American Nazi Party, 39, 56
Andrews, Clark, 80, 116–18
Andrews, Lynette, 117
Animal Farm (Orwell), 93–94
anticommunism, 4, 10, 28, 35, 42–43, 63
antiwar. *See* Vietnam War
Appalachia, 19
Arney, Jim, 80
Asian Americans, 3
atheism, 20, 68
Austin, Tex., 27, 56
automobiles, 179–80

Baldwin, Roger, 62
Baptists, 118, 132
Barkowsky, Eugene, 154
Bentsen, Lloyd, 50, 61
Bible, 124
Bible Belt, 19, 95–96, 156, 176
Birdsong, Mrs. (teacher at La Plata Junior High), 91
Black Like Me (Griffin), 162
Bluebirds, 70

215

Blue Water, Tex., 57
Bonham, Tex., 27
Boomer, Bert, 107
boosterism, 9, 18
Boy Scouts, 124
Boys State, 126
Bracero Program, 109
Bradbury, Ray, 70, 157
Brock, Mrs. (teacher at La Plata Junior High), 155
Brown, Edmund, 39
Brown, Mr. (teacher at La Plata Junior High), 155
Brown v. Board of Education of Topeka (1954), 27, 30, 32, 105, 113
Bruce, Louise Evans, 33–35, 42–43, 46, 194n14
Bugbee, Thomas Sherman, 17
Bush, George H. W., 36, 50

California: 9–11, 28, 39–40, 109; W. Woodward in, 58, 95–96, 111, 141, 168
Canadian River, 4, 17
canals, 179
Canyon, Tex., 17–18, 24, 48
Canyon News, 49
Carr, Waggoner, 37
Carruth, T. Paige, 46–49
Carter, Jimmy, 53
Castro County (Tex.), 5
Catholicism, 20, 54–55
Chávez, César, 109–10
Chicano movement, 109
Childress County (Tex.), 5
Choate, Robert, 39
Christians, 55, 61, 118–19, 140, 195n14
Cíbola, 17
Civilian Conservation Corps (CCC), 23–24
civil liberties, 44, 63, 112, 155–56. *See also* civil rights
civil rights, 2, 13, 112, 160, 169; opposition to, 4, 10, 38, 180; for students, 70, 95, 113, 157; in Texas Panhandle, 13, 44–46, 80, 93; in *Woodward v. HISD*, 82, 88, 173
Civil Rights Act (1964), 36, 55
civil rights movement, 27, 54, 105, 110, 113; opposition to, 15, 41–42, 181; in Texas Panhandle, 20, 40
Civil War (U.S.), 12
Civitan Clubs of Texas, 27
Cold War, 3–4, 24, 29
"Comanche Empire" (Comanchería), 17, 54
communism, 24, 28, 35, 43, 56, 110; in Texas Panhandle, 34, 45, 54, 114
Conkwright, James (Jim): 80, 86–87, 96–97; deposition of, 122–25, 131; testimony of, 160
Connally, John, 36
conservatism, 3; in Sunbelt, 9–10; in Texas Panhandle, 28–42, 49–51, 54–56, 98, 113–14; versus liberalism, 4–7, 11–14, 19, 25, 118, 183–84. *See also* Democrats; Republicans
constitutional rights, 5, 48, 100, 168; and ACLU, 34–35; of Woodward, W., 55, 86, 88, 93, 105, 114, 115, 121–22, 124, 140, 154, 165, 170–71, 174–75, 182
Cooney, Don, 53–56, 165
Cornette, James P., 46, 48
Coronado, Francisco Vázquez de, 15, 17
"Cow Business and Monkey Business" (Haley), 22
Crespino, Joseph, 10
Crystal City, Tex., 2
Cuba, 12
culture wars, 3, 14, 88; in Hereford, Tex., 11, 13, 115, 154, 174, 183–84; in Texas Panhandle, 7, 180–81
Cunningham, Fred, 107
Cunningham, Sean, 25, 50

Daniel, Price, 30–31
Daughters of the American Revolution, 85
Deaf Smith County (Tex.), 25, 113

Deaf Smith Rural Electrical Cooperative, 84
Deep South, 10, 39, 44, 180. *See also* South (U.S.)
democracy, 13, 14, 73, 133, 179
Democratic National Convention (Chicago), 179
Democratic Party, 5, 32, 36, 124; in Texas, 21, 24–29, 92; in Texas Panhandle, 37–38, 40. *See also* Democrats
Democrats, 23, 27, 38; in Texas Panhandle, 7, 20, 25, 29, 30, 37, 40. *See also* Democratic Party
DeMolays, 70
desegregation, 38, 105–107. *See also* integration; segregation
District Court for the Northern District of Texas, 87, 116, 154, 169, 175
Dochuk, Darren, 9–11, 28
Dumas, Tex., 156
Duncan, John, 168
Dust Bowl, 6, 10, 22–23
Duvall, Mary, 68, 69, 91, 92, 145–46; deposition of, 138–41, 149

East Coast, 18
East Texas, 19, 24
Ed Sullivan Show, 41
Eisenhower, Dwight D., 28, 29, 52
equal rights, 46, 47
Equal Rights Amendment, 60, 63
exceptionalism, 9, 13, 15, 21
Exorcist, The (film), 95
Ezzell, Ben, 49

Facebook, 183–84
Fahrenheit 451 (Bradbury), 70, 157
farmers' cooperatives, 109
farming, 6, 40, 148; in Hereford, Tex., 57–58, 108–9; and New Deal, 20–23; in Texas Panhandle, 8, 18, 19, 29, 54, 180
farmworkers' movement, 109
Farr, Mr. (history teacher at La Plata Junior High), 91

Farwell family, 18
FBI (Federal Bureau of Investigation), 47
feminism, 54
Fifth Circuit Court of Appeals, 100, 169, 170
First Amendment, 87, 99, 100, 103, 167, 175
First Baptist Church, 130, 131
Fluker v. Board of Alabama (1971), 100, 103
fluoride, 57
Ford, Cindy, 64, 69, 82, 113, 128, 133, 159
Ford, Henry, 179
Ford Foundation Adult Education, 32
Formby, Marshall, 84–85
Fourteenth Amendment, 73, 87, 99, 167, 175
freedom, 26, 70, 147, 157, 172–73, 179; academic, 32, 101; of speech, 72, 86, 98
Freedom of Information Act (1967), 47
Freeport, Tex., 51
free trade, 4
Frio Baptist Church, 118
frontier individualism, 8, 9, 19, 30, 41

Gartrell, Ruby, 151
gender, 4, 7, 11, 20, 60
Gentry, James H., 80, 130–31
George, Jerry Don, 83–86, 90, 119, 125–28, 129
George, Monica, 129
Germany, 43, 172
Gilded Age, 18
Gilligan, José, 85, 111–12
Goldwater, Barry, 10, 30, 33, 35–38
González, Leticia, 77
Goodnight, Charles, 17–18, 23, 189n4
Gopro Committee, 84, 127–28
Gorman, Benjamin Lee, 19–20
Gossett, Ed, 25
Grapevine, Tex., 161
Grapevine Independent School District, 143
Great Depression, 20–21, 24, 53, 104, 110, 146; migration during, 10–11, 39–40. *See also* New Deal

Great Plains, 10, 23
Great Society, 38
Great War (World War I), 12
Green, Richard, 170, 177
Green, Robin, 67, 73, 185; and appeal, 169; closing arguments of, 165–66; depositions by, 83, 116–28, 130–37, 141–46, 148–52; and hearing of Woodward, W., 80–82, 85–86, 90; and lawsuit preparation, 87–89, 93–94, 96, 99–101, 154–56; and settlement, 171, 177–78; and testimony of Woodward, W., 157–58; at trial, 160–64; and verdict, 166–68. See also Woodward, Wayne; *Woodward v. HISD*
Greenberg, Henry, 32
Griffin, John Howard, 162
Griffith, Thomas Jefferson, 96–100, 167, 177
guardianism, 9, 114
Gulf Coast, 29

Hacker, Andrew, 34
Haley, J. Evetts, 8, 22, 25, 29–33
Hall County (Tex.), 5
Hamlin, Tex., 132
Handbook of Student Rights (ACLU), 70, 98, 113, 157
Harrigan, Stephen, 4
Hartman, Andrew, 6
Hartman, Roy, 60, 67, 76, 182; ACLU, views of, 68–69, 85, 176; deposition of, 142–44, 150; dissertation of, 153, 204n1; and firing of Woodward, W., 64–66, 72, 99, 128; and hearing of Woodward, W., 81, 82; and pretrial, 91, 96–97; testimony of, 160–62, 143; and Woodward, W., relationship with, 61–62, 102, 151, 154–55, 165
Hawaii, 12
Hazlewood, Grady, 25, 37–38, 45, 46
Hendon, Patty, 163
Henry Street Settlement House, 62
Hereford, Tex., 12, 57–58, 75, 81, 109–10, 168, 184; ACLU in, 2, 6, 9, 42, 62–64, 67–69, 86, 110, 124, 141–42, 181; conservatism in, 5, 15, 56, 92–94, 98, 107, 129, 145, 154, 172; culture wars in, 11, 13, 174, 183–84; threats to, 7, 13, 32, 103–5, 108, 112–15, 138, 140, 146. See also Texas Panhandle
Hereford Brand (newspaper), 57; on segregation, 106–7; Woodward, W., in, 112, 123, 128, 156, 170–73, 177
Hereford Chamber of Commerce, 85
Hereford High School, 82–83, 125, 126
Hereford Independent School District, 57–58, 106–7, 113; appeal by, 169–70; and pretrial, 87–88, 93, 96–97; and settlement, 177–78; teachers in, 72, 90, 121, 125, 144, 147–48, 151–52, 154–55; and verdict, 166–68. See also Hereford School Board
Hereford Potato Growers Association, 58
Hereford Reporter, 57. See also *Hereford Brand*
Hereford School Board, 58, 105–7; and appeal, 174–77; depositions of, 116–25, 130–32, 150; and firing of Woodward, W., 62, 72, 93, 99–100, 138, 143–44; and hearing of Woodward, W., 80–81; and settlement, 177–78; and verdict, 170; Woodward, W., relationship with, 94–95
High Plains, 4–5
Hill, Joseph A., 21
hippies, 48–50, 55, 111
Hofstadter, Richard, 12
Holder, Harrell, 171, 177
Holly Sugar, 110
Hoover, Herbert, 20, 29
Huber, Mr. (administrator at La Plata Junior High), 91
Hughes, Robert Patterson (Pat), 95, 112, 182; and ACLU, views of, 68–69, 176; deposition of, 132–38, 156, 158; and firing of Woodward, W., 64–65, 70–74, 124–25, 128, 146–47; and hearing of Woodward, W., 81, 82,

85–86; and Hull, Mike, 83–84, 119, 127; and pretrial, 87–91, 96–100; testimony of, 162–65; and verdict, 169; and Woodward, W., relationship with, 59–62, 92, 94–95, 139, 151, 166
Hull, James, 125
Hull, Mike, 82–86, 90, 118–20, 123, 125–28, 129
Hull House, 62
Hunt, H. L., 28
Huntington, John S., 31

identity, 14, 54, 64; in Texas Panhandle, 7–9, 13, 15–19, 21, 35–36, 43, 50
Indiana, 28, 38
individualism, 17, 23, 26, 31, 180; frontier, 8, 9, 19, 30, 41
individual liberties, 19, 44, 94
individual rights, 14, 70, 113
in loco parentis, 47, 101
integration, 29–30, 44, 105–6. *See also* desegregation; segregation
internet, 182
isolationism, 7–8
Italian POW camp, 108, 114

JA Ranch, 18
Jeffersonian Democrats, 20–21, 22, 25
John Birch Society (JBS), 28–29, 30, 39, 51, 108
Johnson, Lyndon Baines, 10, 27, 35–36, 42–43; as a Texan, 30, 52, 55

Kappa Alpha (fraternity), 44
Kennedy, John F., 27, 35, 36
Kennedy, Robert F., 179
Kent State University, 45
Key Club, 83–84, 85, 126, 128
King, Martin Luther, Jr., 179
Kiwanis Club, 58, 126
Koch, Fred, 28
Kress, 42
Kruse, Kevin M., 6
Kuhlman, Marty, 53, 54, 56
Ku Klux Klan, 52, 120

Lambert, George, 112
Landon, Alf, 20, 21
Langley, Earnest, 80, 106–7, 109; appeal by, 169–70, 174–77; closing arguments of, 165–66; depositions by, 118–19, 141–43, 149, 155; and pretrial, 88–90, 96–97, 124; and settlement, 177–78; at trail, 158–64
La Plata Junior High School, 78, 92, 111, 122; Woodward, W., at, 47, 58, 80–81, 87, 132, 138, 154
Lawton, John, 169
Lee, W. M. D., 18
Levelland, Tex., 34
LGBTQIA community, 3
liberalism, 2–3, 10, 20, 24, 41, 54, 114, 180–81; versus conservatism, 4–7, 11–14, 25, 37, 118, 183–84; cultural, 19, 45, 60, 61, 64, 174; opposition to, 30–33, 35, 50, 105, 110, 112; racial, 115. *See also* Democrats; New Deal liberalism; Republicans
Lions Club, 58, 85
livestock, 21, 22, 57
Llano Estacado (Staked Plains), 4, 187n10
local versus national, 3, 5, 13, 15, 110, 180
Locke, Joseph, 19
Logan, Bruce, 65–68, 99, 158; deposition of, 144–50, 151, 164, 166
Lorentz, Pare, 23
Lusk v. Estes (1973), 103
LX Ranch, 18

Mahon, George, 61
Mailloux v. Kiley (1971), 101, 103
Manion, Clarence, 31
Martin, Danny K., 64, 80, 132, 143, 173
Maryland, 38
Mayer, Margaret, 40
media, 26, 63, 116, 170, 172. *See also* press; social media; television
Mexican Americans, 2, 3, 95, 111–12, 182. *See also* migrant workers
Mexicans, 2, 95, 109, 111–13. *See also* migrant workers

Mexico, 17
Midwest (U.S.), 4, 12, 54
migrant workers, 13, 105, 181, 185; camps for, 109, 111–12, 114–15
Mission, Tex., 2
Model T automobile, 179
Moratorium Day, 49
More, Thomas, 67
Mother's Park, 111
Mt. Healthy City School District Board of Education v. Doyle (1977), 175–76, 177
Murdock, John, 61, 168
Murrah, David J., 189n4

National Association for the Advancement of Colored People (NAACP), 33
National Education Association (NEA), 96, 116, 142, 177, 178
National Farm Workers Association, 109
National Indignation Convention, 30
nationalism, 24, 43
Native Americans, 3, 17
New American Movement, 56
New Deal, 20–26, 31, 53, 54, 110. *See also* Great Depression
New Deal liberalism, 5, 19, 25, 31, 47, 180
New Left, 47, 54, 180
New Mexico, 4–5, 187n10
New Spain, 17
newspapers, 33–35, 102, 183. *See also* press; *names of specific newspapers*
New York State, 34, 95, 96, 141
New York Times, 33
Nickerson, Michelle, 9–10, 11
Nieman, O. G., 173
1984 (Orwell), 94
Nixon, Richard, 36, 37, 50, 169, 179; and Watergate, 61, 64

Obama, Barack, 183
O'Daniel, W. Lee ("Pappy"), 20, 24, 31
Odyssey, The (Homer), 94
Ogallala Aquifer, 4, 57–58

oil and gas industries, 25
"Okies," 10
Oklahoma, 4–5, 17, 187n10
"Old South Day," 44
Orange County (Calif.), 11, 39
Orwell, George, 93–94
Owens, Mr. (Kiwanis Club representative), 126

Paine, Thomas, 45
Palo Duro Canyon, 17, 23–24
Palo Duro High School, 52
Panhandle Herald, 31
Panhandle-Plains Historical Museum (PPHM), 8–9, 180
Panhandle-Plains Historical Society (PPHS), 8, 37
Parkhouse, George, 45
Parkview Elementary School, 105–7
Parkview PTA, 106
Parmer County (Tex.), 5
Pecan Shellers Strike, 110, 112
Pecos and Northern Texas Railway, 57
Pecos River, 22
People's Party. *See* Populists
Perales, Esmerelda, 1–2
Philippines, 12
Phillips-Fein, Kim, 3–4
Pickering v. Board of Education (1968), 100, 102–3
place, sense of, 10, 18, 34, 54, 140
Plains Indians, 17
Plow That Broke the Plains, The (Lorentz), 23
Populists, 4, 12, 63
Potter County (Tex.), 25, 80
Potter County Stadium, 35
Presley, Elvis, 41
press, 35, 38, 47, 116, 123; Woodward, W., coverage of, 168, 172
prisoners of war, 108, 114
Protestantism, 10, 18–19, 55
public schools, 142, 161, 168, 182
public service, 179

race, 23–24, 29, 38; in Amarillo, Tex., 42, 45, 51–53, 55; and equality, 3, 7, 13; in Hereford, Tex., 5, 105–7, 115; Woodward, W., and, 44, 102, 162
radicalism, 2–3, 25, 39–40, 62
radicals, 45, 47, 49, 50, 91
railroads, 12, 18, 57, 179
Rainbow Girls, 70, 90
ranching, 17–18, 19, 20–22, 57, 180
Randall County (Tex.), 25, 31, 39, 45, 80
Rayburn, Sam, 27
Reagan, Ronald, 10, 28, 37–38, 39, 53, 54; and Reagan Revolution, 22, 38
Reconstruction, 12, 36
Red River War (1874), 17, 18
Red Rolling Plains, 4
Red Scare, 45
Reiter, Billy Jo, 168
Republican Party, 50, 124; and conservatism, 13, 28, 35, 36–40; and elections, 10, 20–21, 25, 29, 33. *See also* Republicans
Republicans, 21, 27–38, 40; in Texas Panhandle, 7, 36, 37, 39, 50. *See also* Republican Party
Revolutionary War (American), 45
Rhinehart, John, 47, 48–49
"Rights of Man" amendment, 45
riots, 44, 45, 179
Roche, Jeff, 7
Rockwell, George Lincoln, 39
Rogers, Joe, 114
Romeo and Juliet (Shakespeare), 94
Roosevelt, Franklin Delano (FDR), 20–24, 50, 54–55, 110
Rotary Club, 34, 177
rural versus urban, 3, 6, 12, 26, 183–84
Russell, Bertrand, 43
Russell, Richard, 36
Russia, 172. *See also* Soviet Union

San Antonio, Tex., 110, 129, 144, 149
Saturday Evening Post, 22
segregation, 30, 46, 52–53, 105–7. *See also* desegregation; integration

Sheffy Robbie, 92, 168
Shepperd, John Ben, 27
"Shivercrats," 27
Shivers, Allen, 25, 27, 29
Shoshone, Calif., 58
Sigma Nu (fraternity), 52
Slaughter, C. C., 189n4
Smith, Al, 20
Snapchat, 183
Sneed, Edgar, 46
socialism, 20, 23, 26, 34
social media, 182–83
Socrates, 67
South (U.S.), 4, 10, 19, 53, 106, 181. *See also* Deep South
Southeast Asia, 54
southern plains, 3–5, 7, 9, 15, 17, 44, 187n10. *See also* Texas Panhandle
Southwest (U.S.), 9–10, 39, 109
Southwestern Oklahoma State University, 151, 153
Soviet Union, 28, 43, 94
Spanish, 15, 17
Spanish-American War, 12
Springer, N.Mex., 156
steamboats, 179
Stensland, Per, 32
Sterzing v. Fort Bend Independent School District (1972), 102, 103
Stevenson, Adlai, 29, 52
Students for a Democratic Society (SDS), 46–47, 49, 50
students' rights. *See* civil rights
sugar mill, 110
Sunbelt, 3–4, 9–10, 39
sundown towns, 24
Swisher County, Tex., 5

Tascosa High School, 45, 52, 144
technology, 179–80
television, 44, 179–80, 181, 183
Templeton, Bobby, 170–71, 173
Tenayuca, Emma, 110, 112
tenure (academic), 32–33

Texan Looks at Lyndon, A (Haley), 30, 31
Texans for America, 30, 32
Texas, 8, 17, 24, 38, 45, 55, 86, 88, 99; congressional districts in, 15, 25, 40; conservatism in, 19, 21, 27, 31
Texas Centennial, 9
Texas Civil Liberties Union, 112, 156, 168
Texas Classroom Teachers Association (TCTA), 93, 123–24, 153–55, 178
Texas Democratic Party, 21, 25, 38, 92
Texas Panhandle, 2, *16*, 63, 108–10, 113, 187n10; ACLU in, 43–44, 97, 104, 141; community, sense of, in, 12–14, 17, 180; conservatism in, 4, 18–21, 41–42, 44, 49, 51, 53–54, 56, 62, 113; culture wars in, 7, 180–81; elections in, 10, 20, 25, 29, 30–31, 33–40, 50, 183; and federal government, 21–24, 26, 35, 146; isolation of, 6, 9, 13, 15, 31. *See also* identity; West Texas
Texas Rangers, 29–30
Texas Regulars, 24
Texas State Teachers' Association (TSTA), 142, 154
Texas Tech University, 32–33, 131
Thornberry, Mac, 40
Thurmond, Strom, 10
Tierra Blanca Creek, 57
Timmons, J. Blake, 25
Tower, John, 27, 36–37, 61, 193n58
Truman, Harry S., 29
Trump, Donald, 183
Twitter, 183

unions, 24, 62, 110, 174, 112–15
Unitarianism, 195n14
University of Alabama, 38
University of California, Berkeley, 41
U.S. Circuit Court of Appeals for the Fifth Circuit, 100, 169, 170
U.S. Constitution, 26, 60, 179. *See also* First Amendment; Fourteenth Amendment
U.S. Department of Health, Education, and Welfare, 32

U.S. Supreme Court, 45, 169, 170–71, 175–76. *See also names of specific cases*

Vander Zee, John Dirk, 84
Vaughn, Randy, 160–61
Vietnam War, 179, 42–43; opposition to, 45, 49, 53–54, 55–56, 102
Voting Rights Act (1965), 45, 55

Wald, Lillian, 62
Wallace, George, 38–39
Wallace, Lurleen, 38
Warren, Earl, 31
Watergate, 50, 61, 94
Watts, Calif., 45
Weatherford, Okla., 151, 159, 172
Weatherford Oklahoma School District, 151
Welch, Robert, Jr., 28
welfare state, 26, 34, 194n14
West Coast, 10
Western State College, 153
West Texas, 8, 9, 25, 148–49. *See also* Texas Panhandle
West Texas Chamber of Commerce, 49
West Texas State College, 21
West Texas State University (WTSU), 33, 44–48, 52, 53, 172
Weyrich, Paul, 6
white supremacy, 27, 55
Whitley, Joe, 109–10, 112, 128, 129
Whitley, Pam, 156, 166, 169; and ACLU publications, 63–64, 69, 82, 113, 128, 133; testimony of, 159
Whitely, Sandy, 129
Wichita Falls, Tex., 25, 27, 36
Wiebe, Robert, 12
Willkie, Wendell, 20
Wilson, Kathy, 69
Wisconsin, 38
Witherspoon, Jim, 108–9, 110
Witte Museum, 8
women, 3, 11, 20, 47, 59
Wood, Frederick Charles, 34

Woodward, Audie, 151
Woodward, Halbert O., 154, 159–60, 163, 164–65, 175; verdict of, 166–68, 170, 171
Woodward, Linda, 182
Woodward, Wayne, 56, 79, 151, 181–82; and ACLU chapter, 62–63, 111–12; constitutional rights of, 5, 88, 121–22, 140, 154, 174–75, 182; deposition of, 141–42, 155, 176; early years, 42, 51–53; firing of, 70–74, 89, 146–47, 170–73; hearing of, 80–82, 85–86, 90; and lawsuit preparation, 87–88, 99–101, 53; locals' views of, 54, 107, 118, 124, 131, 132, 148–49, 181; probation of, 64–66; and questioning of authority, 50, 52, 60, 67, 136–37; and religious beliefs, 61–62, 97, 195n14; and settlement, 171; student's views of, 1–2, 58–59, 69, 92, 117, 119, 128, 169; and teaching, 68, 93–94, 101, 103, 133–38, 150; testimony of, 156–60, 176; as threat, 11, 13, 86–87, 95–96, 104–5, 113, 114–15, 138, 158, 183; and verdict, 166–68; at WTSU, 47, 172, 180

Woodward v. Hereford Independent School District (HISD) (1976), 13–14; appeal in, 169–70; charges in, 87–88; defense in, 88–90; depositions in, 116–28, 130–51; judgment in, 167–68; preparation for, 93–95, 99–100, 101; settlement in, 174–78; trial of, 156–68
World War I (Great War), 12
World War II, 9, 23, 24, 108
Wuthnow, Robert, 18

XIT Ranch, 18

Yarborough, Ralph, 31, 36, 50
Young Democrats, 33, 70, 82–83, 84, 90, 92
Young Republicans, 33
YouTube, 183

Zelinsky, Wilbur, 19
Zelizer, Julian, 6
Zimmerman, Ronald (Ron), 80, 120–22, 173
Zimmerman, Zan, 120–21

www.ingramcontent.com/pod-product-compliance
Lightning Source LLC
Chambersburg PA
CBHW031618170426
43195CB00037B/744